CHESAPEAKE LEGACY

Chesapeake Legacy:
Tools and Traditions

by Larry S. Chowning

Schiffer Publishing Ltd®

4880 Lower Valley Road, Atglen, PA 19310

*

To the men and women
who contributed to this project

*

Published by Schiffer Publishing, Ltd. 2010

Chesapeake Legacy: Tools and Traditions was originally published by Tidewater Publishers in 1995

Earlier versions of some of the chapters in this book appeared in the *Southside Sentinel, National Fisherman*, and *Chesapeake Bay Magazine.*

Library of Congress Control Number: 2010921629

ISBN: 978-0-7643-3595-2
Printed in The United States of America

Schiffer Books are available at special discounts for bulk purchases for sales promotions or premiums. Special editions, including personalized covers, corporate imprints, and excerpts can be created in large quantities for special needs. For more information contact the publisher:

Published by Schiffer Publishing Ltd.
4880 Lower Valley Road
Atglen, PA 19310
Phone: (610) 593-1777; Fax: (610) 593-2002
E-mail: Info@schifferbooks.com

For the largest selection of fine reference books on this and related subjects, please visit our web site at
www.schifferbooks.com

We are always looking for people to write books on new and related subjects. If you have an idea for a book please contact us at the above address.

This book may be purchased from the publisher.
Include $5.00 for shipping.
Please try your bookstore first.
You may write for a free catalog.

In Europe, Schiffer books are distributed by
Bushwood Books
6 Marksbury Ave.
Kew Gardens
Surrey TW9 4JF England
Phone: 44 (0) 20 8392 8585;
Fax: 44 (0) 20 8392 9876
E-mail: info@bushwoodbooks.co.uk
Website: www.bushwoodbooks.co.uk

Contents

Preface, vii

1. Hook-and-Line Fishery, 3
2. Shad Planking, 11
3. Salt Herring, 18
4. Tarring Pound Nets, 27
5. Trap-Pole Horses, 37
6. Setting Pound Stakes, 41
7. A Day on the Chesapeake Setting a Pound Net, 55
8. Chesapeake Bay Fishing Bateaux, 64
9. Snapper Rigs, 75
10. A Tale from the Days of Fishing under Sail, 82
11. Menhaden Spotters, 93
12. Catching Catfish in Hoop Nets, 102
13. Fish and Oyster Tales, 111
14. How to Make Shaft Tongs, 118
15. Yankee Skiffs, 130
16. The Oyster Packing Business, 139
17. Clam Rakes, 154
18. Dragging for Conch in the Dead of Night, 162
19. Bottom-Line Crab Potting, 169
20. The Boatbuilders of Tangier Island, 178

21. Sterns on Bay Workboats, 191
22. Winegar's Marine Railway, 199
23. A Longtime Railway Man, 212
24. How to Make a Rope Bow Fender, 217
25. Steamboats and Seafood, 231
26. Steamboat Recollections, 242
27. The Woman's Perspective, 250
28. A Sailing Family, 266
29. Cooking Muskrat, 287
30. Harvesting of Souls, 292
Index, 300

Preface

OVER THE years, I've worked diligently to document the ways of the water.

From time to time, there have been those who have praised my work and others who have criticized it. Some have suggested that my writing is too sentimental and has not always been totally objective toward the conservation and preservation of the Bay's resources.

I must admit that I am sentimental and my writings have reflected a fondness for commercial fishing and Chesapeake Bay watermen. I will not, however, apologize for that.

The truth of the matter is, I like most watermen and I like what they stand for. I appreciate their tradition and their struggle to survive in an occupation that does not fit well in today's fast-paced urban society. Chesapeake Bay watermen are a carryover from earlier days when people had to be extremely self-sufficient just to take care of their basic needs.

In 1981, I was employed at Barnhardt Duck Farms, near Urbanna, Virginia. When the business failed, I, along with others, lost my job. Damon, our oldest child, was a little boy. Peyton, our second child, had just arrived, and Hannah, our third, was not yet born. Although my wife, Dee, had been trained and had worked as an elementary school teacher, she was busy raising children and keeping the household together. I needed something quick to do to keep the bill collectors from beating down my door.

My choice was to work the water, and I decided to catch eels. I read all the propaganda put out by Sea Grant on how many eels could be caught in a pot per day. The agency had conveniently translated it all into dollars and cents, and it looked mighty good to me. I wondered why everybody wasn't doing it.

I went to the bank and borrowed enough money to buy materials to make 120 eel pots and 40 crab pots, and to string two gill nets. The nets and pots would supply the menhaden and blue crabs needed to bait the eel pots. I bought a sixteen-foot Lewis Wright–built flat-bottomed skiff and a 9½-horsepower Evinrude outboard motor. As a boy, I had owned a Wright-built twelve-foot skiff. From that experience, I knew my new skiff would provide a sturdy platform for fishing pots. I also bought some marine plywood, and my father built a holding box for my eels.

To say the least, my experience on the water was an adventure. I learned fast that eels were not going to pay all my bills. I also learned about the age-old system of buying and selling seafood on the Chesapeake Bay. I sold my eels to a buyer from Guinea Neck in Gloucester County, Virginia. He came to my house in a big aerated truck and would haul my eels live to Mount Holly, Virginia. There he sold them to a Dutchman, George Robberecht, who would in turn fly them to Europe to supply a very lucrative eel market. Eels are considered a delicacy in many countries.

Working the water, I learned a lot about life. I was elated the first time I called the buyer to come and get my first load. Over the phone, he told me the price of eels was $1.20 a pound. I'd caught over one thousand pounds in a few days. I thought I was going to make big money. However, when he came to pick up my eels, the price had suddenly dropped to sixty cents a pound. It had something to do with a European glut right then, but the price would go back up, he assured me. The price did jump around a bit, but mostly it hovered around sixty cents and below.

Then there was the time in July when I was the only person around eeling. Most eelers stop fishing in the heat of the summer because catches are down in July and August. They go to crab potting or gill netting and start back up in the fall. I kept fishing in the summer, though, and caught some eels. I had over one thousand pounds in my float. I called the buyer, and he said he would arrive at my place at a certain time the next day. I waited and waited, but he didn't show. When I called him again, he said he would be there the next day. The morning he was to come, there was a red tide (oxygen deficiency in the water), and I lost eight hundred pounds of eel. I toted by hand all eight hundred pounds in plastic bags up the forty-foot hill behind my house and hauled them to the landfill.

What a waste! I kept saying to myself. If I had only known it was coming, I would have opened the door and let them all go the night before.

Even though things were going poorly with the eel business, the gill nets and crab pots began paying off. I was catching more than enough bait for the eel pots. In fact, there were fish and crabs left over. So, I approached several local crab houses about selling crabs to them, but no one was interested. "We've got plenty of crabbers," they all said. So I went to the local market in Urbanna and asked the late Raymond Walton if I could sell my fish and crabs off my truck outside of his store. We walked out in the parking lot and he pointed to a spot. "You can sell all you want right there. Saturday will be the best day," he said. I thanked him and offered to rent the spot, but he didn't want any payment.

On that first Saturday, I headed out at the crack of dawn to fish my nets and pull my crab pots. I wanted to have my catch iced down and the truck loaded so I could get to my spot by 9:00 A.M. I had a good morning fishing, catching over 150 pounds of spot, croaker, and trout and several bushels of hard crabs. I got back to the dock, iced everything down, drove to my spot, pulled out a scale I had rigged up, and waited.

That first day was an education for me in social status. People I had known all my life walked by and looked straight ahead. Some were old classmates who, I would suspect, voted for me to become the Most Likely to Succeed from that 1968 senior high school class. There were others who had followed my track career at the University of Richmond and had written to me in the 1970s when I broke state, Southern Conference, and school records and ran in the NCAA finals in Detroit, Michigan. Some were even related to me, but on this Saturday it was like I wasn't there.

I quickly forgot all about that because people began coming to my truck. They weren't people driving Lincoln Continentals and Mercedes Benzes though. They were people driving old pickup trucks and beat-up cars. They were standing in line and pulling out hard cash with smiles on their faces. They were getting fresh, fresh seafood. I don't know who was more excited—them or me. I knew one thing, though. I could buy groceries that week and pay some bills.

Saturday after Saturday, I spent in the parking lot making more money on fresh fish and crabs than I did working all week on eels. I enjoyed those Saturdays. At my truck, I came to know many people I had seen around all my life but hadn't known by name.

In the 1950s and 1960s, segregation was still a way of life in Urbanna. The public beach had a sign mounted on a telephone pole that read "Whites Only." The local doctor's office had a waiting room for "colored" and one for "whites." The movie theater had a balcony for blacks only, and whites all sat downstairs. In 1964, the schools in Middlesex County were integrated under the "Freedom of Choice" system. I went to school with thirteen black children whose parents were brave enough to send them to the all-white high school. My best fish and crab customers were black, many of whom I came to know and love. Several have been of great help to me since I have gone into the writing business.

One in particular, whom I always call my best customer was Lester Johnson. Lester came by the first Saturday I was in the parking lot. When he came up, I had a pocket full of money and two gray trout left. He looked in my cooler and saw those trout and his eyes beamed. "'I ain't got no money right now, but I'd love to have those fish. If you let me have them, I'll pay you later.'"

Lester was someone I knew. In the spring, he would often stop by my house and sell us watercresses that he had picked from the fields. I had known his father, Alex Johnson. Alex was the first black man I knew who was allowed to sit at the counter at Marshall's Drugstore. He had been a yard man for just about everybody in town. He always had a big smile, and people liked him. There were some black people, though, who said he was an Uncle Tom. I always felt it was men like Alex who laid the foundation for a smoother transition between white and black when integration finally came to the South. In spite of his color, he was accepted because he had a good heart.

I don't know that I would have been so generous at the beginning of the day, but since it was near the end, I gave the fish to Lester. I then packed up and went home. A few days later, Lester came to my door with the money. He had sold a batch of watercresses, he said. Every Saturday, thereafter, Lester would get fish from me whether he had money or not, and he always paid me sooner or later. When I see him now, nearly fifteen years since I stood in the parking lot selling fish, Lester often reflects on that summer. "Larry, you always sold the best fish," he says.

I was able to survive one full season on the water. When I pulled my last eel pot in November, I knew it was over. I loved the peacefulness of the work, the sunrise across the river, the sunset behind Urbanna, and the smell of salt water. But I hated getting stinging nettles in my eyes, the smell of creek mud all through my clothes, and not knowing from day to day if I would have any money in my pocket at the end of the day.

I had mixed emotions on that November day. There was a hint of winter in the air. All the eels, fish, and crabs were gone. What now? I asked myself. As I steered the skiff toward home for the last time, I couldn't help but cry. I waved to a waterman across the way at Payne's Crab House. He couldn't see my tears from there.

That winter I got a job at Southern States Granary. There I hardly made as much in a week as I made on a good Saturday in the parking lot. To bring in extra cash, I bought myself some muskrat traps and leased all the marshes at the headwaters of Urbanna Creek. Before going to the granary, I was up and out in the marshes hours before daylight. In January 1982, black "rats" were bringing $9.00 apiece, and brown, $7.50. Some mornings I'd make more money from my trapping than I would all day at work.

December and January had been good months in the marshes, but something happened in February that would bring my trapping days to an end. Trapping was hard, wet, cold work. Although it was peaceful to be back in those marshes with only a great blue heron or red tailed hawk to keep you company, cold hands and wet feet were an occupational hazard, and my mind was always on the cold. On this particular morning, there was a dusting of snow on the ground and a skim of ice across the marsh. My first line of traps was productive. I had three black rats and a mink. I was always excited when I caught a mink because I seldom did. As I waded through the ice to my next line of traps, I heard a noise that sounded almost like a human cry. When I made it around a bend, I came upon a family of otter working diligently on something in the marsh. They spotted me and dashed away, but not before my eyes caught the eyes of the largest otter. There was hatred in its eyes.

My traps were not designed to catch otter. They were made specifically to kill muskrat and mink on contact. A forty-five-pound otter had gone into the trap and apparently had been stunned or knocked out and had drowned when the tide had risen. As I hauled it over my shoulder through the marsh, I felt sick. As a boy, I had watched a family of otter live and play across the cove. I remembered the sounds of the crying family and the look of hatred in the mate's eyes toward the man who had killed her loved one.

Shortly thereafter, I decided it was time to at least attempt to utilize my education. I began writing for national and regional seafood publications. Several editors have said I am a natural at writing about the ways of the water. "You just seem to know the inside scoop on all that stuff," they have said.

I don't even pretend to know it all, but those months of crabbing, fishing, and trapping were a lesson in life that has helped me with my writing. After having been out there, I can appreciate even more those who depend on the water for their livelihood.

I would like to thank several people for their help on this project. Ray Rodgers has contributed much time and effort in drawings for several chapters. His work is outstanding, and whenever I've needed him, he has always been there to help. I would also like to thank my father, Henry S. Chowning, Jr., for reading each of these chapters for content corrections, and my wife, Dee Chowning, for reading the text for grammatical errors.

There are many others who have encouraged me to continue in the direction of my writings. Paula Johnson with the Smithsonian Institute; Jon Lucy, Mike Oesterling, and Diane Walker with the Virginia Institute of Marine Science; Chris Cornell, editor of *Professional Boatbuilder Magazine;* Willard Lockwood, former editor of Cornell Maritime Press; Fred Gaskins, publisher of the *Southside Sentinel;* and Tom Hardin, managing editor of the *Sentinel;* have all played an important role in my career.

CHESAPEAKE LEGACY

✻ Behind every good story there is usually another good story. While interviewing Woodland Rowe for the chapter on oyster packing houses, he happened to mention his boyhood days working with his father in a summertime hook-and-line fishery near the mouth of the Chesapeake Bay.

Although I was unaware that the fishery had existed, it seemed reasonable enough. Upon further research, I found it had indeed been a small but viable commercial fishery.

1 : Hook-and-Line Fishery

DURING ARCHAEOLOGICAL digs at Jamestown, Virginia, archaeologists uncovered spearheads and fishhooks used to harvest finfish. Early colonial writings and drawings tell a story of Native Americans luring fish to their boats at night by the light of fires built inside hollowed-out log canoes. When curious fish would come close enough to inspect the light, a spear was used to snag the unsuspecting fish.

The English also took up this practice, but one of the first fish management laws in the New World was passed to prevent this style of fishing. The law was promulgated in Middlesex County, Virginia, on March 4, 1678. Court records were quite specific about this prohibition:

> Several of the inhabitants of this county have complained against excessive and immoderate striking and destroying of fish . . . by striking them by a light in the night time with fish gigs.
>
> [These fishermen] not only affright the fish from coming into the rivers and creeks, but also wound four times the quantity that they take, . . . If a timely remedy be not applied . . . fishing with hook-and-lines will be thereby spoiled to the great hurt and grievance of most of the inhabitants of this county.
>
> It is therefore by this court ordered . . . it shall not be lawful for any of the inhabitants of this county to take, strike, or destroy any sort of fish in the night time with fish gigs, harping irons, or any other instrument of that nature.

From the very beginning, hook-and-line fishing played an important role in feeding the first settlers on the Chesapeake. One very large fish-hook was unearthed at Jamestown, which is believed to have been used to harvest sturgeon.

During the first years at Jamestown, colonists experimented with shipping the roe of sturgeon (caviar) to England. This venture failed, however, because salt was used to preserve the roe over the long trip. Interestingly, the roe did not spoil, but the salty flavor of the New World caviar was not accepted by the British nobility—the only segment of the population who then could afford such extravagant taste.

Shortly after this venture failed, tobacco became the mainstay of the New World economy, but the harvesting of fish kept the colonists fed.

Over the centuries, a small but active hook-and-line fishery developed on the Chesapeake. It paled, however, in comparison to the booming colonial haul seine fishery and, later on, the pound net fishery.

New Englanders, on the other hand, found the hook and line to be very effective, according to an 1880s report on the mackerel hook fishery by George Brown Goode and J. W. Collins:

> The men engaged in the mackerel hook fishery . . . were almost exclusively natives of New England. When this fishery was most prosperous (from 1850 to 1870) not less than 10,000 men and boys were employed on

This hand line is typical of the type used on the Chesapeake. Found in Essex County, Virginia, it was used on the upper portion of the Rappahannock River to catch perch and catfish.

Although the hook-and-line fishery paled in comparison with the haul seine and pound net fisheries, it was a viable commercial endeavor on the Chesapeake. Pictured is a fisherman working three lines at once. (From George Brown Goode's *Fisheries and Fishery Industries of the United States*, published in 1887)

board the vessels (schooners) belonging to the American fleet. The vessel engaged in this fishery carried very large crews; in fact larger than have ever been carried by other vessels.

Not infrequently a schooner of 80 to 100 tons would carry twenty men, and, in some instances, twenty-four. Among the crew were generally three or four boys, sometimes five, from ten to seventeen years of age. These boys fished from the extreme ends of the vessel; they were frequently very successful, and by the training in this fishery fitted themselves to assume responsibilities in the fishing fleet at a much earlier age than otherwise would have been possible. At sixteen or seventeen years of age, many of the boys ranked among the first of the crew to which they belonged, and it sometimes happened that the command of a schooner was given to the most enterprising before they were out of their teens.

The Chesapeake hook-and-line fishery was conducted almost exclusively near the mouth of the Bay and did not even approach the scope of the New England fishery.

Log canoes and frame-built workboats were used in the hook-and-line fishery on the Bay, but in New England large schooners were utilized as hand-line fishermen crowded together on deck to catch as many fish as possible. (From George Brown Goode's *Fisheries and Fishery Industries of the United States,* published in 1887)

Marshall McDonald wrote in an 1880 report that in Princess Anne and Norfolk Counties (including the city of Norfolk, Virginia) much of the male population was engaged in fishing, which included hook and line:

> From these counties, three thousand, two hundred and seventy persons are engaged either in the hook-and-line fisheries, the seine fisheries, or the oyster fisheries.
>
> The waters of Lynn Haven Bay abound in hogfish, croakers, trout, and sheepshead, the pursuit of which gives occupation to a number of hook-and-line fishermen from Norfolk and Elizabeth City Counties.

The same 1880 report stated that Elizabeth City County, also near the mouth of the Bay, employed two hundred men in the hook-and-line fishery. The value of the fishery was estimated at seventy-five thousand dollars. "The fish caught in this fishery are consumed mainly at the pleasure resorts lying around Hampton Roads, though some go to Norfolk [fish houses]," he wrote.

In Maryland, a very small commercial fishery developed when dams were built upriver and fish, trying to reach their spawning ground, were trapped at the base of the towering structures.

An 1831 news article in the *Susquehanna Democrat* stated:

> Great quantities of bass were caught in a small eddy formed in the river directly below the abutment of the Nanticoke dam. The fish apparently lay [*sic*] there in schools, and by drawing hooks through the eddy large numbers were caught.
>
> On Thursday and Friday last, a number of fine shad were caught in the same way. One man drew out nine in a day, and sold them for 50 cents each. This is the first instance within our knowledge of shad being caught with a hook.

There is little indication that Maryland commercial fishermen relied too heavily on hook and line, but in Virginia a sizable fishery was established in the early 1800s and lasted into the early part of the twentieth century.

One fisherman who recalls those days of pulling hand lines is Woodland Rowe. Woodland was twelve years old in 1921 when he first went to work with his father, Ralph Hall Rowe, and brother Achilles.

"Papa fished pound nets most of the year, but in the heat of the summer we would go hand-line fishing at the mouth of the Bay near Cape Henry," says Woodland.

Woodland Rowe fished with his father and brother in the 1920s in a commercial hook-and-line fishery near the mouth of the Chesapeake Bay.

"Papa had a forty-seven-foot, three-log canoe. It had been powered by sail when he first had it built, but I can just barely remember when he had a sail in her. Her name was the *Clara F.* and she was built by old man Jim Moore and Alex Hunt of Poquoson. In them days, you could get good timber to build a good boat.

"By the time I got so I could go with them, Papa had cut the mast out and put a twelve-horsepower two-cylinder engine in her. Papa loved that boat and, believe me, boy, she had a many a fish come over her washboards.

"In the summer, we would tie the pound nets up out of the water on poles and let them dry out. It was nearly impossible to keep pound nets clean when the water was hot, so most of the boys around home would tie them up and go hand lining.

"Early Monday morning, we would get in the boat and go to a fish camp at Back River Point at the mouth of Back River near Poquoson. We would never work on Sunday. Papa would get us up just after midnight when Sunday was over and we would take off. He believed that working on Sunday was a sin.

"On workdays, we would get up before day in the morning, have breakfast, and head on down towards Cape Henry and start fishing.

"I remember the first week I went fishing like it was yesterday. I got seasick the first day and begged Papa not to make me go back the next day. I've never felt that bad before or since. The second day, the same thing happened, and all through the first week I kept getting sick. Papa said the second week would be better, and it was. I didn't get sick and I've never been seasick since.

"Uncle Jack Robins was the cook at the camp, and he would cook for several crews. He was from Guinea Neck, too, and was my real uncle. He married my Papa's sister. He never fished. All he did was cook, and he was paid by the crews to do nothing but cook.

"When we fished, each of us would work two lines each. So, we had six lines overboard at once, and I have seen it when we would catch a thousand pounds of spot and croaker each. When they were biting, it's hard to believe, but as soon as you'd catch one fish there was another on the other line. I'd get so tired of pulling them in. It was hard work pulling fish after fish in by hand. My hands would ache at night.

"We fished with string line made from cotton, and we would have one end of the line wrapped around a cork. We used mostly number 8 and number 10 hooks and different weight lead sinkers. If the tide was running extra hard we used a big sinker, but if it was slack water we didn't use as big a one.

"It was not unusual for us to catch three thousand pounds of spot, croaker, and trout in five hours. Now, people might find that hard to believe, but it is the truth. I've seen it when we used all our crab bait and mussels up and had to put little balls of white cotton on the line. When fish were bitin', cotton will catch just as good as crab.

"When we finished fishing, there was always a buy boat ready to take our fish. We would sell to either the *Isaac Fass* or the *Irene and Pearl* [buy boats]. We would get a penny a pound. It didn't matter what kind of fish it was, we always got a penny a pound. When we each caught a thousand pounds in a day, that was thirty dollars and that was good money. In those days, five dollars would go as far as fifty dollars today. Gasoline cost ten cents a gallon and that was high. Thirty dollars a day—that was big money.

"We would stop fishing around noon, sell our catch, and head back to the fish camp. When we would get back, there wasn't much to do, so I'd help Uncle Jack with the cooking. It was hard work fishing and working at the camp, so when night came I was ready to go to sleep. The shanties were primitive, but it wa'n't so bad. People wa'n't used to having as much as they have now.

"I've been sent to the store with two eggs to buy my school pencils. That was when we didn't have a penny in the house, but old man Ben Rowe, who ran the country store, would take my eggs for payment. Can you imagine, a child trading eggs for a pencil today!

"We would fish Monday through Friday and sometimes on Saturday but we were always home before Sunday morning. In those days, if you couldn't go to church on Sunday, you wouldn't leave the yard. That was the old people's attitude.

"We attended old Union Baptist Church in Guinea Neck. There, the children always sat on the front row. I guess the old folks wanted to keep an eye on us. One Sunday, I went to a back pew of the church and sat down.

"Mamma came back and took me back up front, but I got a brainstorm and went to the back again. This time, she dragged me to the front and whipped me good right in front of everybody. To this day, I sit up front when I go to church," says Woodland with a chuckle.

"It is true, there are not as many fish in the Bay as when I was a boy," he says. "Some people think we overfished them, but I don't. I think the bridges and dams have done as much to change the fishing on the Bay as anything. When that Chesapeake Bay Bridge-Tunnel was put across there, the fishing went straight downhill. Those big trucks going across there scared them out of the Bay.

"We had a good time back in those days. It was different times, but it was all right."

✻ *The year 1994 marked the end of an era on the Chesapeake as Virginia officials banned the harvest of American shad* (Alosa sapidissima) *by commercial watermen. The state of Maryland has had a ban on the shad catch since 1980.*

The Virginia ban also marked the end of the annual shad planking sponsored by the Lower Middlesex County Volunteer Fire Department of Deltaville. I started covering the planking for the Sentinel *in the early 1980s and would eagerly await the coming of the event each year.*

I'm sad that it has ended. But, I'm sadder over what it reflects on the state of the shad fishery on the Bay.

2 : Shad Planking

WHEN THE English arrived, shad were being caught in abundance by Native Americans. Indians were using, among other means, stationary nets made from vines and bushes to catch the shad as the fish made their annual spring migration from the ocean into the Chesapeake. Native Americans, welcomed shad in spring as a tasty treat after a long winter of eating dried fish. Fresh fish was certainly a welcome sight.

William Strachey, an early English writer, described the fish in 1612: "Shad, great store, of a yard long and for sweetness and fatness a reasonable food fish; he is only full of small bones, like our barbels [fish] in England." He also noted that Indians preserved seafood by smoking.

Strachey gave a more detailed description of the method by describing how oysters were smoked and dried. "The savages used to boil oysters and mussels together and with the broth they make a good spoon meat, thickened with the flour of their wheat, and it is a great thrift and husbandry with them to hang the oyster upon strings and dried in the smoke, thereby to preserve them all the year."

Shad were cured in a similar manner, he wrote. The fish were attached to an oak plank and hung over the fire.

Interestingly, the English did not at first find the bony shad fish very appetizing. They did, however, learn how to prepare smoked fish on small oak planks from the American Indians.

Around 1700, shad began to appear as a staple on the tables of colonial plantations. Planking the shad was a culinary method of preparing the fish. By the 1800s, the shad fishery was well established on the Bay. One of the best descriptions of planking shad was written in 1837 by a Mr. Howell about the Delaware Bay shad fishery, not far from the Chesapeake:

> The writer has known sixty and seventy wagons supplied [with shad] in a day at Fancy Hill fisheries, six miles below Philadelphia. The great mass are salted like mackerel, and chiefly for domestic use. In the fresh state they are, in the height of their season, one of the most delicious of any of the finny race, and decidedly the best mode of cooking is that called planking, which consists of nailing the fish to a clean oaken plank, previously heated, and setting it before a brisk fire. By this method the juices of the fish are all preserved. They are sometimes treated like hams and are rubbed with fine salt, saltpeter, and molasses, and smoked for a few days, and in this way are very superior to those cured with salt alone.

As towns began to grow along the shores of the Chesapeake, community and church gatherings would include oyster roasts, fish fries, crab pickings, and shad plankings. These social and fund-raising gatherings are still held today in many Bay communities. As they did in the 1700s, the events play an important role in rural and small town life by bringing friends and neighbors together to socialize and enjoy the bounty of the Bay.

The most famous shad planking today is held in Wakefield, Virginia. This gathering is noted for drawing the most famous politicians in the state, who stump the crowds during election years. One shad planking, very similar to the old-time gatherings, is held annually in the Deltaville Firehouse in Deltaville, Virginia. The shad is prepared very much like it was by Native Americans.

A SHAD PLANKING

In April of 1992, some 450 people gathered at the Deltaville Firehouse as firemen smoked nearly nine hundred pounds of shad behind the building over an open fire. Inside the firehouse, others were frying the shad roe. The event has become a curiosity for many people who marvel at the methods used by the firemen to cook such a delicious meal.

"Yeah, it's just like the Indians did it," said fireman Henry Lackey, chef and chairperson of the event. "We've been doing this for fifteen years and a lot of people come around just to see how it's done. We do ours a

Members of the Lower Middlesex Volunteer Fire Department of Deltaville, Virginia, clean and cut American shad for their last shad planking. The fire company has held the annual spring event for many years but decided to stop in 1993 to support a 1994 Virginia initiative to save the species. The state has banned the commercial harvest of shad in Virginia waters.

little different from some people in that they use individual planks for each fish, whereas we use oak boards and are able to get more fish on a board. We think our way is faster and easier.

The traditional oak planks or boards allow the fish to be cooked close to the fire. "Oak can stand more heat than pine or some of the other soft woods," said Lackey. "If we used pine, it would catch fire."

Nails are driven through the underside of the board, and the fish are attached by pushing the flattened shad through a nail point on the board.

CUTTING THE FISH

The fish are cleaned and iced down the night before the shad planking. The heads of the fish are cut off, the fish are gutted, and the roe is removed

Before smoking the fish, firemen dip them in a special sauce.

(photo 1). After the cavity is cleared, a cut is made from the top of the fish, down one side of the backbone just to the top of the tail (photo 2). When the fish lies open flat from the cut, it is ready for the plank (photo 3).

THE RECIPE

Before being attached to the board, each fish is dipped in a special sauce. It took some arm twisting, but Lackey finally spilled the beans and gave out the recipe . . . or at least he gave out the one he wants the public to know about. There is another secret recipe, only to be fed to firemen, he later admitted.

The recipe came from a retired U.S. game warden who would not give out his source of the recipe. The sauce recipe is as follows: For every 60 pounds of shad, mix 6 quarts of lemon juice, 2 pounds of butter, 2 tablespoons of black pepper, 2 ounces of paprika, 1 ounce of Tabasco sauce, 2 ounces of La Choy soy sauce, and 8 ounces of Lea & Perrins Worcestershire sauce. Throw it all together and heat until it boils.

Each fish is dipped in this special sauce and then attached to the oak plank, which has been brushed thoroughly with cooking oil to keep the fish from sticking.

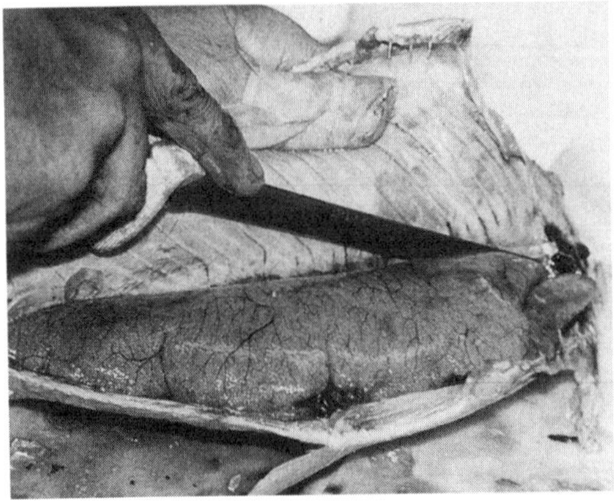

Photo 1

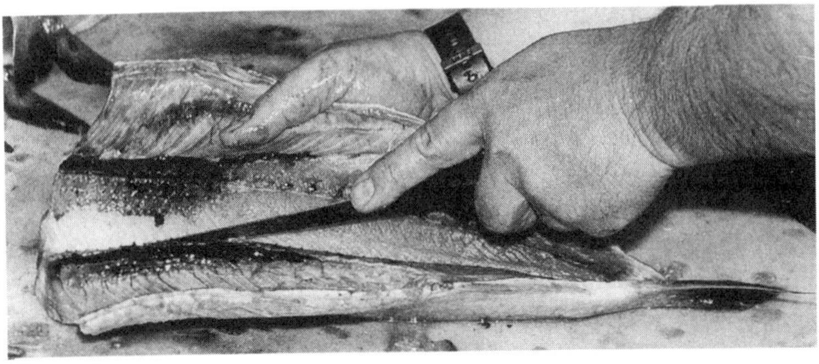

Photo 2

Photo 3

The cut shad are shoved through nails hammered into oak planks. The boards have been coated with vegetable oil to keep the fish from sticking. The planks full of fish are placed close to the fire and are smoked for hours.

From 8:30 A.M. until the hungry crowd begins arriving at 4:30 P.M., the fish cook on the open fire. Firemen baste the fish with the sauce every twenty to twenty-five minutes.

"The key is cooking it slow," said fireman Bobby Faulkner. "They say lemon juice helps to cook the bones out of shad, but the only real way to get rid of all the bones from shad is to throw it away," he mused. "Actually, the lemon juice and the butter give it most of its flavor."

The fire is constantly nursed along with slabs of pine and poplar. The wood came from a sawmill in King and Queen County. Slab wood is not easy to find, said Faulkner, because almost all sawmills use chippers now to grind up slabs into wood chip mulch.

To feed the multitudes, the firemen purchased 875 pounds of shad, which were caught by one York River fisherman in a stake gill net.

All the customers seem to enjoy the event. "We come to this every year and enjoy it just as much as the year before," said one participant, with his stomach full.

"I feel the firemen deserve a lot of credit," said Lydia Rock of Deltaville. "They are preserving a part of our heritage that people need to remember."

As in many culinary ventures, however, you can't please everyone. After eyeing the shad, one youngster asked for a hot dog. That's understandable: It took the English a hundred years to develop a taste for American shad.

Pine slabs are used to fuel the fire, and as it burns, a fireman wearing a gas mask bastes the fish with a sauce every twenty to twenty-five minutes.

The finished product drew hundreds of people to the annual Deltaville Shad Planking.

* *The idea of doing a story on salt herring goes back to* Harvesting the Chesapeake. *It was one of several ideas considered for that first volume, but I opted to save it for this second one. I'm glad now that I did, because I may not have gone to Mrs. Bettie James or Mrs. Louise Gray for their help on this chapter. Both of these wonderful women taught me at Middlesex High School and are much admired and respected by many for their contributions to community life.*

3 : Salt Herring

THE FIRST written mention of salt was in the Bible about 2,300 years ago, in the book of Job: "Can an unsavory thing be eaten, that is not seasoned with salt?"

For early settlers along the Chesapeake Bay, salt was a treasured commodity. John Smith and others who settled on the shores of the James River found fresh fish in abundance during warm-weather months, but in the winter, very few fish were caught.

Good refrigeration was still centuries away, so the main means of preserving fish and other meats for winter was by salting. Good salt, however, was not easy to find.

In *The Bounty of the Chesapeake,* James Wharton referred to the differences between the northern and southern colonies: "It was different in New England and Canada. There the fishing was good year round. . . . The cool temperatures over many months of the year made the catches much less perishable and conditions favored an organized fish salting industry.

"The New England salt fish industry blossomed and the best salt in the world was brought there from Lisbon, Portugal, to help the northern industry grow."

This was not the case in Virginia, though. Lack of good salt for preserving fish was an ongoing problem for Chesapeake Bay fishermen. Early laws established by Great Britain for only the southern colony contributed greatly to this. The mother country ruled that southern plantations could get commodities from other countries only if they were not manufactured in England. If manufactured in England they had to come from England. Salt was a British commodity. The problem was simple: British salt was not as good for curing fish as Portuguese salt.

This law was in direct response to Virginia's loyalty to the beheaded King Charles I. The southern colony was the last of Britain's colonies around the world to relinquish support of the fallen king. After the British Civil War, Oliver Cromwell, the new "protector" of England (1649–1658), placed restrictions on the southern colony so "it might never . . . give him further trouble. To this end, he thought it necessary to break off their correspondence with all other nations," Robert Beverley wrote in 1705 in *The History and Present State of Virginia.* A variation of this law remained on the books until the time of the American Revolution.

In the 1770s, George Washington faced the same problem of not being able to purchase good salt from other countries. He wrote in one of his business letters that Liverpool salt was inadequate for the curing of fish. Lisbon salt was the proper kind.

SALT MAKERS

Early on, the colonists tried to establish their own salt supply in the New World, and salt makers were sent to Virginia to build saltworks up and down the coast. As early as 1620, saltworks were built at Cape Charles on the Eastern Shore to take salt from the sea, wrote Beverley.

Salt-evaporating houses were located close to the ocean and Bay. The seawater was evaporated by being channeled into a large basin where natural evaporation could take place. Later, the water was channeled into large pans. A wood fire was built to hasten the process.

Solar evaporation was also a method used to make salt. One of the early "salt ponds" was constructed between what is today Fox Hill and Buckroe Beach in Hampton, Virginia. To this day, it is still called the Salt Pond. In 1776, this area was converted into saltworks where solar evaporation was used to convert the salty water into salt.

These early saltworks were scattered up and down the Bay and produced some salt but not nearly enough to feed a growing nation. Today, salt mines and salt wells produce most of the salt in the United States.

SALT HERRING

Salt herring and corn bread for breakfast were standard fare for most rural Virginia homes from the 1700s well into the twentieth century. Also, salt fish was a staple for most plantations located near a river or the Bay. These

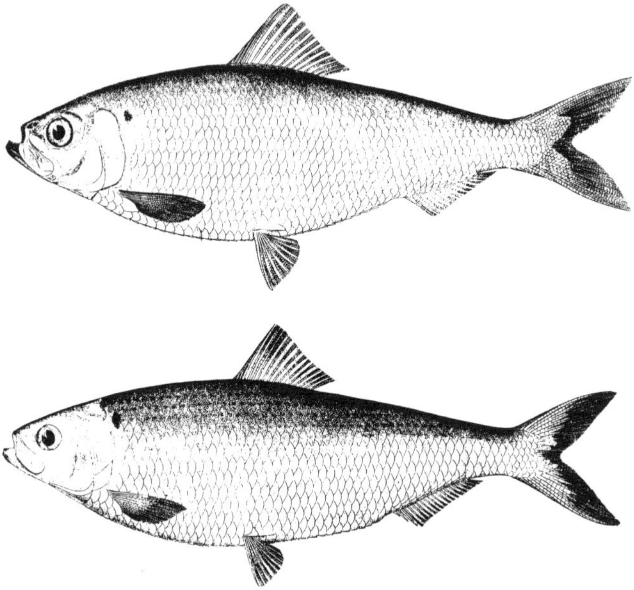

Branch herring (*Clupea vernalis,* Mitchill) (upper) and glut herring (*C. aestivalis,* Mitchill) (lower) are two species of herring caught on the Chesapeake that have for centuries been salted down and enjoyed by people living on the Bay. (From George Brown Goode's *Fisheries and Fishery Industries of the United States,* published in 1887)

mini-communities had to feed a growing slave population. Salt fish was one of the answers to this problem. In colonial times, haul seine shore nets were the main gear used to catch the millions of branch and glut herring that made their way up the Bay to spawn in the early spring.

Slave labor was utilized to catch the fish and cure them in salting houses on the plantations. On some plantations, each slave was allotted so many fish a month. At Mount Vernon, Washington allotted twenty salt herring a month per head.

Before the American Revolution, Virginia salt herring became known worldwide, as large sailing vessels would carry the herring to the West Indies and exchange the kegs of herring for rum and other merchandise. Rum was so plentiful in the southern colony that it was rationed to slaves, wrote Wharton.

The Virginia love of salt herring was passed on from generation to generation from colonial times right on up to the twentieth century. For

Since the early 1700s, herring has been salted down and used as a staple breakfast food in many Tidewater homes. This crock has been used for salting fish since the mid-1800s at Walboro, the family home place of Mrs. Bettie James in Saluda, Virginia. From use, it has hundreds of small hairline cracks. A piece of wire is wrapped around it to help hold it together.

both freeman and slave, salt herring was the food most favored for breakfast in Tidewater Virginia.

BETTIE JAMES AND LOUISE GRAY

Bettie James, ninety-four, was born in 1899 at her grandfather's farm just outside of Saluda, Virginia. Mrs. James still lives at Walboro, the family home, built by Philemon T. Woodward in 1852. The family's favorite breakfast food was fried salt herring roe mashed up with butter and spread over batter bread. The family recipe for salt herring was passed down from Grandpa Purkins.

Louise Gray was born in the family home place, Lewisville, in King and Queen County at the turn of the twentieth century. She grew up on the farm and at least twice a week ate salt herring for breakfast.

The following interview on salt herring was held on August 12, 1993 with Mrs. Gray and Mrs. James at Mrs. Gray's home in Saluda:

Mrs. James: "Every spring we would salt roe herring, and most people who have ever had our recipe think it's the best in the world. We would buy two hundred roe herring and put them up in [wooden] kegs or stone jars. Stone jars are better because the brine won't leak through the seams.

Not only were meat houses such as this one used for curing and storing pork and beef, but crocks filled with salt herring were stored in these houses through the winter. When the breakfast menu called for salt herring, it only required a quick trip to the backyard meat house to produce enough fish to feed the family.

One of the main staple foods for slaves was salt herring. At Mount Vernon, George Washington allotted twenty salt herring a month per head. At Walboro, salt herring was eaten regularly by the slave family that lived in this slave house still standing on the farm.

The family recipe for salting down herring is still used by ninety-four-year-old Bettie James, who lives in Walboro, her family home place just outside of Saluda, Virginia. Mrs. James's grandfather had Walboro built in 1852.

"The recipe calls for 200 roe herring, 1 quart of King Po-t-rik molasses, ½ pound of black pepper, 2 ounces of red pepper, 2 ounces of salt, and 2½ pounds of dark brown sugar. Mix all the above ingredients and warm on the stove.

"The key is not to remove the roe from the fish. We had a way of cutting the herring so when we pulled off the head, the entrails would come out, leaving the roe inside.

"Clean the fish, scale them, cut off their heads and tails, and draw the fish. Put the fish in a tub of salt water that will float an egg and soak overnight. Drain the fish on a board and pack them in the mixture.

"In the keg or crock we would alternate a layer of salt, layer of fish, and layer of mixture. Continue until all the fish have been treated. When the crock was full we would tie a cloth over the top to keep flies out.

"This was Grandpa Purkins's recipe, and he did love salt fish. When Mamma would cook, she would take the roe and mash it up with butter and put it on batter bread or biscuits. Lands, was that good!"

Mrs. Gray: "Some families used lard tins to salt their herring in, but the tin would rust and the fish would get a rust on them. The stone jars were better.

Bettie James

Louise Gray

"When the fish would get down some in the crock, we would take an old plate, one with a crack in it that we weren't using anymore, and put it on top to keep them down in the brine.

"The brine went down because when we took the fish out, we gradually lost some of it. When it would get low, the weight of the plate would keep the fish down in it.

"Our fish were stored in the smokehouse along with other meats.

"We cleaned our herring differently. We scaled them and cut the head off and left the tail. We split the fish evenly beside the backbone so they would lie flat. The guts and roe were removed.

"Then we would put a handful of salt and fish—some more salt and fish, some more salt and fish, some more salt and fish, et cetera, until the crock was full.

"Mamma would take the roe and put it in a pickle jar and salt it. She would take some salt, put it in the bottom of the jar, and then put roe down—salt and roe, salt and roe, et cetera—until the jar was full. We used the fish and roe separately.

Mrs. James: "We salted fish and roe all together. When you cut the fish head, you pull it around and it pulls the entrails out and leaves the roe. We don't split anything. The entrails would come out the front and leave the roe right in it.

"Then we would cut the tail off a little bit and soak them [the fish] overnight, and the next morning, we put them in the recipe."

Mrs. Gray: "We liked the fish flat because when we fried them they would cook down so crisp and nice that you didn't know that there were any bones in them—except the backbone.

"We would get our fish from Bowlers [Steamboat] Wharf [on the Rappahannock River in Essex County]. We were about eight miles from Bowlers and we would go over there in horse and buggy or wagon. Sometimes the fishermen would come around home in a horse and wagon selling herring."

Mrs. James: "Most of our fish came from the Rappahannock and York Rivers. We used to have a lot of hired hands on the farm, and they would have to be fed. And they helped with the cleaning of the fish. We salted the fish on our kitchen porch. There was a big chicken coop off the ground with a shelf on the back of it in our backyard. They would bring them [herring] and scale them on that chicken coop and then haul them up on the kitchen porch for salting. All our salt came in sacks from Neale's Store [general merchandise store] in Saluda."

Mrs. Gray: "Salt herring was standard breakfast food in rural Tidewater Virginia. We would buy a hundred fish for two cents apiece. The big farmers couldn't feed their hands much cheaper than that. They would give maybe a half a fish to a person. It was salty. You didn't want to eat large quantities.

"During slave times, the slave owners had the responsibility of feeding them. Salt herring was a cheap type of food."

Mrs. James: "When I lived over in Mathews County near Mobjack Bay, there was a place where they pickled herring. There were these big vats with brine and something else in it, but I don't know what it was.

"I was told that people in bars in Baltimore would eat this pickled herring while they drank beer.

"The herring were cut in slices, and the vats were bigger than this room." Mrs. Gray's living room was a good-sized room.

Mrs. Gray: "We depended on salt fish for winter food, just like storing vegetables in a hill. We would put potatoes, turnips, and other things and cover it up with straw and earth.

"We stored our grain. When the flour gave out, we would take some wheat and have it ground up at the gristmill.

"We were a typical rural family trying to achieve self-sufficiency—trying to have enough food to run us through the winter.

"Salt herring was just a standard thing. I think it goes back to the 1700s."

Mrs. James: "We usually had a cook who would cook it for us. She would soak the fish overnight to remove some of the salt. The next morning, she would dip it in cornmeal or flour and fry it up in lard to get it real brown. It was good eating. We ate salt fish two or three times a week with hot biscuits.

"Eating salt herring for breakfast was just a way of life for us."

✻ *In 1989, I made several trips to Gwynn Island in Mathews County, Virginia, to complete the chapter on pound nets for* Harvesting the Chesapeake: Tools and Traditions. *Wilson Rowe graciously helped me with that chapter.*

On one of my visits to Captain Wilson's home, he said to me, "Come on, let me show you something." We walked across a field and there he showed me the "kittle" (kettle) his father, George Vernon Rowe, had built over seventy years before to tar his pound nets.

I swore then, if I did another book similar to Harvesting the Chesapeake, *a chapter on tarring nets would be part of it.*

4 : Tarring Pound Nets

Pound nets were introduced on the Chesapeake Bay around 1870 by George Snediker of New York and Charles Doughty of New Jersey. They constructed the first successful net near the mouth of the James River. By the 1880s, the pound net was being used up and down the Bay. Its success as a gear form changed forever the way fish are caught on the Chesapeake.

Since nets remained in the water for months at a time, each one had to be coated to preserve it from rot and fouling. During the early part of the twentieth century, watermen dipped their cotton or Manila hemp nets in coal and gas tar. Coal tar was very thick and used primarily on new nets to give it an "extra" good coating. Gas tar was thinner and used to coat older nets that already had a good coat of coal tar.

When tar was applied to a net, it was heated in large cast-iron pots. On Gwynn Island, these pots are referred to by local watermen as kittles (kettles).

As other antifouling paints and preservatives were developed and watermen began using nets made of polypropylene, fishermen stopped using coal and gas tar. They began to use copper-based paints and asphalt-based preservatives, many of which do not require heating.

Wilson, Shelly, and Julian Rowe of Gwynn Island are three watermen who still tar their nets and use a kittle that is nearly seventy-five years old. Once a year in February after the brothers have mended all their nets,

This "kittle" was built to tar pound nets over seventy years ago by George Vernon Rowe on Gwynn Island in Mathews County, Virginia. It is still being used by his sons, Wilson, Shelly, and Julian Rowe. The three brothers have carried on the tradition of harvesting fish in pound nets, passed down to them by their father and grandfather. Pictured are, from left, Julian Rowe, Scott Bergman, and Buddy Mitchell waiting for the tar truck to arrive to haul the tarred bays off the drain board and out into a field to dry.

they heat up the old kittle and dip their nets in the tradition of their forefathers.

CAPTAIN WILSON REMINISCENCES

"Oh my golly, my daddy built this kittle when I was a young boy, probably seventy, seventy-five years ago. He went up the river [Piankatank] and got the pot off a big farm and came back and built the drain board and firebox into it.

"When I got grown, I had to get my own kittle because sometimes it was too wet to get to Daddy's. Yeah, and there were so many boys using his kittle that I didn't always get to use it when I wanted. I've still got my old kittle pot. It's turned upside down out there under the trees.

"During one winter, I've seen the day when fifty nets were tarred in Daddy's kittle. There were plenty of other kittles on the island, too, but Daddy would let anyone use his who wanted to. In those days, what your neighbor had was yours and what you had was your neighbor's.

"A many a time, I had to use my own pot to tar my nets. When I'd do that, I'd pull a wagon up with my horse by the pot and haul the net up in my old Studebaker truck. [The wagon was used as his drain board.]

"One time, Daddy, another man, and me were tarring a net at his kittle. It was before we started using trucks to haul nets to the field. We pulled Daddy's horse and wagon up by the drain board, put the tarred net in the wagon, and that horse got in a mire. All four feet went down in the mud, and the horse's belly was touching the ground. We should have known better because it was wet as I don't know what.

"There we were with a load of net on the wagon and the horse up to its belly in mud. We unhitched the wagon, and Daddy went and got a long board and shoved it under him. I got on one side and Daddy was on the other, and we pulled up on the board and finally got the horse out of there.

"I guess we tarred nets there for fifty years with just horse and wagon. Sometimes we would use two horses to pull the wagon. It would depend on how far we had to go to find a field to dry in. Sometimes we would have to go a ways to find one without nets already in it.

"Years ago, all we did was tar our nets, but later on we would tar in the spring and put copper to it in the summer. My granddaddy (Isaac W. Diggs) and all them old fellows only fished in the spring and early summer. They would fish a couple of deep-water shad nets in March and then put out their other nets in April. They'd quit the end of June and go do something else. He raised a big garden because there was always family and a house full of company there. He didn't care how many. He loved people.

"We put nets out in February to catch Labrador herring and shad, but my granddaddy wouldn't put a net out before March 21. He'd say, 'It ain't no need to put it out before line gale.' I don't know what 'line gale' means. I guess it means the sun crosses some kind of line. [It is the first day of spring, or vernal equinox—when the sun crosses the equator, making day and night of equal length.]

"Lord Jesus, there must have been 100 to 150 nets here on the island then, and what a sight it was when they were spread all over the fields. In those days, you could hardly find a spot to put your net.

"When copper paint came along, we started fishing in late summer because it would keep grass, barnacles, and dog stones off the net better than the tar."

Pound net fishermen use net copper—cuprous oxide—and other preservatives today to keep nets clean in the summer. Fishermen still prefer copper paint, but copper has been banned because of its detrimental effect on the environment. The Rowes use their kittle for summertime treatment, too, but the cuprous oxide is not heated. Some fishermen use the oxide for spring and summer treatment.

"There used to be three kittles right here within one hundred yards of one another," says Captain Wilson. "I don't know of anywhere else on the Bay where watermen are still using the old kittles like ours." Some fishermen dip their nets by hydraulically hoisting them off a flatbed truck and lowering the net down into a very large pot, made from fuel oil tanks, cut in half.

"Everybody used to use that old coal tar. It was damn thick stuff. You know how molasses is when it has been set out in the cold? Well that coal tar was just as thick. Sometimes you could hardly get it out of the barrel," continues Captain Wilson. "It was so thick, I would have to add a little bit of kerosene or fuel oil to thin it down. Granddaddy and Daddy didn't do it [tar nets] a damn bit different, except they didn't have the pickup truck.

"Daddy loved his horses. Topsy was the name of one that we had for a long time. She was a good horse. She was pretty as a picture. You could roll marbles down her back. [There was no sway in her back.] Topsy knew just where to walk and what to do, whether she was plowing a field or hauling a net wagon. But you had to watch out because all at once she'd run away and the devil couldn't catch her," laughs Captain Wilson.

"I had a nice net wagon. The last one I bought was brand new. I bought it over Mathews [County] Courthouse and towed it home behind my car. It had metal shaft tongues. She's around here somewhere on this island right now.

"The old net wagon Daddy used to use went back to my granddaddy. It's no telling how many hands it had been through. We rebuilt the wheels, framework, and every darn thing on her a many a time. It had wooden shaft tongues on her. Sometimes when we would back the horse and wagon up to the drain board, the horse would step on the tongue and snap it right in two. Good horses, like Topsy, would know to lift her foot off before she broke the tongue.

"Yeah, by Jesus, I used to have a time with horses. We had one that would run away and kick you, too. The man who sold him to me must have doped him up. The day he brought him over here for us to see, he would do anything. He went in the field and plowed and cultivated. We hooked the tar wagon to him, and he hauled a net from down the shore.

"He looked half-asleep all the time, though, and I should have figured he was doped up. By Jesus, a week later he started perking up and every day he was different. Daddy would say, 'We must have fed him something bad or maybe we fed him too much.' Finally, we had to get rid of him. We told the people we sold him to the truth about him. We weren't the type to cheat anybody, even though that guy cheated us.

"Yeah, boy, the days of tarring nets the old-fashioned way are just about over. What you saw today is a tradition that goes back to when the first pound net came here. Like I said, we ain't doing it much different from the way my daddy and granddaddy did it," says Captain Wilson.

FUELING THE FIRE

It is a warm, cloudy day when Captain Wilson and four other men go about the task of tarring his pound net in a pot full of Net-Set, an asphalt-based preservative. Some watermen, rather than heat the Net-Set, thin it with mineral oil, gasoline, or white kerosene. For Captain Wilson, firing up the "ol' kittle" is the only way to go.

At eighty-one years of age, Captain Wilson has tarred many a net in his lifetime and watched his father tar nets. He can remember when his father built the kittle in the backyard when Wilson was just a small boy.

As Buddy Mitchell stirs the hot tar in the kittle with a wooden paddle, Captain Wilson is on his hands and knees looking down the fire hole to make sure the red oak used to fire the kittle is burning hot enough. To keep the fire contained in the hole, a metal barrel top is used to cover the opening.

Before lighting it off, the oak wood was dipped in fuel oil. The fire was started with old newspaper and straw. It took about 1½ hours to get the fire hot enough. The reason it took so long was because rainwater had gotten into the fire hole, says Captain Wilson.

Buddy has lived on Gywnn Island most of his life and has worked with Wilson for many years. He suggested Captain Wilson mix pine wood with the oak to help get the fire hotter. "Nothing burns better than dry pine, but oak burns slower," says Buddy.

"It's warming up. I think I got it," says Wilson. "It don't make no difference the type of wood just so it ain't wet."

HISTORY OF TAR POTS

The tar pot is made of cast iron. Wilson's father took his boat up the Piankatank River and bought the pot from a farmer sometime in the 1920s.

Captain Wilson says most tar pots used on Gywnn Island came from farms. Big cast-iron pots were used in hog killing to scald hair off the hogs and "womenfolk used to boil lard into them and cook things," he says.

"My grandmother would cook cabbage outdoors in a big old cast-iron pot," says Captain Wilson. "They were big old forty- to fifty-gallon pots. She didn't cook no three of four pounds of cabbage either. I've seen her cook fifty pounds of cabbage. We had a big family, and anybody who came to her door was welcome to a meal. Plenty of folks came, too."

A wooden paddle is used to stir the Net-Set, and a touch of kerosene is sprinkled every so often on the fire to keep the blaze hot enough. The firebox is dug out under the pot, and a barrel top is used as a cover over the firebox. Buddy Mitchell is stirring the tar, while Captain Wilson Rowe checks the fire.

Once the net is tarred, it is dragged up onto a drain board. The drain board is slanted so tar, dripping off the net, will run back down into the tar pot.

The pots were also used on wash day to wash clothes. "My grandmother would boil the clothes in water, then rinse them out, wash 'em on a washboard, put them back in the pot of boiling water for a little bit, ring them out by hand, and hang them on a long clothesline that was strung between two giant oak trees in her backyard.

"The pots were all-purpose, but when we put tar in them, they wa'n't much good for anything but tarring," says Wilson. "It wa'n't easy to get that tar off a pot, so everybody had a pot for tarring, a pot for washing, and a pot for cooking."

DRAIN BOARD

The Rowes' kittle is unusual in that it is complete with a drain board, firebox, and chimney. Years back, most watermen fired their pots on an open fire and used a horse wagon as a drain board.

The Rowes' drain board is made of wood, built on stakes, and slants toward the pot. When the net is tarred and pulled up on the drain board, Net-Set, dripping from the net, runs down onto the drain board and back into the pot.

The net is loaded into a tar truck and stretched out in a field. Shelly Rowe drives the tar truck as Scott Bergman guides the net from the back of the pickup truck out onto the ground.

"We try to save every bit of tar we can," Wilson says. "We used to pay about $5 for a barrel of coal tar. A barrel of Net-Set cost us about $135. We don't want to lose a drop of that."

A roller is built into the front edge of the drain board, just above the pot, to allow the men to pull and roll the net up onto the platform with ease.

TARRING THE NET

"I like the fire so hot that when you touch the chimney it will burn the glove right off your hand," says Captain Wilson.

When the fire is hot enough, a pickup truck full of net is backed up to the tar pot. First, Shelly tars his dip net, a long-handled net used to dip fish from the pound head. After he sets the dip net aside on two barrels in the woods nearby, the crew pulls the pound net bays off the truck and drops the net into the hot tar. (A bay is a section of a pound net that helps direct fish into the pound head; see page 63.) After it lies in the tar for several minutes, Julian and Scott Bergman, standing on the drain board, pull the net out of the kittle and up onto the drain board.

After the net drains for several minutes, Shelly starts the tar truck. The truck starts with the sound of several small repetitive explosions. The

The nets are stretched out in the field and left there for several days to dry.

Wilson Rowe sits on a cast-iron tar pot he once used for tarring nets. At eighty-one Captain Wilson is still going out every day during the fishing season to work his pound net.

exhaust pipe on the Chevy is dragging the ground. The old truck has tar from one end of it to another. Its main purpose obviously is to haul tarred nets, not for "Sunday-go-to-meeting day."

The tarred bays are dragged onto the truck and hauled to a field, where they are spread out to dry. The hedging, pocket, and rest of the net are all tarred and hauled the same way.

After all the net is tarred and hauled to the field, all hands go out and spread the different parts so it will dry evenly. With the job done, Captain Wilson dumps water down the kittle chimney to kill the fire.

* *I was out on a pound net boat in 1989 on the Potomac River doing a story for* National Fisherman, *when Captain Eddie Gaskins suggested I do a story on trap-pole horses.*

I was amazed to hear horses were still being used to haul pound poles from the forest on the Northern Neck. When I got off the boat, I drove straight to Brown's Store in Northumberland County and hiked a good mile back into the woods where I found Ralph Thompson, his horse Midnight, and several other men cutting and hauling poles. There was quite a surprised look on their faces when I walked up on them with a camera around my neck.

This chapter is a good example of how old traditions of the Bay's fisheries have survived almost into the twenty-first century.

5 : Trap-Pole Horses

THE HORSE has played an important role in the evolution of the seafood business on the Chesapeake and throughout the United States. Before good highways, trucks, and railroads came along, the horse and wagon was the best means of transportation for fishermen to distribute oysters, fish, and crabs.

During the 1700s, 1800s, and early 1900s, a horse was as commonplace in a waterman's household as a pickup truck is today. When not hauling a wagon load of oysters to market or a freshly dipped pound net down the road to the landing, the family horse was being used to plow and till the garden or to pull the family buggy to church on Sunday morning. A good horse was not taken for granted.

Today, there is still a place for the horse in the seafood industry. Virginia forests abound with spruce and pine. These trees grow tall and straight and have been used by Chesapeake Bay watermen for years to hold the twine for the Bay's pound net fishery. (A pound net is a stationary trap formed of nets supported on stakes.)

Years back, pound nets were used extensively up and down the Chesapeake. This provided a lucrative business in February and March for local woodcutters. A good timberjack could fell one hundred poles a day. With a good horse, he could haul them from the woods and have them ready for market.

Most timberjacks had a horse trained just for pulling trap poles out of the woods. Today, one such horse is named Midnight. At thirty-three, Midnight is one of the oldest trap-pole horses still working. She belongs to Meade Hinton of Northumberland County and is worked by timberjack Ralph Thompson.

MIDNIGHT AT WORK

On this particular February day, I find Ralph and Midnight working far back in a stand of pine near Brown's Store. It is cool and sunny. Sweat mats Midnight's coat under her horse collar. The smell of a horse at hard work is a treat few experience today.

On a break, Ralph talks about his mare and all the hard work she has done over the years. "When she was young, she could pull a hundred poles a day," he says. "She can still pull fifty-five to seventy-five poles a day."

Trap-pole horses are still worked in several areas around the state. Virginia forests are dense and thick, and a horse can go up and down a ravine, through a briar patch or between trees, all the while pulling a pole, says Ralph.

"They haven't found anything that can do it any better than a horse," says Ralph as he holds Midnight by a rope rein. "How are you going to

This early twentieth-century photo shows fishermen near Fox Hill, Virginia, standing by a horse and wagon used to haul fish from the beach to a waiting trolley car. The trolley car hauled fish caught by area pound net fishermen to processing plants in Hampton, Virginia. (Courtesy of Charles Elliot)

Horse and wagon were used during the early days of this country and well into the twentieth century to haul fish to market. This line drawing from the 1800s shows the horses helping to haul a seine net ashore. (From George Brown Goode's *History of the American Menhaden* published in 1879.)

get a tractor through a wood as thick as that?" he asks, pointing to the nearby forest.

Demonstrating Midnight's ability, Ralph and the horse go back into the woods and show how the mare can maneuver about while dragging a sixty-foot pole. With a series of commands, he makes the horse pull a pole up a hill and down into a thicket so tightly covered with brush and trees that a gnat would have trouble squeezing through. Effortlessly, the large bay workhorse pulls the pole up onto the logging road and beside a large pile of cut logs.

When Ralph gives the command, "Gee, gee," the horse turns to the right. When he yells, "Haw, haw," Midnight turns left. "Come up" commands the horse to go ahead, and "back" means for her to back up. When Ralph yells, "Ho, ho" the horse stops in her tracks.

These days fewer fishermen use deep-water nets, which require at least fifty-five-foot poles; horses were used extensively when pound nets were being placed in deep water. When watermen began working in twenty- to thirty-foot depths, timberjacks were able to pull the smaller poles out by hand.

"Midnight is one of the best there has ever been," says Ralph, who has looked after the horse for sixteen years. "All she is used for is to pull pound poles. A good trap-pole horse is hard to come by. We have a young one now that we are trying to break for pulling poles, but it's not an easy job."

In 1993, Midnight was sold, and Ralph was asked to "fetch her" from the barn and lead her onto a truck to carry her away. "I was hoping to be

One of the last functions of the horse in the seafood business is the transporting of pine trap poles from the woods. Trap-net fishermen purchase some new poles each year, and trap-pole horses like Midnight are essential to the business. Here, timberjack Ralph Thompson of Northumberland County, Virginia, works Midnight as he has for sixteen years. Midnight recently retired at the age of thirty-five.

away on that day," says Ralph. "I thought she might put up a little fight, but she went right up on the ramp, and into the horse trailer, and he drove away with her. She was a lady to the end. I watched the truck go down the lane, and then I went in the house and cried."

✻ *When I was a boy, there were several pound nets set nearby in the Rappahannock River. On warm summer days, I'd often go out to the nets in my twelve-foot wooden skiff. I'd carry along my dog, Blitz, a Chesapeake Bay retriever who loved going along so much he would swim behind me for miles if I didn't let him aboard.*

Certain times in the summer, riders (doublers) would swim into the river and position themselves on the poles, just right for the plucking. (A rider is a female and a male blue crab that attach to one another when mating). I'd carry a crab net and basket to catch and hold the jimmies and sooks that were unlucky enough to have taken a rest on a pole just as I would come along.

It was some years later that it dawned on me those poles were more important to the men who were fishing the pound nets than to me. When considering this chapter, I remembered those days and what an important part they played in my growing up. It seemed only appropriate to include a couple of chapters on setting a pound net.

6 : Setting Pound Stakes

SETTING POUND stakes is a yearly chore for watermen working in the Chesapeake's pound fishery. The style of net used by Bay fishermen has changed very little since it was brought here in the 1870s. One thing that has changed, though, is the method used to install pound stakes.

Pine and spruce stakes are used to hold the stationary pound net in place. Each net uses 125 to 200 stakes, and the ways of installing poles vary from area to area. In the beginning, mauls and strong arms "as big as stove pipes" were the main tools employed to drive the poles into the bottom. These worked fine as long as the nets were being placed in shallow water or on a soft bottom. Later, as watermen began setting nets in deep water and on hard bottoms, fishermen concocted various forms of mast, boom, and block-and-tackle configurations to help with their task.

STRONG ARMS AND MAULS

Shelton "Shelly" Rowe of Gwynn Island, Virginia, a pound netter for over fifty years, knows something about installing pound poles. Shelly's grandfather, Ike Diggs, worked pound nets on Gwynn Island as a young man in the 1890s. All he ever used was a maul. Shelly has one of Ike's mauls, and, on occasion, he uses it himself to help set a pole.

Before the turn of this century, the maul was the main tool utilized in the pound net fishery to set pound poles. Shelly Rowe holds a maul his grandfather used to set poles in the 1890s. The maul is made from the stump of a hickory tree. The ends were smoothed down but the bark was not removed; there is still some bark left on the sides. Shelly says of his maul, "It's a man killer, and you've got to have some arms on you to handle this boy."

"My grandfather didn't know any different; he always used a maul," says Shelly. "When I was a boy, a lot of watermen used mauls. In my day, there were several fellows down near Hole-in-the-Wall [near Moon, Virginia]. They would drive by hand, and what they could not drive by hand they would pump and drive by hand at the same time." Pumping is a technique still used today. A water hose is lowered down near the pole, and when the running water hits against the bottom, it softens the mud around the pole.

"I've seen them stand on boxes, one fellow on one side and one on the other, and just drive them right down," says Shelly. "Sometimes they stand on the washboards or in the bottom of the boat. It just depends on how high the stake is up. One on one side and one on the other, and they would never miss a stroke. Never miss a stroke.

"The type of bottom tells you what you need to use. If you've got mud bottom in shallow water, you can drive it in by hand, but if you've got pipe clay mixed with sand, you can drive by hand but you've got to pump, too. Now, we got a spot up the Bay where there is pipe clay mixed with gravel. All you got to do is put them in about eighteen inches and they will stay there forever. Last year, we made the mistake of putting some in three feet and at the end of the year, we couldn't draw them out. We hit them about 250 to 300 pile driver licks to get them down. That was too many damn licks, I can tell you that."

Virginia law requires pound pole stakes to be taken up each year at the end of the fishing season. Shelly says he contacts the Virginia Marine Police when he is unable to draw the stakes. "I always call the inspector about those poles. I couldn't draw them to save my life. I do get them up eventually. I wait for the worms to eat around the bottom, and then I break them off."

PILE DRIVERS

Another tool used to install pound poles is the pile driver. Early pile drivers were similar to those used today by some Chesapeake Bay watermen. The only difference now is that gasoline and diesel engines provide the power to hoist the driver up into the air and drop it down onto a pole. Early on, the driver was hoisted by hand.

Shelly has one of the oldest pile drivers on the Bay. Most of his poles are installed by driver. "My daddy and I started using a pile driver because of those deep-water nets. We had two deep-water nets in thirty-two foot of water. The nets were just inside the ship channel, and the poles were fifty-five feet long. You'd best believe, we didn't want to drive them by hand. It was on mud bottom, and we had to put the poles in the bottom eight to ten feet to hold them.

"Those were good catching nets. We would set it in February to get those early runs of herring and shad," says Shelly. "They were good

A pile driver is one of the oldest methods of driving pound poles into the bottom of the Bay. The main components of the rig are the wooden runner, steps, and driver. The runner (or track) extends over the washboards on the starboard side of the boat and guides the driver (a 550-pound iron weight) onto the top of the pole. The steps support the runner and are attached on the port side at the base of the pile driver and reach upward to the top of the runner. The base of the wooden pile driver extends across the boat and is bolted to the washboards to keep it steady in rough seas.

The driver, a 550-pound iron weight, sits in the runner. A very strong rope is used to move the weight up and down.

summertime nets, too. We caught a lot of what we called hook fish—croaker, spot, trout."

The pile driver on Shelly's vessel is stationed so it is worked from the starboard side of the boat. The main components of a pile driver are the runner, steps, and driver. The wooden runner (or track) extends over the washboards on the starboard side of the boat and guides the driver (an iron weight that can weigh as much as 550 pounds) onto the top of the pole as it is being set. Wooden steps support the runner and are attached to the port side of the boat at the bottom and to the top of the runner.

A wooden fair lever (a device shaped like an H with a hole in the middle) is used to hold the pole in place. The fair lever attaches to the runner, and the pole fits through the hole. On some pound boats, a large truck brake and a modified automotive clutch start and stop the reel, which is used in hoisting the weight up into the air. A foot pedal controls the reel, and a hand lever puts the reel in gear to lower the driver. Shelly's driver is powered by a World War II–vintage Wisconsin air-cooled engine.

When Shelly first got started in the pound net business, he would drive poles with a 100-pound driver that was hoisted up by hand; later, a two-cylinder donkey engine was used to hoist a 250-pound driver. There was no clutch or brake system then. The rope was put around a winch head that ran off the main engine.

Shelly's forty-eight-by-fourteen-foot *Maid King* is a classic Chesapeake Bay pound boat. Built about seventy years ago by the late Lennie

A rope tied to the driver extends upward to the top of the runner and runs through a pulley and back down between the steps to another pulley attached to a forward bulkhead. The rope then leads to a winder.

A wooden fair lever is used to hold the pole in place while it is being driven into the bottom. A line tied to one side of the fair lever keeps the loose side from falling overboard when a pole is being positioned in the runner.

Smith of New Point, Virginia, the *Maid King* is one of the last of its kind left on the Bay. Most pound boats—usually built in the 1920s—have been restyled for other fisheries.

Shelly's vessel was built shortly after watermen began installing internal-combustion engines in their boats, and the *Maid King* has several characteristics of early commercial sailing vessels. The most noticeable is the rudder steering-stick system.

"When I got the *Maid King,* she was about gone. I took her and fixed her up by putting piece by piece back in her. You'd spend a barrel of money if you tried to fix her all at once. Christ, a whole damn barrel full," he says.

"I just patch her up to keep her going. I'm real easy on her. When I go out there to draw stakes and it gets rough and snatching on her, I just come on home. I know she won't take but so much. Sometimes I don't know how she takes what we put on her."

DANGEROUS WORK

"It's a lot easier to put stakes in with a pile driver, but I tell you the truth, I'd rather do it with a maul," says Shelly. "I've always been scared of that sucker. Whatever she hits, she cuts off."

Shelly Rowe shows how a fair lever is positioned in the runner.

Shelly holds up his right hand, showing a finger that has been partially cut off. "She hit that finger right there, and I've got no feeling in it to this day," he says. "It was real rough the day we were out there, and I was trying to hold us in close to the pole, and I got my finger in there someway."

"That rig on the *Maid King* is just like what my daddy used years ago. The first time I used one of these was with my daddy. The net was up on old Haven Bar right straight to the east of Hole-in-the-Wall. It was halfway between the shore and the ship channel, in about thirty feet of water. That was a hard place to keep a net. The tide was always running strong. Me and my daddy had three nets. We had two deep-water nets and a shallow-water net. The shallow one was in twenty-two feet of water. The one I got now is in eighteen feet.

"This is hard to believe, but when I was a boy, there were a hundred shallow- and deep-water nets behind this island. Now, there is one. Mine!

"Hard to believe, ain't it?"

A MODERN METHOD

Another fisherman who uses a different style of rig is Eddie Gaskins of Ophelia on the Northern Neck of Virginia. Eddie works two nets on the

The winder is powered by World War II–vintage Wisconsin air-cooled engine. A large truck brake and a modified automotive clutch start and stop the reel. A foot pedal controls the reel, and a hand lever puts the reel in gear to lower the driver. The capstan on the side of the reel is used to pull the anchor or to pull old pound stakes out of the bottom.

The *Maid King* is a classic deadrise pound boat. It was built in the 1920s by Lennie Smith of New Point, Virginia, not long after the transition from sail to combustion engine took place, as evidenced by the steering stick on the stern. This is a typical steering stick found on sail-powered work-boats. Later on, wheels mounted inside the boat and side-mounted sticks took the place of the stick-rudder steering system. Shelly Rowe uses the *Maid King* to drive poles in the spring and to "snatch" the pine poles out of the mud when the fishing season is over. The vessel is rigged with a pile driver to set poles by.

Potomac River and one on the Chesapeake Bay. He can set six hundred poles in a week if the weather is good. He does this in February before fishing begins in March and April. To drive the poles, Eddie uses a mast with two booms on his vessel.

Eddie's modern driver is made from a pipe capped at one end and with handles attached to either side. Two men stand above the pound pole, guiding the driver as it hits the stake. A rope attached to the driver goes up to a block on the boom and down to a winch head on the main engine. One man guides the rope on the winch head while others handle the driver.

When the Bay bottom is soft, Eddie's rig will drive the poles with little trouble, but on hard bottom, the poles are driven and "blown" into

A more modern method of setting pound poles is demonstrated on the *Martha Virginia*, owned by pound net fisherman Eddie Gaskins. Here, the crew of the *Martha Virginia* set stakes in the Potomac River.

the bottom. Also, small-diameter poles placed close together are used on hard bottoms because bigger poles are more difficult to set.

When the poles are blown in, a water hose is tied to the bottom of the pound pole, and 1¼-inch Jabsco pump hooked to the main engine pumps water to the hose. The flowing water helps to work the pole down. Once the pole is set, a trip line releases the hose, which is pulled to the surface, leaving the pole in the bottom.

Eddie uses thirty- to forty-foot-long spruce and pine stakes that are eight inches in diameter on the butt and three to four inches on the little end. A point is made on the bottom of the pole with a chain saw, and all knots are chopped and smoothed with an ax.

The bark is left on the poles. Some fishermen use copper paint on the lower ends of the stakes, but not Eddie. He says that he doesn't see any reason to use the paint, because by the time he gets the poles set, most of the copper has been knocked off.

At the pound site, Eddy drops four anchors to keep the boat running straight up and down the Potomac River. One anchor is taken straight out

Captain Eddie Gaskins holds a stake steady as crew members pound the pole into the bottom. The driver is made from a capped pipe that is raised and lowered by power from the main engine.

The bark is left on the stakes, and a point is cut into the bottom of each one with a chain saw. All knots are chopped and smoothed out with an adz. These poles are ready to go into the water.

from the bow in a skiff and dropped overboard. Another is carried out from the stern, and two others from the port and starboard sides. During rough weather, a fifth anchor is often used.

Once the first pole is set, a string is used as a guide to position the rest of the poles. "A lot of people think you just come out here and put the poles wherever you want, but there's a lot more to it than that," says Eddie. "The way a pound net is set, many times determines whether or not it will catch."

POLE HUNCHER

Although Eddie never used a maul to drive a pole, he does recall driving a pole or two by hand. He used a tool called a pole huncher. The metal tool has a vise in the middle that screws down on the pole. Handles extend from either side so two men can lift the tool and pole up and down and work it into the bottom.

The work was mostly done by hand, but Eddie recalls when power was utilized. A rope was extended from a winch head, up to a block and tackle at the top of the mast, and down to where the men were working.

The rope was tied around the stake and pole huncher. As it was raised and lowered by power from the main engine, two men held onto the handles to keep the huncher positioned over the hole. "We would hold onto the handles, and when it went up in the air and came down, it was as good as riding a roller coaster," says Eddie.

"The way we do it now is a lot better than using that old pole huncher," he says. "It took a lot of experimenting to get to where we are today."

Before gasoline engines were used to help drive stacks, some watermen on the Potomac River used a pole huncher. This viselike tool allowed fishermen to hold the pole steady while two watermen, one on one handle and one on the other, would lift and shove the stake into the bottom.

✻ *Initially, I had planned to write about setting pound stakes and nets in one chapter. But after spending the day with Eddie Gaskins and his crew aboard the* Martha Virginia, *I realized each task merited its own chapter.*

I first met Eddie in the early 1980s. Over the years, he has been a great help to me in my efforts to record and preserve the ways of the water. His success as a Chesapeake Bay waterman is a tribute to hard work, traditional upbringing, and an astuteness to bring together the best of the old and new ways of working the water.

7 : A Day on the Chesapeake Setting a Pound Net

ON THIS April day, there is a foggy haze over Ellyson Creek just off the Little Wicomico River on Virginia's Northern Neck. Captain Eddie Gaskins and his crew are aboard the *Martha Virginia,* heading out toward the Chesapeake Bay to set a pound net.

Eddie already has two nets set on the Potomac River that he has been fishing for several weeks. He plans to set this net in the Bay at a point near where the Maryland and Virginia lines connect, just across the Maryland line.

Eddie is a thoughtful, friendly man in his late forties. His face bubbles with energy, and his soft-spoken, easygoing manner is refreshing and indicative of a man content with his life.

He grew up in Ophelia on the Northern Neck and is a third-generation pound netter. He won't admit it, but he is one of the more successful pound netters on the Bay. This is partly due to his progressive approach to marketing, but mostly because he's a damn good fisherman. Eddie has his own walk-in freezer, which enables him to hold his fish and wait for better prices. He also markets most of his own fish rather than selling wholesale to a fish house. This way he cuts out the middle man and is able to get more for his catch.

Eddie's freezer and piers are located in Ophelia, just down the road from Sunnybank, where a quaint two-car cable ferry crosses the river.

The age-old tradition of setting pound nets on the Chesapeake in the spring involves hours of labor and knowledge that goes back hundreds of years.

His waterfront property has been in Eddie's family for many years. It belonged to his grandparents and has been passed down from father to son.

HEADING OUT

As the *Martha Virginia* and its captain and crew head out toward the Bay with four seine skiffs under tow, Eddie talks of his life as a Chesapeake Bay waterman: "When I was in my twenties, I was crab potting in the spring and summer and crab dredging in the winter and fall," says Eddie. "One day, Nelson Mitchell from over in Irvington [Virginia] came to me and asked me if I wanted to go pound netting with him. I did, and I've been doing it ever since. I bought Nelson out about twelve years ago and went on my own.

Eddie Gaskins of Ophelia, Virginia, fishes pound nets in Maryland and Virginia waters. He is a third-generation pound netter and one of the more successful fishermen on the Chesapeake.

"When I started with Nelson, he was getting old and he needed someone he could count on to help him. From the start, we agreed that I would buy him out one day, and when he was right much older I reminded him about that.

"He was one to always hold his words, but I could tell he didn't want to give it up right yet. So I told him, 'Why don't we become equal partners and every year we can renew our contract until you are ready to sell?' That's what we did until he got too old to fish.

"One day, he came to me and said it was time for him to quit. I'll never forget the look on his face. He didn't cry. Nelson wouldn't cry, but there was a painful look on his face.

"Nelson died nine years ago, and I owe an awful lot to that man. I had worked in the pound net business some as a boy, but he taught me the ways of the trade."

WEATHER, GROWING OLDER, AND CHILDREN

"It's been rough weather this spring," continues Eddie. "I told my wife this morning, I would be glad to get this spring behind me. Every day it's either been blowing a gale or it's a thick fog."

While keeping a close eye on the four skiffs, he switches topics. "I always heard the old boys say, 'Do what you're going to do when you're young because your time is short on this earth,'" says Eddie. "We've lost a lot of good watermen this year.

"Frank Lewis was just fifty-two years old when he dropped dead of a heart attack. We're going to miss him. He was a good waterman and a good man.

"It wasn't so many years ago, I thought I'd never die. When you are young, you don't always think clear. You start thinking clearer when you have children of your own. I got two sons and I tell them all the time, 'Go to school, get that education, and don't go in the water business.'

"The water business is a rough life in some ways. I've thought a lot about trying something else, but I can't come up with nothing. You see, we are so few now and the sports fishermen are so many that we don't count for much anymore. They've got a lot of political clout.

"Some people don't look at what we do as a business, but if they had to pay all the insurance and other things I've got on my men and my boats, they would think it was a real business.

"When my father was a boy, all he had to do was work the water. Even if he did find something else, he always knew the river and Bay were there to support him if things didn't work out. It was a type of security that I don't have anymore.

"I look at my two boys, Edward and Paul, and I tell them, 'Get that education!' Education is just like the river was for my father and grandfather; it is something you can count on to help support you when other things don't work out. My boys may fish for a living, but I want them to be able to have a way out if things fall apart. I don't see too many ways out for me. I guess I'm in it for the long haul. I remember Nelson's look on his face the day he told me he was quitting. I hope I never feel that bad.

"Boy, this fog is something," he remarks as he slows the engine of the *Martha Virginia* to get her and the skiffs through the narrow jettied channel of the Little Wicomico that opens into the Chesapeake Bay.

"This is a rough spot," he says, referring to the mouth where the river and Bay meet. "Last spring, we were coming out when one of those little square-nosed skiffs was rolled over in the channel. The young people were in the water, and an old man was hanging to the bottom of the skiff that was floating upright. We got the young people, and I yelled over to the old man, 'Can you swim?'

"Yeah, but I ain't going to let go of this boat,' he said. We got him in the boat and got the skiff over to the shore."

GOOD FISHING SO FAR

Eddie maneuvers the boats through the narrow channel and heads out into the Bay. "Everyone thinks fishing has been bad, but we had a good year last year," he says. "There were plenty of spot out here and more flounder the last two or three years than anyone has ever known of around here."

"Bluefish have dropped off, but I can remember a time when it was real unusual to catch a bluefish," he says. "Rockfish are everywhere now. We threw back two thousand pounds on Monday." Rockfish or striped bass are protected in Maryland and Virginia and can only be caught during commercial seasons.

"It was hard on us at first to throw them back. It would make you want to cry, but it doesn't bother us now. We've gotten used to it," says Eddie. "We landed one hundred and some boxes [a box holds one hundred pounds] of bunkers [menhaden] yesterday in the two nets."

A large portion of Eddie's business is the sale of bunkers for bait to crab potters and to fish houses that sell the bait to potters.

SETTING THE NET

"The fog has shut in on us," says Eddie. "Some days we can't see the shore part [leader] of the net because it's so foggy." As Eddie goes past a large raft of bufflehead ducks, he says, "There have been more ducks this year than usual." A pair of cormorants sails past the *Martha Virginia.* "There have been plenty cormorants too."

"I see a pole," says Eddie. "I hope it is the right one. It would really be something if you had to put it in your book that the captain got lost out here."

"Yeah, that would be something," says Wayne Gough, one of Eddie's crewmen. Wayne was captain of a menhaden fish steamer on the Gulf of Mexico before he started working for Eddie last season.

Eddie, Wayne, and the rest of his crew, Bret Mitchell and Kendal Deihl, arrive at the stakes around 8:30 A.M. They had installed the leader

Eddie pulls the seine skiff as his crew release and fasten the seine to the poles.

portion of the net the day before. The leader mesh extends from the water surface to the bottom. The top of the mesh is tied to the hedge poles with half hitches. A solid half-inch chain runs along the bottom of the leader to hold it down.

Today, they will install the pocket, pound, and heart and will have completed the task by 2:30 P.M. The six-hour job starts with Eddie in a sixteen-foot pound skiff powered by a twenty-five-horsepower Yamaha outboard engine. He tows the four seine skiffs full of net out to the pound pocket. Although the *Martha Virginia* is just a few hundred yards away, she is barely visible. The fog seems to have swallowed her whole.

The pocket is installed first. The three crew members are in a large skiff. Eddie tows the skiff close to the pound stakes, and a crew member reaches out with a gaff and pulls the seine skiff inside the pocket. They start by tying the top of the net to the stakes on the north side. The tide is running north to south; its flow will help stretch the pocket across to the other stakes.

"Let's hope the tide stays like this," says Eddie. "If it does, we will be finished in a hurry. It can be mighty hard work when the tide and wind are working against you."

Once they tie off several stakes, Eddie secures the larger skiff to his skiff and begins to pull it across the pocket, stretching the net as he goes.

The crew helps by shoving the net overboard as it stretches across the pocket. Round grab chains, tied to the bottom of the net, are slid over each corner stake to help hold the pocket in place.

Eleven grab chains are used altogether. Six are used in the pound, and five in the pocket. The net is tied to the stakes with an eight-foot becket. A becket, made of half-inch nylon line, is tied to the top of the net and to the pole. This holds the pocket in place and allows the men to pull the net up and tie it off to check for holes and other problems.

Once the pocket is tied down, Eddie goes back to the *Martha Virginia* and brings the pound net and some Diet Cokes for the crew.

The pound head and heart are put in place the very same way, with Eddie pulling the net across the pound head and beckets and grab chains used to hold it in place. On the heart, or bays, the lines are tied directly to the top of the net with twine.

PORCH MONKEYS

The men all work hard without taking a break for lunch. "We got the tide helping us," says Eddie. "We've got to move as quickly as we can. These boys know their business. When you are putting a net down, you don't want a bunch of porch monkeys out here helping you."

Eddie and the crew all laugh. One of the crew members yells over to Eddie, "You're going to get it now, calling those city folks porch monkeys."

"Well, that's what they are," replies Eddie.

"A hundred years from now, people are going to read this and laugh about me calling them porch monkeys," says Eddie. "It's just like they call them chicken-neckers up in Maryland because the city boys use chicken necks to work a trotline."

MORE ABOUT THE NET

While the crew tie the top of the bay to the stakes, Eddie, using beckets, ties support lines on the north side of the net to sixteen brace poles. There are only six brace poles on the south side because the worst weather comes from the north. "The north side needs all the support it can get," says Eddie.

There is also a battery-operated light on one pole to keep night traffic away from the stationary net. The nets on the Potomac and Virginia portion of the Bay require a reflector, but pound nets in the Maryland portion of the Bay must have a light.

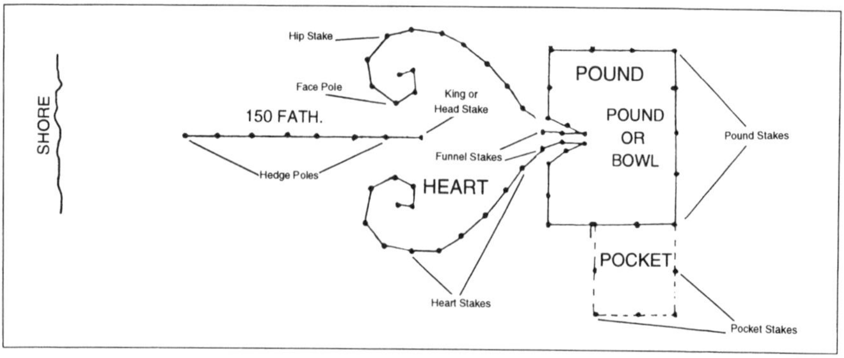

Diagram of a pound net with a pocket and one heart, or bay. The bay leads into a funnel, which leads into a pound bowl, or head. This style of net is used by Eddie Gaskins and his crew. A pocket net is easier to fish than one with just a bowl because the pocket is smaller and lighter, says Eddie. This makes it easier to haul the fish from the pocket into the seine skiff and requires less labor. (Courtesy of the Virginia Institute of Marine Science)

"I don't know if the light helps or not," says Eddie. "Some boys down the Bay say the light hurts because people in boats will run to a light at night.

"One thing for sure, it doesn't always help. We had a barge go through this one four years ago. It was a mess. When it happens, the first thing you do is get a lawyer. The day before you carry them to the courthouse steps, they will settle, but not before that day," says Eddie.

"Not everyone uses a pocket in their nets," says Eddie. "Our style is an old style of doing it. Walter Coles Burroughs [a Mathews County, Virginia, fisherman] said pocket nets don't catch nothing. I guess he figures I've been starving to death all these years," laughs Eddie.

"The advantage to a pocket is you don't need as many men to fish it because it is smaller. When you fish just the pound head, you need a lot of help to pull up all that net." The pound head is at least twice as large as the pocket.

On the bow of Eddie's skiff is an electric winch. It is used to pull the corners of the net tight when the tide is "flying" and to help pull up pound stakes at the end of the season. "We started using the winch several years ago," says Eddie. "When I told Walter Coles about it, he laughed. Later on, he tried one and said it was the greatest thing since loaf bread."

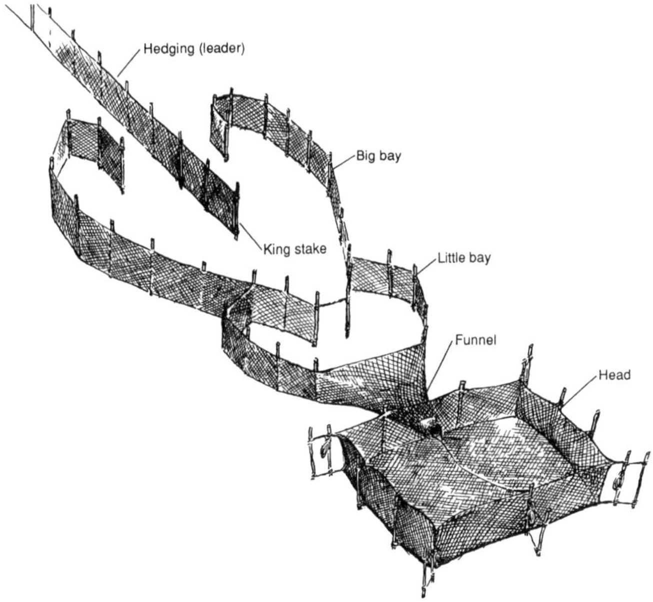

Diagram of another style of pound net without a pocket. It also has two hearts, or bays, a style seldom seen on the Chesapeake today. Gaskins says this style is harder to fish, but some watermen on the Bay prefer using just a pound head. (Courtesy of the Virginia Institute of Marine Science)

JOB DONE: HOMEWARD BOUND

As the day wears on, the fog lifts. The tide remains steady and aids the watermen's work all day. When the job is done, Eddie and his crew head for home. "Everything went smooth today," says Eddie. "We've been out here when the old Bay would nearly beat us to death."

During the trip home, Eddie talks about his wife, Diane. "The first fifteen years of our marriage, Diane kept me afloat. I wouldn't have made it fishing if it wasn't for her. It took several years to build this business, get the freezer, and establish myself," he continues. "Without her help, I couldn't have made it."

Diane was a bank manager for many years before stopping her outside work to raise a family. "We are a very traditional family," says Eddie. "Most watermen are that way."

Back at the dock, Eddie and the crew clean up from a day's work. A laughing gull perches on a piling nearby, and an osprey soars high overhead. The afternoon is still young as Eddie and crew drive away. Tomorrow they'll go fishing.

✳ Several months after I published an article about two Mathews County, Virginia, boatbuilders in the October 1991 issue of National Fisherman, *I received a letter from Charles Elliott, the grandson of a boatbuilder down in the Fox Hill area of Hampton, Virginia. Charles related to me a story of a very lucrative pound net fishery that existed off the Grandview/ Buckroe beach area from the 1880s to the 1950s and the unusual boats that were used by fishermen in that fishery.*

I was certainly intrigued by Charles's letter and decided to make the trip to his home at Buckroe to find out more about these boats. He graciously shared with me his extensive knowledge and photo collection of the boats and people of old Fox Hill.

8 : Chesapeake Bay Fishing Bateaux

SHORTLY AFTER the old Works Progress Administration (WPA) was formed in 1935, a group of naval architects and draftsmen joined this government program. The WPA was started to help put the nation's work force back on the job.

The draftsmen were given the task of documenting the many types and styles of commercial fishing vessels used throughout the country. The compiled drawings were part of the "Historic American Merchant Marine Survey." One of the drawings was of a Chesapeake Bay fishing bateau built in 1920 by Matt Elliott of Fox Hill, Virginia.

Interestingly enough, the use of "Chesapeake Bay" as part of the name is somewhat inappropriate, as the total length of the Bay's shoreline, if unraveled, would cover eight thousand miles. The bateau, however, was mainly utilized on a stretch of beach about six miles long, designed exclusively for the fishermen who worked that shoreline.

The boats ranged in length from twenty-five to thirty-two feet. The blunt-end skiffs were designed to easily be maneuvered through the rough surfs of the Grandview/Buckroe beach area and to be hauled up on the beach with relative ease.

The fishermen of Fox Hill had access to some of the best fishing grounds on the Bay and also to an excellent market. A fish processing and packing house was located on the beach, where a trolley car would come daily from Hampton, Virginia, to pick up the fish. The fish were hauled

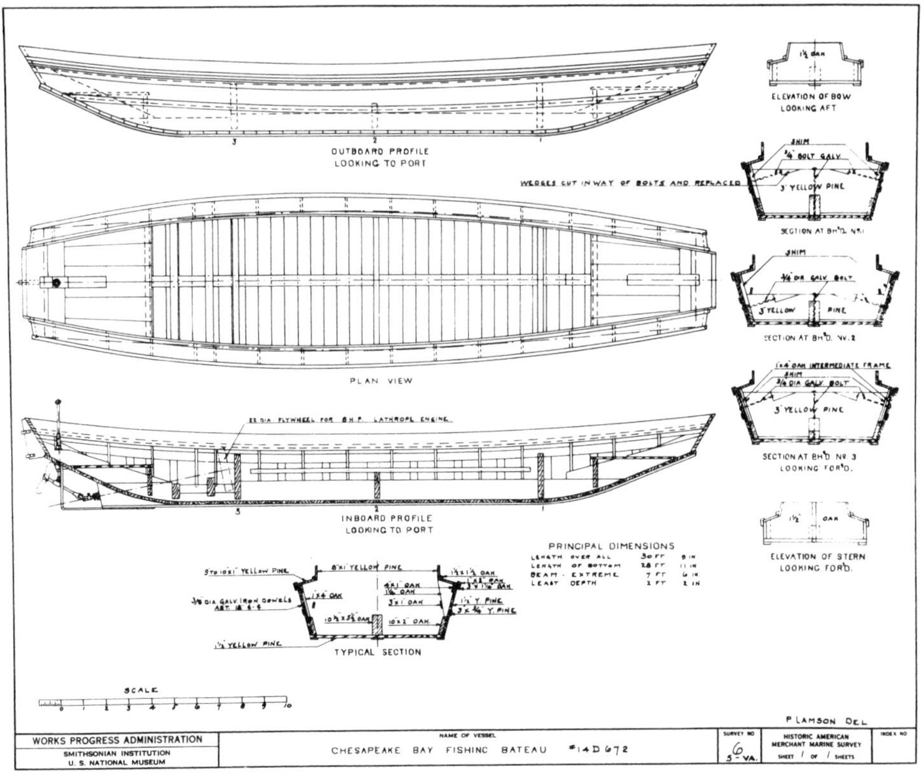

These drawings made in the 1930s by the Works Progress Administration (WPA) offer a blueprint of just how Matt Elliott built his pound net bateau. (Courtesy of the National Museum of American History, Smithsonian Institution)

to the city's steamboat dock and carried by steamboat to markets in Washington, D. C.; Baltimore; Philadelphia; and other eastern ports.

With their nets just off the beach and their market right at their doorstep, fishermen of Fox Hill did not need the long (over forty feet) deadrise-style vessels used by other pound net fishermen up and down the Bay. In the smaller bateaux, fishermen were able to travel quickly to and from their pound nets.

The bateau was a small, sturdy scow with raised stern and bow. It could be dragged through the surf onto the beach and could quickly be hauled up onto shore loaded down with 125 bushels of fish (the payload capacity of the boats).

The Grandview/Buckroe beach area is near the mouth of the Chesapeake. The beach is so situated that when northeasters roar through the capes and into the narrow mouth of the Bay, the storms are funneled right to this stretch of beach. The wind and sea come with such force that it would make it impractical for fishermen to build mooring docks along the shore. Therefore, the bateau was designed to be hauled up onto shore daily.

When fishermen first started using the skiffs, the boats were powered by sail. When there was no wind, long oars were used to get the fishermen to and from their fishnets. Around the turn of the twentieth century, gasoline engines were introduced in the bateau. One-cylinder engines, also known as one lungers or donkey engines, were the main power plants.

In the old sailing rigs, a rudder and tiller stick were designed to be removed when the boats were hauled ashore. The steering rig was held in place by sockets. When power came, fishermen kept the same type of steering and tiller system, but the prop shaft and propeller presented a problem. Fishermen had to come up with some method of raising the shaft and propeller when they hauled the boats up—often loaded down with fish—onto the beach.

To remedy this problem, watermen installed a universal joint in the shaft. A handle was also attached to the shaft that extended up through the boat. An L-shaped adjustable metal strut was designed to hold the

These fishing bateaux were used from the 1880s until the 1950s to harvest fish from pound nets in the Grandview/Buckroe beach area near the mouth of the Chesapeake. The boats were also used to install pound poles, as evidenced by the pile drivers mounted on the bateaux. (Courtesy of Charles Elliot)

These boats were built and designed to be pulled up daily on the beaches of Grandview and Buckroe. As shown, a track is made from flat boards. Round poles were laid down on the track, and the boat was rolled and pulled up onto the beach. Before combustion engines, horses and mules were used to haul the boats. Later, donkey engines were utilized. This photo of pound net fisherman John Price (foreground) and an unknown companion was taken on Grandview Beach in the 1930s. (Courtesy of Charles Elliott)

The strong surf along the Grandview/Buckroe beach area was not conducive to the building of small piers to moor traditional-style workboats. Therefore, the Chesapeake Bay bateau evolved to accommodate the needs of a very lucrative pound fishery in that area. (Courtesy of Charles Elliott)

shaft in place and allow it to be raised and lowered. The bottom of the L strut was attached to the skeg and extended aft, while the top extended up and was attached to the bottom of the raised stern. The shaft went through the strut.

When fishermen hauled their boats up to the surf, the engine was shut down, and the rudder and tiller were pulled out and laid upon a seat. To raise the shaft and propeller, they would simply pull up on the handle. Then the entire crew would jump out of the boat, guide the bateau toward shore, where a steel cable, attached to a block and tackle, was secured to a metal ring in the bow.

The other end of the line was attached to a capstan or windlass up on the beach. The windlass had a pound pole anchored into the top so that two ends of the pole could be used as handles for the fishermen to wind the line up onto the capstan. Three men on each pole would walk the spool around and around, winding the line and pulling the boat up on the beach.

On the beach, planks were laid down to form a track, and poles were laid down on the planks so a boat could be rolled with relative ease. Later on, gasoline donkey engines replaced man power, and steel cable replaced rope.

In the 1930s, U.S. government records showed that there were over 160 pound nets located off the beaches of Grandview and Buckroe and 90 percent of the men living in the Fox Hill area worked in the pound net fishery.

CHARLES ELLIOTT

Charles Elliott of Buckroe Beach was born and raised in Fox Hill. His grandfather was Matt Elliott, whose boat was used by the WPA as a model to make the profile drawings of the bateau. Matt built boats most of his life near Harris River in Fox Hill.

Charles's father was a Fox Hill waterman and Charles's first recollections are of the men and boats on the beaches of Buckroe and Grandview.

"I've seen a bateau come ashore so filled with fish that you could lay a boat hook across the boat and the hook would dip in the water," says Charles, "but I never heard of one sinking.

"You see, fishing was really big when I was a boy here in the 1930s. About then, the beach front on Grandview came up for sale. It was part of the Grandview Development Corporation. The fishermen all got together and bought up all the beach and set up fish camps along the shore.

Charles Elliott, the grandson of Matt Elliott, a longtime builder of Chesapeake Bay fishing bateaux who built his skiffs in the Fox Hill area of Hampton, Virginia.

"One of my earliest recollections is riding my tricycle down to the camps and watching the boats come in loaded down with fish. In the early years, there were horses and wagons waiting for the fishermen, and later, trucks went right down on the beach.

"The fish were loaded onto wagons and hauled to a fish packing house just up the beach. Once packed in boxes, fish were loaded onto a flat car of a streetcar that would come almost to the packing house. Fish were hauled to Old Point Comfort and hauled out by way of Bay Line steamers to the big cities.

"My God, seafood was big in Hampton back then. When I was growing up, all of downtown Hampton was built on fish and crab packing. Most of the big, old, beautiful homes, like you see up in Reedville, [Virginia], were built with seafood money."

FISH CAMPS

"My greatest thrill as a child was us children going to eat at the fish camps. The cook was the first one to jump out of the boat right when they were coming ashore, and he'd have about a half-bushel of fish in a basket. He would have already cleaned them coming in.

"He'd go in the shanty and light up the wood cookstove and start frying fish. Most all the fishermen loved fish, and they all loved molasses and biscuits. And at the start of every season they would buy a brand-new five-gallon gas can and fill it up with molasses and keep it in the shanty.

"I remember asking one of the cooks, 'How long does the five gallons of molasses last?'

"'Not as long as you think it will,' he said.

"On warm summer days, they'd eat outdoors either under a big tree along the edge of the water [or on the screened porches of] some of the shanties. Wherever they ate, there was always a big rickety table, and for chairs they'd use little barrels or empty fish boxes or bundles of old and new nets that were just sitting around.

"I never met a fish camp cook who wasn't good at fixing up a meal. They fixed fried fish, sliced tomatoes, baked beans, iced tea, hot biscuits, and the best rice pudding I have ever eaten.

"The shanties in the camps were about sixteen by sixteen feet—all one room with tin roofs. Inside, there was usually a cast-iron wood cookstove, fish boxes full of scrap wood used to fuel the stoves, [and] a rough kitchen table. More fish boxes were nailed to the walls to serve as shelves to hold can goods, and a box also sat on the floor for a washstand. A washbasin set atop the box, and a bucket of water for drinking and washing up before meals sat next to it on the floor. There were also bunks to sleep on for fishermen who came from Mathews and Gloucester Counties to help fish.

"You see, there weren't enough fishermen in Fox Hill to work all the nets, so watermen came from other areas to work, and they lived in these shanties. The men around home went to their own houses at night to sleep.

"As a small boy, I loved to go and listen to the stories the fishermen had to tell. One time I asked an old fishermen, 'What's the biggest fish you ever caught?'

"He went inside and brought out a broom and drew a big circle in the sand with the stick end of the handle.

"When the circle was complete, he said to me, pointing to the circle, 'That was the size of its eyeball.'

"I about laughed until I cried," says Charles smiling.

"I remember another time, they were talking about eating soft crabs and ice cream together and they all agreed it would kill you," he says.

"You know, watermen are superstitious. I guess somebody around here died when they ate a soft crab with ice cream, and then everybody must have thought it would kill you."

CATCHING FISH

"In 1934, medium croakers were bringing a quarter of a cent a pound. That was twenty-five cents for a hundred pound box of fish. It don't sound like much, but fishermen were making loads of money because they were catching loads of fish.

"I've heard stories of one boat catching fifteen hundred boxes in one set [150,000 pounds]," he says. "One of my neighbors was a partner in one of the rigs, and he made seventy-five thousand dollars in one season. Now, boy, that was a lot of money in those days.

"I know another fishermen in the 1920s who bought his house from one night's catch of hard heads [croakers]. People don't believe it, but the Bay was solid full of fish.

"I remember one time right before World War II, the Navy was doing some target practice off the beach, and they warned the fishermen not to go out because they might get shot.

"Do you think that would stop them with all that money out there? No way! They went right on out there with machine guns blasting all around them and fished their nets.

"I used to go out with them sometimes, and you know fishermen, they love to argue. They would argue on who was the strongest, and they would fill bushel baskets with seine weights to see who could lift the most," he recalls. "Another time, they got to arguing over who could eat the most soda crackers without drinking water. The crackers are real salty."

"Another time one of our boys bet a Guineaman [from Gloucester County] that he did not have enough nerve to piss on the head [spark plug] of a Lathrop engine. When he did, it knocked the hell right out of him," laughs Charles. "It about killed him!"

"The old pound netters had names for their nets. There was one net called the Lane Pound, and it was set in the same place for over one hundred years," says Charles. "It was called that because it lined up with the road that led to the beach."

Other names of nets were the Old Rock, Pink Periwinkle, Black Sow, Rainbow, John Peter, and George.

"The nets were in lines [parallel with the beach], and the first row off the beach was called the first header. The next row was second header, then third header, and so on as the lines ran all the way out to the boat channel. I don't exactly know how many rows there were.

"Can you imagine 160 nets on that six-mile stretch of beach?" he says. "It was an amazing fishery."

FISHERMAN'S SON

"My papa was a fisherman and a crabber. During crabbing season, I would peddle down to the beach on my tricycle to carry him salt for his trotline. He would keep the trotline in a tub of brine during the day to keep his bait from spoiling.

"Papa did a lot of crabbing at night because at certain times during the season, school crabs would come, and for some reason, those crabs would drop off the line in daylight. I don't know why that was, but the only way to catch them was to crab at night.

"I'd come down to the shore in the dark and look out where the moon would make a ray of light across the water. I would watch for his boat to appear in the ray. When I saw him, I would holler and wave my hands to get him to see me.

"One night when I went with him, it got real chilly and I got real tired. In the boat, there were crab barrels, and my father turned one down lengthwise, put his coat up in it, and told me to crawl up in it to get warm. Before long, I went to sleep. At dawn, the other fishermen wanted to know where I was, and Papa pointed to the barrel.

"To this day, there are still some old friends of mine that kid me about that barrel," he says with a smile.

"They were hard times, though. I can remember Papa coming in from a night's work having caught one barrel of crabs—worth a dollar a barrel.

"Besides crabbing, Papa would oyster, clam, and net for rock [striped bass]. He would hand tong for the oysters and clams, and Papa had a special tong for oysters and a special one for clams. The clam tongs had longer teeth than oyster tongs. He would also rake for clams."

BOATBUILDING AND FISHING TRADITIONS

"My grandfather was not the only boatbuilder in the family," says Charles. "My first ancestor to come to Fox Hill was Obediah Elliott in the 1790s. After the Revolutionary War, a number of families came to this area to find a better life. [Obediah] came from the Eastern Shore of Virginia where he had been a boatbuilder.

"Obediah probably came here because of the shipyards. In those days, Fox Hill was noted for its shipyards that were scattered along Harris River. Many sloops and schooners were built here. One of the boats Obediah built was a schooner named the *Only Daughter.*

"The pound net fishery is not the only fishery that is famous here at Fox Hill. In 1867, Captain Elijah Reed [the father of the Chesapeake Bay menhaden fishery] came down from Brooklin, Maine, to harvest menhaden, and the first place he set up was not far from here in a place called Factory Point.

"That's where he built a fish factory. The fish were cooked in large kettles and spread on wooden platforms built above the sand. The fish would dry, and oil would drain into a trough built around the edge of the platform. The oil was barreled and the rest of the fish was loaded onto schooners and shipped up the Bay for farmers to use as fertilizers.

"He stayed a little over a year before the boat traffic and storms drove him to the Northern Neck of Virginia, where he started another factory."

Reed later became the namesake of Reedville, Virginia, where the Yankee sea captain settled and established the menhaden fishery that is still a very important part of the lower Northern Neck's economy to this day.

"When I was a boy," says Charles, "there were old-timers here in Fox Hill who said they could remember the odor from the factory. When the wind was blowing from the north and east, the smell was terrible, they would say."

THE FISHERY DECLINES

The fishery began to decline drastically in the 1950s when the supply of fish could no longer support the Fox Hill fishery. "I know there are many reasons for the decline of fish on the Bay, but one has to be waste," says Charles.

"You talk about pollution, I've seen pinhead [small] croakers piled up on the beach this high [holding his hand above his head]. They only sold the best. Didn't they?" remarks Charles, shaking his head.

There were also natural causes that hurt the Buckroe/Grandview fishery. "The 1933 August storm took everything away from here," recalls Charles. "I remember the wind picked up a pound boat and threw it up on top of a building at the Buckroe Amusement Park. After the storm, every pound net out there was gone. You can imagine the devastation to

Frank and Hugh Horton and an unknown fishermen work a pound net from a bateau off Buckroe Beach in 1938. (Courtesy of Charles Elliott)

the fishing community, because a lot of the fishermen owned five and six nets. They had to start over. The main thing that killed the fishery, though, was lack of fish to support it.

"There is only one pound net off Grandview and Buckroe Beach today, and that is being worked by a part-time fisherman. His ancestors were fishermen, and he is just carrying on the tradition because he loves it.

"It's unbelievable to me that the fishery is gone, and all the boats—they're gone, too. I've got pictures of the last one dying up in the marsh over near Harris Creek [River].

"I tried to get a museum to get it up before it died, but no one wanted to take it. It is hard for me to understand. I guess people have just forgotten what fishing and the boats meant to all the folks who used to live here at Fox Hill."

✻ *I first heard the word "snapper rig," while interviewing a Tangier Island waterman in the early 1970s. I was unaware then of what it meant—so I inquired.*

In 1986, when I was asked by a National Fisherman *editor to do a story on the small menhaden snapper fleet of the Chesapeake, I didn't have to ask what it meant.*

9 : Snapper Rigs

FOR OVER a decade now on the Chesapeake Bay, a small fleet of independently owned boats, or snapper rigs,* have been purse seining for menhaden, which are sold for bait to local blue crab watermen and other fishermen elsewhere on the East Coast.

Bait dealers on Virginia's Northern Neck have rigged up a hodge-podge of fishing vessels to harvest the menhaden. They've taken classic Chesapeake Bay deadrise buy boats, North Carolina and Gulf shrimp trawlers, and Maine sardine carriers and outfitted all of them with the most modern purse seine gear available. The result is a very efficient fishing fleet.

Several things seem to have contributed to the emergence of this fishery on the Bay. Historically, stationary pound nets have been the main supplier of bait for Chesapeake Bay crabbers. Even before the invention of the crab pot by B. F. Lewis of Harryhogan, Virginia, in 1928, crab trot-liners were going to the pound netters for fish to bait their lines.

These pound nets, however, were actually designed to harvest food fish, and for the watermen who operated them, the sale of bait or scrap fish was only a sideline, albeit a nice one. Menhaden, bluefish, and small croakers (pinheads) were among the species they sold to the trotliners. Generally, there was plenty of bait to go around, especially since many trotlining watermen preferred eel and caught their own.

With the introduction of the crab pot and the general growth of the blue crab industry, however, things began to change. The need for reliable

* The origin of the word "snapper" as it relates to small menhaden fishing boats has been lost to time. Some watermen, however, think it may have come from a size comparison of a snapper bluefish to a snapper menhaden vessel. Snapper blues are smaller than a fully mature bluefish, and snapper menhaden boats are smaller than the large company-owned menhaden fish steamers.

sources of fresh bait for crab pots grew tremendously. At the same time, due mainly to increasingly high start-up costs and low harvest, pound nets were declining on the Bay. It was to fill this gap that the snapper rig fleet began fishing in the mid-1970s.

The first to gear up was Kelley Seafood of Northumberland County on Virginia's Northern Neck. Company president, Jimmy Kelley, says he decided to get into the bait business in 1974 to meet the needs of local blue crab fishermen. He started buying menhaden from pound net fishermen on the Eastern Shore of Virginia and block-freezing the fish. "This just didn't work, because we never knew how much bait we were going to get," he says. "So, we decided to try and catch our own."

Kelley's firm has grown into one of the largest on the Bay. He now supplies bait to Maine lobstermen, Gulf of Mexico crawfish fishermen, and crab fishermen on the West Coast. "About 75 percent of our bait goes out of state," he says. "Most of it is sold on the East Coast and the Gulf of Mexico."

During the early years of his bait operation, Kelley used the *Yeomac,* a sixty-five-foot Chesapeake Bay deadrise buy boat. He strung a two-hundred-fathom purse seine, rigged up a purse boat, and started catching menhaden. His was the first small purse seine seen on the Bay in many years.

Since the Northern Neck is the home of the two largest menhaden firms in the nation, Zapata Haynie and Ampro Fisheries, purse seining is

Bait dealers have converted a wide range of fishing vessels for purse seining, including this former shrimp trawler.

The techniques used by the snapper rigs working the Chesapeake Bay are very similar to the methods of the much larger corporation-owned operations. One of the main differences, however, is the use of one purse boat by the snapper rigs instead of two by the corporate boats. Purse boats like the one pictured are used by snapper rigs and are the workhorses of the operation. They must carry the entire seine and are loaded down with heavy gear to manipulate the net.

certainly nothing new to the Chesapeake region. During the days of sail and steam, snapper rigs fished for menhaden and sold their catch to local processing plants. Most of the plants were small kettle operations that processed the fish to extract oil. It was discovered in the 1800s that fish oil from menhaden had many applications. Many small kettle plants were started primarily to supply a growing demand for the fish oil to fuel lamps in homes.

But as the menhaden industry grew, the situation changed significantly. Soon, economic conditions made small catches unprofitable. At the same time, the cost of outfitting and operating high-capacity menhaden steamers and purse boats grew prohibitive. Together, these factors signaled the end of the small, independent snapper boats on the Bay.

Their disappearance, however, proved to be temporary, as the present reemergence of the snapper rigs revives a tradition that goes back well beyond the turn of the century. Understandably, though, the return to small-scale purse seining has been something of a learning process for those involved, including pacesetter Jimmy Kelley.

Kelley had experimented with a small purse net as a teenager and knew the principle of how it worked. Making the gear pay off for his business, however, was another story. "We tried several different types of nets in the beginning," he says. "I even bought nets from the big companies, but they didn't work real good for us because of the deep bunt."

As a result, Kelley developed his own purse seine, a design that has become the standard among modern-day snapper rigs. "You see, all our fishing is done right here on the Bay, and we don't need a deep net," he says. The larger companies fish on the Bay and up and down the East Coast, in some very deep water. "We designed a shallow-water net that has a tapered bunt," Kelley explains. "This way, when the net is pulled in tight, all the fish are up, ready to be sucked on board. It also makes the ring line less likely to foul."

Besides Kelley, several other bait dealers have seen the purse net as the means to an end, and there are now seven vessels working the Bay. With the exception of the nets, the gear on the snapper rigs is basically the same as that on the larger company-owned menhaden steamers.

When these bigger vessels make a set, they begin by casting off two forty-foot aluminum purse boats that are lashed together, each carrying half of the huge net. The forty-footers are directed—as a pair—to a school of fish by a spotter pilot, flying high overhead. At his signal, each purse boat splits away and begins a large semicircle. In the process, the twine zings over the side of each boat, followed by the purse line, which runs through rings at regular intervals along the bottom of the net.

When the circle is completed and the purse boats are linked once again, a hydraulic winch, or cathead, is used to drop the "tom" overboard. Made of lead, the tom weighs about one thousand pounds; it slides down the purse line, both anchoring the end of the line and holding the net on the bottom. As the tag end of the purse line is wound up on a purse boat winch, the lower edge of the net bunches up against the tom, closing the seine and preventing the escape of the encircled menhaden.

The suction hose from a hydraulic fish pump is lowered into the net full of fish, and the menhaden are transferred to the hold of the larger boat.

Having dropped a sea anchor to hold tension on the end of the net, a snapper rig's purse boat circles a school of menhaden at top speed, streaming the seine aft as it goes.

The tom is then hauled up, and the power blocks on both purse boats begin to draw in the net, reducing the size of the circle. When the net is as tight as the power blocks can make it, the steamer comes alongside.

When the larger vessel is in position, the purse boats form a triangle, with their sterns against the big boat and their bows against each other. A gaff hoist is lowered, lashed to the twine, and hauled up to tighten the net further. Finally, a fish pump hose is lowered into the net, and the menhaden are transferred to the fish hold aboard the steamer.

Snapper rig operations have modified this system somewhat to reduce cost. The biggest difference is their use of just one purse boat, which approaches the school, drops a sea anchor to hold one end of the net, and then continues to circle the fish while feeding the seine overboard. And, since the nets used by the snapper rigs are smaller than the seines carried by the company-owned steamers, the lead line itself

A snapper rig's single purse boat is alongside the larger boat (not pictured), using its power block to harden up the catch.

keeps the twine on the bottom during pursing, thereby eliminating the heavy tom.

Kelley says, however, that some Maine purse netters use two small toms, which he thinks might work better than the technique used in the Chesapeake Bay. Other than the tapered bunt, the single purse boat, and the lack of a tom, the rest of the snapper rig's operation is basically the same as that of the larger steamers.

Kelley recently added the 65-by-16-by-6½-foot wooden vessel *Nereid* to his operation. Built in Rockland, Maine, in 1937, the *Nereid* carried passengers and supplies between the ports of Thomaston, Boothbay Harbor, and Port Clyde. Before being converted to a sardine carrier in 1957, she also regularly made the run to rugged Monhegan Island, off the Maine Coast.

Dale George is the boat's captain. For eighteen years, he was the skipper of a larger menhaden steamer owned by Standard Products of Kilmarnock, Virginia, known today as Ampro Fisheries. But in 1985, when Standard opted not to fish the Atlantic coast, George and a couple of hundred other pogy fishermen found themselves looking for work.

"The gear on the snapper rig is a lot like the big steamers," says George. "But fishing the *Nereid* is a lot different from fishing the larger boats. It's harder work, because you don't have as much help and there is only one purse boat." The *Nereid* carries a crew of five: four of them man the purse boat, while the mate stays with the larger vessel as the set is made.

There are other contrasts, as well: The big company steamers hold over a million fish, whereas the *Nereid* carries about one hundred thousand. Some snappers have refrigeration, but the *Nereid* does not and cannot stay out long. On a recent day, the captain and crew of the vessel made three sets of between thirty thousand and forty thousand fish each, then headed for home.

Although those numbers may pale in comparison to the mammoth catches of the company-owned menhaden steamers, they represent hard evidence that smaller bait purse seiners are both effective and efficient. The return of the snapper rig marks the revival of a traditional fishery on the Bay. It isn't often that this happens. But traditions can be revived. The snapper rig is the proof in the pudding.

✳ *Shortly after* Harvesting the Chesapeake: Tools and Traditions *was published in 1990 I received a letter from John Frye, author of* Men All Singing, The Story of Menhaden Fishery. *He was very complimentary of my book and alerted me to the historical significance of Chapter 7, "A Striker for Menhaden." He said he was unaware of the snapper rig fishery that worked the Bay under sail at the turn of the century and that I had uncovered an aspect of the menhaden fishery unknown to most Bay historians.*

Steam power was introduced to the menhaden fishery in the 1850s, and Frye and others had thought that there was no one left alive who could remember, firsthand, fishing for menhaden under sail.

At the same time I was researching the chapter, Melvin Dize, who had worked aboard a sail-driven snapper rig, shared with me this story about two other young men who had crewed another such rig.

As a boy, Melvin was a crew member aboard the Twilight. *He died in 1992 at the ripe old age of ninety-four, perhaps the last living soul to have worked aboard a sail-driven menhaden vessel. This story is dedicated to his memory.*

10 : A Tale from the Days of Fishing under Sail

THERE WAS a fine mist rain falling. It was an early autumn day. The air was still warm, but the chilling drizzle portended the onset of a colder season. The leaves on the fruit trees in the orchard were mottled, displaying summer green mixed with speckles of orange and yellow. The foliage would peak in a few days.

The orchard was in the middle of Tangier Island and had been planted so many years ago that no one could remember just when. The land beneath the apple and peach trees had the distinction of being the highest point on the island. For generations, families who owned the orchard had buried their dead beneath the fruit trees in the hopes of preventing a strong northeaster from flooding the land and unearthing the caskets.

On this day, the island was once again going to renew that tradition. It was in the afternoon, after the fishermen had finished harvesting their nets, that the small funeral procession walked down the narrow lane from

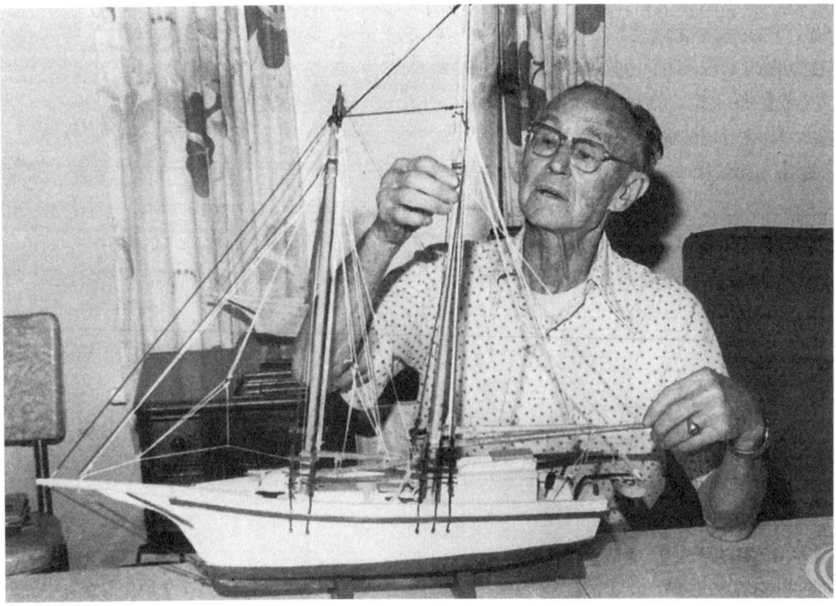

Melvin Dize was one of the last men alive to have fished aboard a sail-driven snapper rig.

the small white clapboard Methodist church onto a sandy footpath that led to the orchard. It was Willie Cooper's funeral. A teenager, Willie had lost his life in the hold of the sailing pungy *Amanda F. Lewis.*

As the procession moved down the path, several men carried the wooden coffin on their shoulders while small children and dogs ran alongside. When they reached the short path to the cemetery, the minister began to sing:

> Abide with me: fast falls the evening tide;
> The darkness deepens; Lord, with me abide;
> When other helpers fail, and comforts flee:
> Help of the helpless, O abide with me!

The group huddled in close to hear the last rite. Several children sat on a rusty wrought-iron fence around the grave site as the Reverend Thompson spoke of hope and prayed for Willie's salvation. The minister's message was short, and when it was over the crowd left quietly. Willie's mother, Mrs. Cooper, waited until all were gone before going over to the four men who were to lower Willie's body into the ground.

"Jonah, is it six feet deep?" Mrs. Cooper asked the tallest man there, whose arms were as big as stovepipes.

"Yes, ma'am," he said.

"Is there any water in the hole?"

"No, ma'am, there's no water in the hole," he answered.

For a moment, Mrs. Cooper placed her hand on the coffin and wept as she prayed silently. "Why, Lord? Why? . . ." she gasped.

The Reverend Thompson, who was at the edge of the path, saw her pain and walked over to place his arm around her.

"Pack the dirt down good, Jonah. I don't want my baby to float back into the sea that took him from me," said Mrs. Cooper.

"Yes, ma'am."

"It's made of oak, ya know," she said touching the wood again on the coffin lid. "I got it special from the western shore. It's the best. I hope it will last ya, Willie." She looked off into the distance.

The Reverend Thompson gently pulled her away from the coffin and walked her toward her home on the other side of the island. The men waited until the two were out of sight before lowering the coffin down into the hole and covering it with dirt. When it was filled, Jonah and his men packed the earth down well, just as Mrs. Cooper had requested.

It was the autumn of 1918.

In the spring of 1918, the ospreys had built their nests, and laughing gulls were chattering all over Tangier Island. Many of the men from the island were already off to the Eastern Shore of Virginia to trotline for hard crabs; others were working fish pound nets in the Bay. A group of youngsters were down on the steamboat dock, passing time and waiting to see who would arrive on the boat. They sat on fish boxes and leaned against pilings that held up the pier.

"Hey, boys, you'll never guess what I'm gonna be doin' this summer. I've got me a job on the *Amanda F. Lewis* and I'm going to fish for menhaden in the Bay," said a blond-haired, blue-eyed teen named Willie Cooper.

"They tell me that those fish stink some kind of bad," said Mel Parks, who was leaning up against a piling. "They make fertilizer out of them because they ain't no good for anything else."

"Mel, you're just jealous because you didn't get the job," said Marty Jones, a very large young man for his age. "I'm gonna be on the *Amanda,* too."

Willie and Marty were best friends. They had lived next door to one another ever since Willie was six. Willie and his mother had moved into the narrow two-story cottage on Heron Gut after his father had frozen to death hunting ducks over on Watts Island.

"I'm going to be the tom man," said Marty, chewing on a broom straw and flexing his muscles as he leaned against a piling. Marty's arms and legs were as strong as a bull's.

"You ain't that strong," said Mel. "Beside, big ol' Charlie Brooks is the tom man on the *Amanda*."

"Who isn't strong enough?" bellowed Marty as he picked up Mel with both hands and held him high over his head.

"Let me down! Let me down!" Mel screamed.

Marty let him down, and Mel took off to hide behind a heap of oyster shells on shore.

The *Amanda F. Lewis* and the *Twilight* were sister pungy sailing ships that were scheduled to leave the following morning to fish for menhaden in the Bay. The fish were gathered by use of a purse net. Then a tom, or large weight, was thrown overboard to close the purse when the fish were trapped. The tom man, who threw the tom overboard, was usually the strongest man on the boat.

"Here she comes," yelled Willie. The old steamboat was heading toward the dock.

Mel came out from behind the shell pile with a handful of oyster shells. "Yeah, when she leaves, we can skip shells at her to see who comes the closest," he said.

"Forget it, Mel, we're too old to be skipping shells now," said Willie. "That's kid stuff."

The only person to get off at the landing was ol' Moe, a black man who worked aboard the steamboat. He carried some chickens in a coop for someone on the island.

After the vessel left, the boys swam for a while and then went into Joshua Tom's little confectionery for a Coke and a piece of hard candy. Willie and Marty lingered for a short while, then headed for home.

"We're going to be bunking together, aren't we, Willie?" Marty asked.

"Sure! Are you a little scared?" Willie asked.

"No! Are you?"

"Nope!" said Willie.

There was a long pause as the boys ran up Captain Peter's little hill toward their homes. Marty put his arm on Willie's shoulder and confessed, "Willie, I'm going to tell ya the truth. I'm a little scared, but don't tell nobody."

"So am I," admitted Willie.

They both grinned and ran home.

That night, Willie ate some fresh trout that Captain Peter had given them. The old captain had rather taken to Mrs. Cooper since Willie's father passed on during the big freeze.

Willie slept lightly his last night at home. The anticipation and excitement of working on the pungy was a lot for a young man to handle.

Just before dawn, Willie hurried downstairs for a breakfast of salt fish and corn bread. His mamma gave him one last hug and a grass sack filled with clothes, a razor, and a few other necessities. Mrs. Cooper told Willie to shave each day and not to come home looking like a bum. She also insisted that he stay away from those wicked western shore women.

Marty was already waiting by the picket gate outside Willie's house. Willie leaped over the fence and the boys ran side by side down the path to Captain Gab's house. Gab, the skipper of the *Amanda F. Lewis,* had hired the boys to work with his summer crew.

They reached the captain's home all out of breath. Mitch Dize, first mate on the *Amanda,* was standing in the yard smoking a pipe when the boys ran up.

"Ho there! Don't rush! The captain's still eating his breakfast," said Mitch.

Mitch puffed on his pipe for a second. "Well, now, they tell me you boys are going fishing with us."

"Yes, sir," answered the boys.

"Well, I know you'll both do just fine. Go on down to the dock and wait for us in the purse boat. The other men are already aboard the *Amanda* getting ready."

Willie and Marty walked down the hill to the captain's dock and boarded the purse boat. They sat very still, looking out at the coal oil johnnies (kerosene lanterns) dimly lit on the sailing vessels anchored in Cod Harbor. Both boys could hardly contain their excitement. Marty's eyes were stinging from lack of sleep.

"Good morning there, mates," came a stern voice from the dock. It was Captain Gab. He was a stout old fellow who had trouble getting into

The *Amanda F. Lewis* was one of the last Chesapeake Bay pungies to work the Bay and one of the last sailing vessels to be used in the menhaden snapper rig fishery. (Drawing by Dr. A. L. Van Name, Jr.)

the little boat. After Mitch and the skipper were aboard, Gab told the boys to row out to the *Amanda.*

The captain and first mate talked as the boys rowed. "We'll head on over to the western shore of Virginia," said Gab. "Some of the other boats are going over that way, too."

As they approached the sailing vessel, the boys strained to see her lines. The old pungy had pleasing lines, with two tall raking masts and a thin main topmast that was bowed slightly forward. She had a fancy bowsprit and a carving of the vessel's namesake on her stern. Metal rods were attached to the stern, positioned over the face of the carving to protect it from the yawl boat that was suspended from the davits. A carved wooden anchor sat atop the gold ball on her foremast.

In the days and weeks to come, the boys were to learn every inch of the vessel. Their hands became firm and hard from pulling the seine day after day. Marty had proven himself the strongest aboard the *Amanda* early on and had been made the tom man. Willie was responsible for lighting all the coal oil johnnies aboard the vessel and also helped Marcus cook the meals on a large cast-iron cookstove. Marcus was a large black man who had been working aboard sailing vessels some forty years. He had harpooned whales during his youth in New England waters and had even captained a schooner on the Chesapeake before hiring on as the *Amanda*'s cook. Most of the crew respected Marcus.

The boys found that the thrill of landing a large school of menhaden made the time fly by. When catches were good, the crew spent time in Reedville, Virginia, where the fish were sold to the Edward's plant.

When fishing was poor, the *Amanda*'s crew stayed on the Bay, and the boys passed the hours on deck singing with the men or listening to the tales of the old seamen. Willie and Marty slept and ate with the crew in the hold of the vessel.

The fish that were caught were stored in a large box-type structure built on deck. Many nights, the boys would awaken to wipe from their faces the fish juices and water that had seeped through the seams in the deck. Still, they loved their work.

"In your boats! In your boats!" came a yell from the crow's nest high atop the mast.

"It's a big one!" Mitch screamed. "The water is purple with them!"

There was a mad scramble on deck as the men jumped into the two purse boats that were tied to the stern of the pungy. The boats were loaded with net.

"We'll be in Reedville tonight," said Willie excitedly.

A smaller striker boat was sent out first to help herd the fish into the seine and to guide the purse boats in making the set. Captain Gab was in one purse boat and Mitch was in charge of the other. The two boats, side by side, approached the school as the striker directed the set with hand signals. When all were ready, the purse boats separated.

"Let her go!" Gab screamed as the net flowed smoothly over the sides. The purse boats encircled the school as the striker, on the opposite side of the circle from the purse boats, pulled the cork line to keep the net stretched tight.

"We got 'em," Mitch yelled.

"All right, tom man, let her go," yelled Gab.

Marty lifted the tom high over his head and threw out the weight into the water. As the tom hit, water splashed all over the crew in the other purse boat.

"Doggone!" screamed Mitch. "You got us again, tom man."

Ol' Marcus brought the *Amanda* up beside the purse boats. The men strained bringing up the net full of fish. When everything was ready for loading, Marty and Willie boarded the *Amanda* and climbed to the top of the mast. This was the fun part for the boys.

There was a large dip net on deck that was hooked to block and tackle and attached to the masthead. Willie reached the top first and caught the rope. After the dip net was lowered into the school, Willie let go of his foothold and sailed out into the air with the rope in hand.

"Yee, ha!" he screamed, as he flew through the air. His weight raised the net full of fish up on deck, where several men guided the silver mass of fish into the wooden box. Marty made the next jump. This was done over and over until the set was all stowed on deck.

The *Amanda* and the *Twilight* both made several sets that day. When the boats were filled with menhaden, they sailed for Reedville. Although the crew was tired from fishing all day, there was much left to do when they arrived. The menhaden had to be shoveled into wheelbarrows and hauled to the local plant, where fish oil was extracted for paint and other products.

It was after dark before the two vessels were completely unloaded, so Shad Crockett, the skipper of the *Twilight,* and Captain Gab decided to stay in port for the night. Gab ordered his men to stay on board the *Amanda* so that he could sail early the next morning for Wolf Trap Lighthouse.

"Willie, you look tired," said Marty.

"Yep," said Willie. The boys went below, spread their blankets out on the deck floor, and fell fast asleep.

Just before daylight, Marty and Willie went back up on deck to light the coal oil johnnies that had blown out during the night. The sails were hoisted, and the *Amanda* caught a fair breeze toward Wolf Trap. The *Twilight* was not far behind. Just after dawn, Willie helped Marcus serve breakfast to the men and afterward went up on deck to throw bread crumbs to the black-headed laughing gulls that waited each day for handouts.

The morning passed without a single sighting of fish. At 10:30 the men went down into the hold for lunch. The spotters remained atop the masts, and Captain Gab stayed at the helm. They would eat after the crew was finished.

Twenty-some men crowded around the makeshift tables in the hold. "I bet you money that before I finish this grub, they'll spot a hundred thousand fishes," said Marty to one of the crewmen nearby. Others talked of home, but most just ate. The hold was hot from the summer heat and the fire in the stove. The men did not tarry but ate quickly and went back up on deck to cool off. There were buckets and rope tied to the rail of the *Amanda,* which were used by the men to cool down.

Before Captain Gab went below for his lunch, he ordered the men to drop anchor and to let up some of the sail. "It's no sense looking high and low for fish when there ain't none," he said.

The hours passed slowly that windless day. The crew spent most of the day trying to keep cool by throwing buckets of water on each other. At 4:30 in the afternoon, Willie went below to help Marcus fix supper.

The *Twilight* was anchored close by, and across the way, Captain Shad noticed a sudden change in the weather. The sky was black toward the southwest, which often meant a summer squall was coming. "Is everything tied down good there, Mate?" Shad asked one of his crewmen.

Shad gazed over at the *Amanda F. Lewis.* A frown came across his face. The sail on the vessel was still partly raised. "Give me the horn, Mate!" snapped Shad.

The entire crew of the *Amanda* had gone below to eat supper. No one saw the sky turn black or noticed the wind beginning to blow. They heard the horn blowing but thought it was just a passing steamboat.

"They've got to get the sail down," cried Shad as he blew the horn again as loud as he could.

Still there was no response from the *Amanda.* Suddenly, as so often happens on the Chesapeake, the wind came from nowhere and filled the old pungy's sail, causing the vessel to rock back and forth. Then came a gust that struck with a powerful force.

"My God, they've capsized!" screamed Shad.

The Bay water rushed into the hold. The men were thrown about. Arms and legs, chairs and gear went everywhere. Some men were fighting the water as they tried to get to the hatch.

Marcus's deep voice bellowed above the screams of the men. "Let her fill, boys! Let her fill!" Marcus knew that if the vessel filled, the crew could then swim out easily.

Marcus's voice seemed to calm the desperate men. The shouts and cries quieted as Marcus instructed them not to panic. When the water filled the hold, the men were able to swim to the top. The purse boats of the *Twilight* were waiting on the surface. Against the gusting wind, Captain Shad and his crew fought the weather to gather the crew of the *Amanda.*

Captain Gab was the last to come up from the hold. There was blood running from a gash on his face. Captain Shad asked Gab how many men were aboard.

"Thirty-two," Gab answered.

"Count off," commanded Shad.

As the last bubbles of air rose from the hold of the vessel, the men began to count. Some were holding onto the sides of the purse boats because there was no room left inside. The first count reached thirty-one.

"Maybe someone counted the same number twice," said Shad. "Count again."

But they still came out one man short. "Who's missing?" Gab asked.

Marty sat near Marcus in the bow of the forward purse boat. "Willie, Willie!" Marty began softly, then started screaming "Willie! Where's Willie?"

Marty leaped up on the gunwales of the skiff and started to dive back into the sea. Suddenly, a hand reached out and pulled him back into the boat. It was Marcus. Marty struggled to get loose, but Marcus held tight. Finally, Marty gave up and began to cry. "Oh, boy, boy, boy," said Marcus as he held Marty close against his chest. Several others wanted to try to find Willie, but they all realized it was too late.

The wind stopped as quickly as it had started. The Bay was calm again. Captain Shad told the men to bow their heads as he prayed for

Willie. The men all went back to the *Twilight.* The sails were hoisted and the sad journey back to Reedville was under way. Marty sobbed as he watched the *Amanda* bobbing upside down from the stern of the *Twilight.* Marcus came over and put his arm around him.

"I've seen it happen so many times," said Marcus. "A young boy lost to the sea. Why couldn't it have been an old buzzard like me? No! It's always the young buck who's got so much to live for."

The old man paused and walked over to the water barrel. He got himself a drink. "Death ain't never easy, boy," he said to Marty. "I know Willie was your friend, but you gotta go on. You're damn lucky to be alive yourself. All we can do now is pray for Willie. It's in God's hands."

Marty watched until the hull of the *Amanda* was out of sight. The laughing gulls howled overhead hoping for a handout, but Marty just stared into the horizon.

The *Amanda F. Lewis* was raised several weeks later. Willie's body was found beneath the heavy cookstove. He was apparently trapped as the stove rolled over on him when the vessel capsized.

* *As I buckle my seat belt on the Cessna aircraft making ready to take off from Hummel Airfield in Topping, Virginia, the pilot points to a bag and asks if I am prone to getting airsick.*

"Not that I know of," I respond.

There is a grin on his face when he says, "The last three guys I took up said the same thing. If you are ever going to, you will today."

Throughout the day that carried us from Virginia into North Carolina and back again, three thousand feet in the air, tilting one way and then the other to get the best possible visibility, the radio on the plane keeps blaring.

Toward the end of the trip, I realize that not all of the conversation between the fish spotters was over where fish were located, but instead over whether I would make the entire trip without getting airsick!

Finally, I hear the pilot say, "This guy is going to make it. He's looking at the water—not into the horizon."

When stepping off the plane at the end of the day, I feel some satisfaction in making the entire trip without getting airsick.

11 : Menhaden Spotters

"There she blows," was sung out from the mast-head.

"Where away?" demanded the captain.

"Three points off the lee bow, sir."

"Raise up your wheel. Steady!"

"Mast-head ahoy! Do you see that whale now?"

"Ay ay, sir! A shoal of Sperm Whales! There she blows! There she breaches!"

"Sing out! Sing out every time!"

"Ay ay, sir! There she blows! There—there—thar she blows—bowes—bo-o-o-s!"

"How far off?"

"Two miles and a half."

'Thunder and lightning! So near! Call all hands."

—*Etchings of a Whaling Cruise,* J. Ross Browne, 1846

Over the centuries, fish spotting has primarily been done from a crow's nest that was set atop the highest mast. Sailing vessels roamed the high seas for whales and fish. On the Chesapeake, one of the few fisheries that has required a fish spotter is the menhaden fishery.

Years ago, menhaden (or bunkers, as they are locally called) were enjoyed by some as a table food. In those days, fishermen could easily catch the amount needed to feed those who were able to acquire a taste for the oily fish.

The demand for menhaden, however, began to grow around 1811, when Christopher Barker and John Tallman of Rhode Island began extracting fish oil from menhaden by boiling the fish. It was discovered that menhaden oil was as good a fuel as whale, dolphin, and porpoise oil used in oil lamps. Before electricity came into use, oil lamps provided light in many households throughout the country. Since hunting menhaden was a sight less risky than capturing the giant mammals of the oceans, demand for the oily bunkers skyrocketed.

In 1867, Captain Elijah Warren Reed from Brooklin, Maine, came south to the Chesapeake and began catching menhaden with the intent of extracting fish oil. It was the beginning of the modern-day menhaden fishery on the Chesapeake.

Early menhaden steamers had a platform at the top of the mast for spotters to look out over the water. The *William Floyd* here bears a spotter atop the mast and another atop the pilothouse. (From George Brown Goode's *History of the American Menhaden*, published in 1879.)

Throughout the history of the menhaden fishery on the Bay, many individuals have contributed to its evolution. One name, though, that deserves particular attention is that of John Armistead Palmer, Jr.

John Frye, in his history of the menhaden fishery on the Bay, *The Men All Singing,* devoted an entire chapter to this man who founded Palmer Fisheries of Reedville, Virginia, in 1921. Frye noted that Palmer was the first to use an airplane to spot fish. Before Palmer got the notion to get a bit higher in the air, the highest vantage point for fish spotting had been the top of a masthead or a high bank near the shore. Frye wrote that "Palmer concluded that Chesapeake Bay bunkers were really too deep most of the time for the captains to spot them efficiently in the traditional way from the crow's nest, and also that the fish boats would have to range farther, even outside of the Bay, to find fish and thus needed quick information on distant schools."

Palmer first got the notion that an airplane could be used to spot fish when he watched a Curtiss flying boat named *Kingfisher* glide high overhead one day. The plane had been brought to Reedville to take passengers up in the air for a dollar a minute. Frye wrote that shortly thereafter, Palmer approached the U.S. Navy about using one of their planes as an experiment to see if fish could be located from the air. The

Before the airplane came along, the crow's nest, atop the mast, was the best place for fishermen to spot fish. (From George Brown Goode's *History of the American Menhaden,* published in 1879.)

When menhaden fishermen were fishing in waters where there were high banks along the shoreline, spotters were stationed on land and would signal directions to fish boats by waving a cloth. (From George Brown Goode's *History of the American Menhaden,* published in 1879.)

Navy and the Federal Bureau of Fisheries agreed to give it a try. Morse code would be used to relay fish locations to the fish boats. That was the beginning of the modern-day menhaden spotters.

John Palmer, unfortunately, did not make it in the menhaden business. After several successive bad fishing seasons, Palmer Fisheries eventually closed. Palmer, however, made a lasting mark on the industry that stands to this day.

According to Frye, "John Armistead Palmer, Jr., had too many good ideas that put him fifty years ahead of the menhaden industry."

FLYING HIGH SEARCHING FOR BUNKERS

A haze lies across the Chesapeake Bay as pilot Charles H. Williams III peers down three thousand feet from a Cessna 182 RG aircraft, searching for a school of menhaden. Scanning the Bay is what Williams does for a living as chief spotter pilot for Zapata Haynie Corporation of Reedville. With his head against the side window, he dips and turns the plane, trying to obtain the best possible visibility. Then suddenly—there they are!

The airplane was first introduced as a means to spot fish on the Chesapeake Bay in the 1920s by John Armistead Palmer, Jr., of Reedville, Virginia. A modern-day spotter is Charles Williams III, who at the time of this photo was head spotter pilot for Zapata Haynie Corporation of Reedville. Today, Williams is general manager of Ampro Fisheries, also of Reedville. The Cessna 182 RG aircraft was used by Williams to spot menhaden in the Chesapeake and up and down the Eastern Seaboard.

To unfamiliar eyes, the blue waters of the Chesapeake look about the same, but to Williams's trained eyes the shaded color and rippled water mean fish big enough to make a set.

The blue menhaden boats race to the site. Williams directs the operation from the air, fielding questions over his radio concerning the size of the school and the fish in it.

"Where are they, Charles?" comes another crackling question.

"You're going in the right direction," replies the spotter. Williams estimates how many boat lengths they are from the fish and gives that information to the steamer captain. There are fifty or sixty in the school, meaning fifty thousand to sixty thousand fish.

Suddenly the steamer, a half-mile away from the fish, begins to slow down. The two purse boats streak through the water side by side. Williams makes several course and speed corrections along the way, and the captain and the pilot discuss the best positioning for the set. Consideration is given to wind direction, tide, fish movement, and sea conditions.

The pilot positions the two purse boats as the set is made. Each boat splits away, forming a large circle. Williams signals each boat, referring to one as the big boat and the other as the little boat, even though they're both about thirty-six feet long. The big boat is so called because it has the captain or first mate aboard.

"Hold the little boat off," he says, in an obvious move to cut the fish off so they can't escape the purse nets. The big boat has already circled behind the fast-moving school.

"Start the little boat around," signals Williams. As the purse boat moves in front of the swimming school, there is no escape.

When they are one steamer-length away he says, "Port a little."

"Steady."

"Get all ready."

"Let 'em go!"

The fish are caught.

Williams puts his radio mike down and looks at the horizon for a moment. The job is done for now, and they've made a good set. "You get a great feeling when you make a good set," he says. "But you feel just as low as you feel high when you go out and have a poor day."

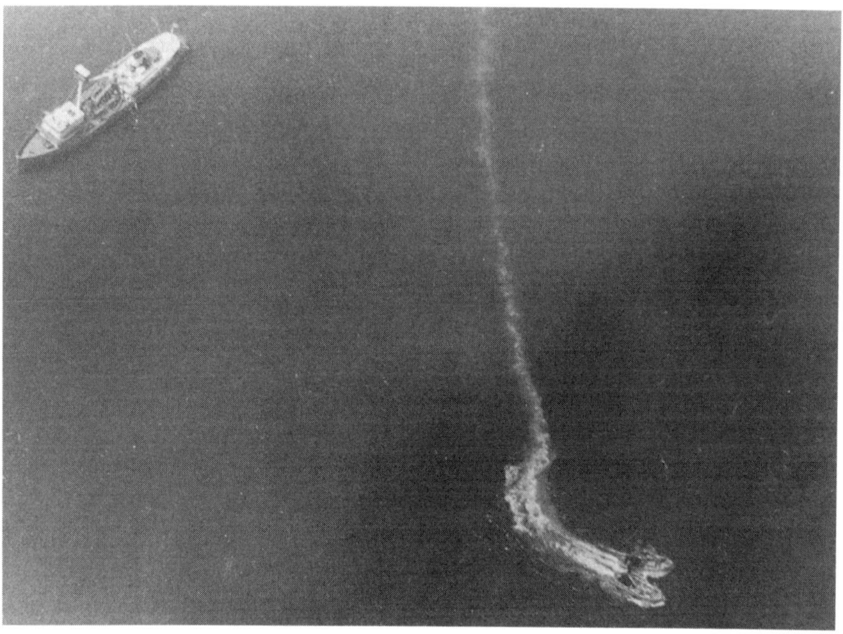

At three thousand feet, Charles Williams radios the boats and alerts them to a school of fish ahead. He directs the two purse boats racing side by side to the location of the fish.

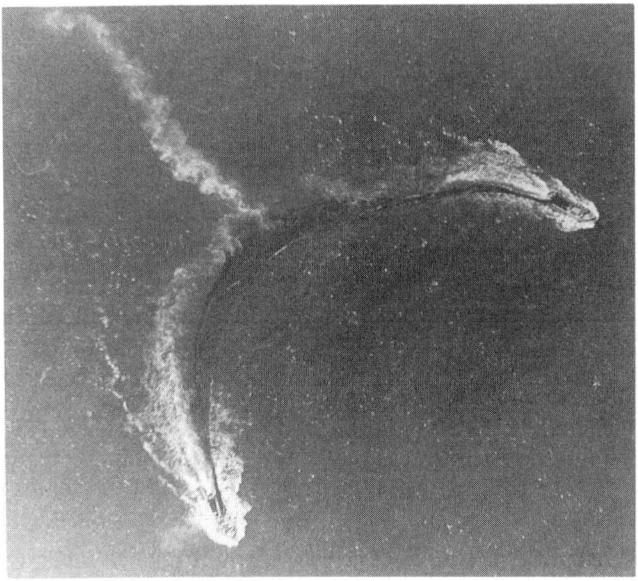

As the purse boats streak through the water, Williams makes course and speed corrections, and when the school of menhaden is in sight, the purse boats split away to encircle the fish.

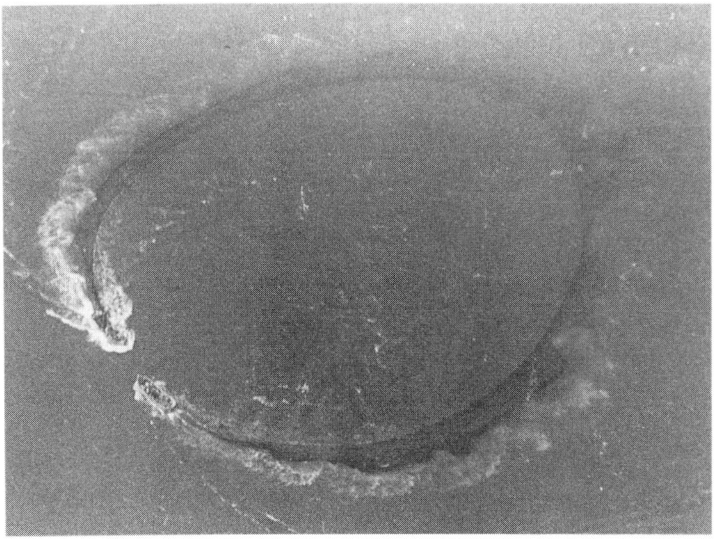

The menhaden purse net is towed into a wide circle so the fish are cut off from escaping. Once the set is made, Williams is off again, tracking down the next school of menhaden.

Williams has been a spotter pilot with Zapata Haynie for thirteen years. His father and grandfather had been in the menhaden business as fish boat captains. Charles started out crewing with his father during his high school days. So, after a four-year stint in the Navy, it seemed only natural for him to follow in the fishing tradition. But somewhere along the way, he decided to take to the air instead of the sea.

"If I weren't doing this, I'd be working on the water," he says. "I enjoy working on the boats; it's a good life. But I enjoy spotting, too."

As chief pilot for Zapata Haynie, Williams is on salary and uses a company airplane. Other company pilots, however, use their own planes and most are paid a commission—so much per thousand fish. "This gives them an incentive to find the fish," says Williams. "It's kind of like farming: You're paid for what you reap."

A good set is one hundred thousand fish, and a good day's work is 1.2 million. "When you get a set that has twenty thousand to twenty-five thousand fish in it, it's almost not worth the work," Williams says. "The wear and tear on the boats may not be worth it." A record year for Zapata was 1984, when 500 million fish were hauled to the Reedville plant. All were caught on the Atlantic coast, which included the Chesapeake and Delaware Bays and New Jersey, New York, Maryland, and North Carolina waters. The same year, 1.2 billion fish were caught by Zapata Haynie's vessels in the Gulf of Mexico.

"It runs hot and cold. Some days you might not have a hundred thousand fish to a boat, and other days everybody is loaded," says the chief pilot. "You have to be cunning to get the boats in the right position. It takes a considerable amount of skill to be a good fish spotter."

Another mark of a good spotter is whether he can tell the size of the fish from up high. "We can generally tell if the fish are three or seven inches long from three thousand feet away by the amount of whip." The whip, explains Williams, is the white streaks across the water surface caused by the flicking and splashing tails of the menhaden.

The pilot explains that the same size menhaden often school together. "We have problems after a strong northeaster. The little fish are pulled out of the creeks and estuaries and mix with the big fish. Since the small fish gill [get their gills caught] in the nets, this creates added work for the crew, who have to shake and pick the small fish out by hand."

"Bluefish are the only fish that give us much trouble because they school like menhaden," says Williams. "If we were to set on blues, it would be a mess because they have teeth and will eat up a net. A net costs over twenty thousand dollars, so that's the last thing we want to do."

Zapata Haynie's planes are spread out across the Bay. Three planes fly out of Reedville, and one flies out of Hummel Field in Topping, on the south side of the Rappahannock River. Planes also fly out of Yorktown, Portsmouth, and Norfolk.

"This way, we don't have all our eggs in one basket," says Williams. "If things are foggy on one part of the Bay, we can have boats and planes working in another part without much delay."

Williams starts his day at five o'clock in the morning and finishes after dark. Spotters work five days a week, and the Zapata Haynie pilots take turns working on Sundays. The steamers do not fish on Saturdays or Sundays, but on Sunday, a spotter flies from Cape Hatteras, North Carolina, to New York to locate fish so that on Monday morning the boats can be positioned in the best locations. The captains of the steamers are generally at home on Sunday monitoring the pilots, says Williams.

The Sunday pilot also has to fill out a fish report that relates tide and weather conditions, fish sightings, and sizes of schools. When Monday morning rolls around, captains, crews, and other spotters have a good idea of where the best fishing might be.

The season on the Chesapeake runs from the third Monday in May to the third Friday in November. After this, Williams and the menhaden fleet must leave Virginia waters. They then travel up the coast, as far north as New Jersey and New York, or south to Cape Hatteras. Fishing stops during the winter months because the vessels are not equipped to handle freezing weather and because menhaden are a migratory resource, says Williams. June, July, August, and September are the best months for menhaden fishing on the Bay, he says.

Williams thinks one of the major concerns of the menhaden industry today is loss of fishing grounds. "The fish we catch are in shallow water, and a high percentage are within three miles of the coastline," he says. "It's important that we don't lose any more fishing grounds. . . . All users of the inland and coastal waters must learn to live together so it won't place undue burden on anyone."

Charles Williams recently left Zapata Haynie as its chief spotter pilot to become general manager of Ampro Fisheries of Reedville, the nation's second largest menhaden firm.

✻ *In 1989, I was casually talking with John "Chip" Collamore III of Hulls Unlimited East, a fiberglass boatbuilding firm, in Deltaville, Virginia, when he told me about a boat he had recently completed. It was built for the Maryland catfish fishery on the Sassafras River.*

"You ought to go do a story on my boat," he said.

I told him that I was unaware that Maryland had much of a catfish fishery but that I would look into the possibility of doing a story on the boat. My investigation revealed that there was, in fact, a very large catfish fishery, and instead of doing a story on the boat, I decided that the fishery itself was more the story.

I thank Chip for giving me the tip that led to this chapter and also for introducing me to Albert "Buffalo" Strong, who graciously agreed to take me out for a day of fishing on the beautiful Sassafras River.

12 : Catching Catfish in Hoop Nets

THE EARLIEST of English writings about the New World mentioned catfish. Captain John Smith, in 1607, listed catfish as one of the fish in the New World that he was "acquainted with."

In 1705, Robert Beverley wrote in *The History and Present State of Virginia* that catfish were in abundance on the Chesapeake Bay. That same year, the unknown author of *Narrative of a Voyage to Maryland* wrote that "there is also the catfish which I believe is so called from its short thick chubbed head like a cat also with whiskers on each side of its mouth. It is a good fish but eats much like an eel and [is] found mostly in muddy water."

Anne Royall, in 1826, was not very complimentary of Chesapeake Bay catfish when discussing the fruit, fish, and meat market in Alexandria, Virginia, in *Sketches of the History, Life and Manners in the United States*:

> The market of Alexandria is abundant and cheap; though much inferior to any in any part of the western country except for beef and fish, which are by far superior to that of the western markets. . . . Their exquisite fish, oysters, crabs and foreign fruits upon the whole bring them upon a value with us.
>
> Their fish differ from ours, even the same species. Their catfish is the only sort in which we excel; they have none that answers to our bluecat, either in size or flavor, and nothing like our mud-cat. Their catfish is

> from ten to fifteen inches in length, with a wide mouth, like the mud-cat of the western waters; but their cat differ from both ours in substance and color; they are soft, pied black and white. They are principally used to make soup, which is much esteemed by the inhabitants. . . .

MODERN-DAY FISHING

Throughout history, catfish have been highly sought by commercial fishermen. In recent years, however, many people who enjoy the taste of catfish are serving up pond-grown cats. As crop farmers throughout the South began to use small fishing ponds on their property for growing catfish, many experts speculated that the commercial catfish fishery across the nation would suffer greatly. The prophets weren't too far wrong; many states have seen drastic declines in effort by commercial watermen to harvest cats.

An exception, however, is the state of Maryland. In 1980, commercial watermen in Maryland landed only 110,500 pounds of catfish. By 1985, those figures rose dramatically to 1,274,000 pounds and the annual catch has been over 1 million pounds every year thereafter. Catfish is now the number-one finfish caught in Maryland waters.

The main reason for this increase in catch is that a reliable, seasonal market for catfish has developed in several midwestern and southern states. Interestingly, this market has not come from the platters of big-city restaurants. Instead, Maryland cats are used to stock pay lakes, that is, ponds where hook-and-liners might pay eight dollars for an hour or so of fishing and be practically guaranteed of catching a fish.

BUFFALO STRONG

Albert "Buffalo" Strong, Jr., of Chestertown, Maryland, has been harvesting cats from the state's waters since 1970, as did his father in the sixties. "Buffalo" is a nickname that his grandfather gave him as a child. "I guess because I used to watch westerns on the television all the time," he says.

Buffalo says that 80 percent of his yearly harvest goes to stock ponds in Ohio, Indiana, New York, Pennsylvania, and Kentucky. "This market is great from April to Labor Day. The problem with the pay lake market is that it is slow after Labor Day and we do some of our best fishing in the fall," he says.

Buffalo says aquaculture and fish farming have hurt commercial catfish fishermen, particularly in retail and wholesale markets, where the fish are sold for food. "One of the advantages they have over us is that we can only supply fish when we can catch them. If they plan it right, they can supply fish to the market year-round."

"We have an advantage over them when it comes to the pay-lake market because those pond-grown fish have been trained to feed. As one man in Georgia who owns a lake told me, pond-grown fish will bite on a cigarette butt," says Buffalo. "Our cats are a lot more choosy when it comes to eating and are harder to catch because of it. Let's face it; the man running the lake doesn't want all his fish caught up the first day."

Another contributing factor to this steady market has been the price of Maryland cats. For fish sold to the live market, the price has stayed around forty cents per pound at the dock, while farm-raised catfish generally cost sixty-five to ninety cents per pound. The "dead market," where fish are shipped on ice to buyers and then sold to retail stores, offers less than half of the forty-cents-per-pound figure.

There are problems, however, that go along with harvesting cats for a live market. The number of days of fishing is limited by the availability of a truck with live tanks that picks up the fish. Buffalo says channel cats do not survive particularly well for days at a time in floating boxes. During the fall, fishermen often get only a couple of days a week of fishing because the market is simply not there. "There are days when we just sit by the telephone waiting for a call," Buffalo says.

Watermen working other Chesapeake Bay fisheries don't have the same problems. Many crabbers, oystermen, and other fishermen sell to buyers and leave the wholesale or retail marketing of the product to them. Naturally, watermen must worry about whether their processors and buyers can sell the product, but they don't have the headaches of trying to establish and hold on to markets.

"This is a tough part of the business for all of us," says Buffalo. "Last year the market was real good, but this year we lost a big buyer in Chicago who was hauling eighteen thousand pounds a week from us—that's two or three days of work a week. Then, a lake in Georgia went out of business [with the owner] owing us money."

"But we were lucky," he adds. "Rainbow Lakes, a firm that owns pay lakes in Ohio and Indiana, doubled its weekly order. So, it worked out all right."

On this particular day, Buffalo has a market for four thousand pounds of catfish. His catch goes to Virginia Live Fish Company in Chester, Virginia, where the catfish will be prepared for food consumption. "The only reason I have this market is because no one else is fishing. They all start back the first of October," Buffalo says. About fifteen catfish rigs are being worked from the Chester River to the Sassafras River, with more farther up in the Susquehanna, he says.

FISHING

Buffalo works the entire upper Chesapeake Bay and owns three boats. On this September day, Buffalo has over two thousand pounds stored in a live box and hopes a good day of fishing will fill his order of four thousand pounds. With his mate, Mark Elburn of Rock Hall, Maryland, Buffalo sets two lines of hoop nets in the Sassafras River just off from Turner Creek, where he moors his boats and keeps his live boxes. This area has not been worked since much earlier in the summer, so fishing should be good.

Each of Buffalo's boats work sixty to seventy nets in the fall and about thirty in the summer, when it is hotter and thus harder to keep the fish alive. The hoop nets on this day are baited with crushed horseshoe crab, but the bait type often varies with the time of year. In the spring, surf clams are best because they are soft and catfish feed by sucking. Since the fish are not as active in the early spring when the water is still cool, clams are an easy meal.

Menhaden are sometimes used. "We try it all," says Buffalo. "In the spring, we drive all the way to Cape May, New Jersey, to get clam bellies

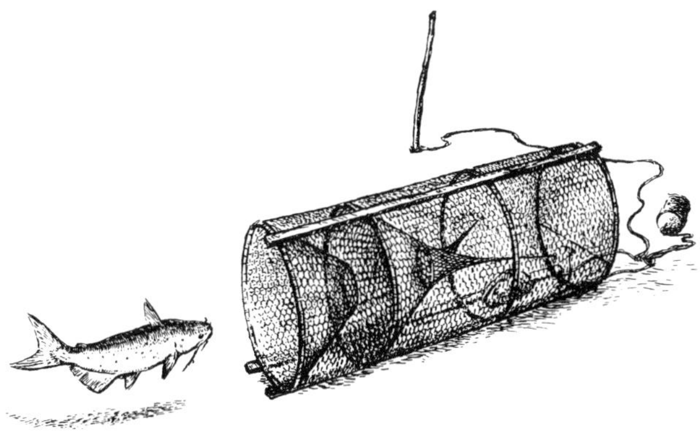

Hoop nets such as this one are used to harvest catfish on the Chesapeake. (Courtesy of the Virginia Institute of Marine Science)

Stepaside II was built specifically to harvest catfish on Maryland's Sassafras River. Waterman Buffalo Strong had the fiberglass boat built in Deltaville, Virginia, in 1989.

[surf clams], and in the fall we get our horseshoe crabs off the trawlers in Ocean City, Maryland. We usually start catching a few cats in March, but this year we didn't catch many until the end of May. It had us worried for a while, but August was a better month than usual. So, it all worked out."

The circular hoop nets measure 8 by 3½ feet with two interior chambers. The hoops themselves are made of fiberglass, a material that has been used for several years. "Before then, we used wooden hoops, and we would always have to carry a bunch of extras because so many would break in two. Fiberglass hoops hold up a lot better," says Buffalo. The mesh size is four inches in the front and three inches in the tail.

Rods made of PVC pipe run the length of the nets and are used to keep the gear stretched out straight. This setup is also relatively new, as Buffalo used oak strips just a few years ago. Although he uses hoop nets exclusively, other watermen use fyke nets to catch cats, which are set in shallow water near a shoreline. (A fyke net is a cylindrical fish net, similar to a hoop net, that is anchored in position or secured to stakes.)

About nine hoop nets are strung together at about seventy-five-foot intervals and tied together by a long rope. When the boat approaches the line, Buffalo tosses a grapple iron over and snags the rope. As the boat moves forward, the line is pulled over rollers positioned amidships and on the stern. When each hoop net surfaces, the mate unties the end of the fish net and dumps the catch into a basket, which is attached to a small mast/boom configuration. The rig swivels so it can be turned

Buffalo Strong (right) and his mate, Mark Elburn of Rock Hall, Maryland, fish the circular hoop nets in the spring, summer, and fall.

Fish are dumped from the hoop net into this basket. The basket is attached to a small mast/boom configuration that swivels to allow Buffalo (right) and Mark to easily dump the fish into a live box on deck.

Mark Elburn stirs the fish to help keep them aerated. On this day, Buffalo had over two thousand pounds in his live tank. There was so much weight, the vessel began to list.

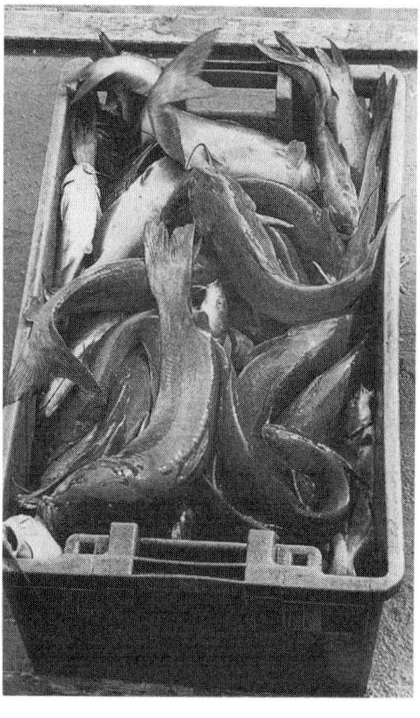

These channel cats caught from the Sassafras River will end up in a pay lake somewhere in the Midwest.

toward the inside of the boat, where the fish are then dumped into a large live tank.

A three-horsepower pump aerates the water to keep the fish alive. There is room on the deck for two tanks, but on this day there is only one. "Later in the fall, we'll put the other box in," says Buffalo. "One day last fall we caught forty-five hundred pounds in nine pots."

The trap is rebaited and thrown overboard, and the boat moves on to the next one. After the first line of nine pots was fished, it is clear that the fishermen have more than their two thousand pounds. In fact, the forty-two-foot *Stepaside II* begins to list toward the side of the loaded live tank.

Buffalo also has enough fish to fill a five-hundred-pound order for a Washington, D. C., fish market. The rest of the pots are left in the water. "The fish will keep until we can get back to them," he says. "The water quality here is much better than it was a few years ago. We can tell because the fish live a lot longer in boxes than they used to."

The entire trip took just a little over an hour. "It's not like this every day. It was so good, you would almost think we staged it for the camera," he says.

These wooden live boxes hold the catfish until Buffalo gets enough to make a load. Once he gets a load, fish are transferred from these boxes into a live-haul truck and hauled throughout the country.

UNLOADING

Back at the dock, a large flatbed truck with sixteen compartments filled with circulating water is waiting. The fish in the live tank on the boat are now emptied into a floating live box. A small door built into the starboard side of the vessel, when opened, allows fish to fall into the waiting box, which measures about six by twenty feet. Some boxes are made completely of wood with plastic-coated wire on the bottom, while others have wire all the way around.

The full live box is dragged to shore, where the fish are weighed and transferred to the truck. Another truck arrives hauling three-hundred-pound blocks of ice for the fish compartments. "They like to keep the temperature at fifty degrees [Fahrenheit] so the fish stay alive on the whole trip," says Buffalo. "When they go to Ohio and Indiana, it takes fourteen blocks of ice."

The work done, the truck driver writes Buffalo a check for $1,920 for forty-eight hundred pounds of catfish.

The winter months aren't as profitable for the fishermen. "We can't fish in the winter because they stop feeding when the water temperature gets down around fifty degrees," Buffalo says. "My wife owns an insurance company in Chestertown, and it really helps out after the cats are gone."

✻ *One of the more popular chapters in* Harvesting the Chesapeake: Tools and Traditions *is "Haul Seine Tales." The chapter includes stories of big fish catches during the 1940s and 1950s.*

As I researched this book, fish and oyster stories seemed to always come into the conversations. Some were so good that I could not resist.

13 : Fish and Oyster Tales

FIELDING DICKINSON of Loretto, Virginia, fished fyke, gill nets, haul seines, and pound nets above the salt line on the Rappahannock River near his family home place of Wheatland. The fresh water of the Rappahannock historically has provided some good fishing for catfish, perch, striped bass, and shad. Fielding recalls two stories. One has little to do with catching fish, but the other tells of a big catch he and his partner landed in the 1950s.

AN EMBARRASSED YOUTH

"I was about ten or twelve years old when this happened," recalls Fielding. Growing up, two of my favorite people were two colored folk, Uncle Al and Aunt Blanche. I had known them all my life because Aunt Blanche was the cook at Wheatland and Uncle Al was a handyman around the place. He knew how to cut up meat, lay the ice down in the icehouse, and shape the locust [fence] poles just right. He was a wise old apple.

"They lived over on the next farm in a two-room house. One side of the house was an old, low-ceiling log cabin where Aunt Blanche had her kitchen. I can tell you one thing, some of the best cooking in the world came from that little cabin. A typical breakfast was muskrat, fresh fish, sausage, corn bread, and eggs. You put all that stuff on the table and you had a feast.

"They had an adopted boy, Ernest, who I played with all the time. When we grew up, Ernest and I fished [commercially] together.

"One day, I was over there and Uncle Al was out digging worms for a fishing trip. Uncle Al and Aunt Blanche were great hook-and-line fishermen.

"He said to me, 'Come on, go fishing, boy. We need someone to help Ernest row that skiff over to Maple Creek.' To further entice me, he said, 'Blanche has cooked up some good food.'

"I couldn't turn down some of Aunt Blanche's food, so I said, 'Yeah, let's go.'

"They had a great big seine skiff with two sets of oars, and Ernest and I had a time rowing that skiff. Aunt Blanche was a fussy woman. The whole way over, she was telling us to keep the boat straight. I can see her now with that great big straw hat, holding that bamboo fishing pole in one hand and a bean can full of worms in the other.

"We got over to Maple Creek, and they started fishing. They were catching mostly catfish and an occasional perch, when I got the feeling I was going to have to pee.

"They were catching fish right and left. I knew nobody would want to go ashore. There was a duck blind just over yonder. I said, 'Aunt Blanche, what's in that duck blind over there?'

"'Hush up, boy, I'm catching fish.'

"I kept trying to hold it. Finally I said, 'Aunt Blanche, I got to go ashore for a minute.'

"'Boy, have you got to pee?' she asked.

"'Yes, Ma'am!'

"'Then hang your minnow right over the side of this boat and do it. Ain't nobody going to look at you, and besides, we're catching fish right now.'

"I was embarrassed, but I did it," he laughs.

FISH THAT DIDN'T GET AWAY

In the early 1950s, Fielding and Earnest were fishing for a living in the Rappahannock not far from Saunders Steamboat Wharf. This story is about their first day ever fishing a pound net. They caught a big catch of rockfish.

"We had always used haul seines, gill nets, and fyke nets, but one day we decided we'd buy a pound net," says Fielding. "Ernest and I went to Mathews County [Virginia] and bought a net for seventy-five dollars from an old boy down there. We also paid him twenty-five dollars to come up and show us how to set it. Neither one of us knew how to do it."

Mathews County, in the Mobjack Bay area, was where the first pound nets were successfully used on the Chesapeake Bay in the 1870s.

"We cut the poles and he showed us how to lay off the bays and put the net on the poles.

"The first day we fished was the first Saturday in April. We caught 5½ tons [11,000 pounds] of rockfish. We didn't even try to save the perch and herring that were in the net. We loaded everything we could in our skiff and then had to get these gill netters from across the river, in eighteen-foot skiffs, to come over and help.

"We pulled the skiffs up on the bank, and I drove my 1949 Dodge pickup truck down to the landing and filled her up. We sold the fish to old man Roberts at Nomini Creek for four and a half cents a pound [for a total of $495]. The day before I had gotten six cents a pound.

"We thought we were going to get rich, but the next day we didn't catch hardly anything. You can't ever tell about the river. Just when you think you can is when it will make you into the biggest fool in the world!"

A DEADLY OYSTER BATTLE

Over the years, there has been much written concerning the oyster wars of the Chesapeake. The oyster battles between Virginia watermen and Maryland Oyster Police on the Potomac and the battles between Bay watermen and Yankee oystermen are well documented.

For years, though, I have wondered about the neighborhood battles. I had heard tales of neighbor fighting against neighbor over oyster grounds, particularly in Virginia, where private grounds can be leased.

This story, related to me by Ruby Lee Norris of Topping, Virginia, tells something of what it was really like. I have a feeling that just as many people were killed over the years in these little neighborhood skirmishes as there were in the big battles.

"Now let me tell you," she begins, "there is a story in this world from this area about oyster battles. This is a story that I heard from my family members.

"One of the men in our neighborhood is supposed to have been defending oyster shore down on Scroggins Creek on the Piankatank River. This other fellow was encroaching on his territory, and the two of them had a big gun battle. And this neighbor of my family's shot the other man and killed him. Dead!

"Our neighbor was hauled into court for murder, and everybody in his family, on both sides, had to go his bail. It was five thousand dollars. This happened in 1911, and at that time, five thousand dollars would probably equal a million dollars today. There were a lot of people in his family, though. They pooled their money and property and appeared before the court and went his bond. Everybody came to his defense, even those in the family who couldn't stand him. Family pride, I suppose.

"When they came to trial, it went on for several days, but the jury cleared him because they proved that it was self-defense. This happened in 1911; I was born in 1915. I started school in 1921 when I was six years old with specific instructions to stay out of the way of these people.

"There was an undeclared war between the two families. They silently had little battles going on as kids. I remember that one time they stole a lunch, and I had to give the poor girl half of my sandwich. Another time, one of them stepped on the foot of the enemy who was standing in line by me going into the classroom after a recess break.

"There was no more killing, but the little battles went on until enough time passed that the death of the man was forgotten."

MURDER AMONG SHUCKERS

Over the years, Woodland Rowe has told me many stories about life at J. W. Hurley & Son oyster house in Urbanna, Virginia. This story is about a sad situation, but it reflects the rough and tough life of being an oyster shucker in the 1930s.

"Shuckers were a rough class of people," recalls Woodland. "I don't mean to say there weren't those who were good people. Many were hard-working, God-fearing people. Some of the finest folks I knew worked there, but most shuckers came up the hard way. They didn't have nothing given to 'em, I'll tell you that. They earned every penny they got.

"One of the worst things I remember happening was when George Carter killed his live-in girlfriend on Saturday night down at the old Long House near Burtons [steamboat] Wharf."

"The Long House was an apartment-type shanty house where shuckers rented rooms during the oyster season. Many of them came from far distances and had to find a place to stay in town.

"George and his woman got to fighting over something, and he took a board, hit her in the head, and knocked her down a flight of stairs. He hit her several times until she didn't move, and then he took gasoline, poured it over her, and lit her off.

"It was an awful sight to see," says Woodland shaking his head. "George was able to evade the law for several weeks. During that time, I had to come in early from buying oysters to drive shuckers home. A lot of them would walk to town, but everybody was scared to death of George. So during that time, I would go from house to house, and they would ride in the back of Mr. Hurley's truck.

"Finally George came out of hiding and tried to get a waterman up in Remlik to take him across the river. The waterman told George he had to work on his engine for a while, but he would take him across. In the meantime, a man was sent to get Sheriff Beverley Segar.

"When Mr. Segar drove up, George was sitting on the dock waiting. George put out his hands to be cuffed and said, 'Well, I guess you got me, Mr. Segar.'"

SOME WORDS OF CAUTION

This story was told to me by a ninety-four-year-old who asked that his/her name not be used.

"There was an oyster grower named Jake, who had oyster grounds on Mobjack Bay in Mathews County, Virginia. A Guineaman* was stealing his oysters, and word came that he had been seen out on Jake's ground taking oysters as fast as he could tong.

"Jake was furious. He ran to a corner in his kitchen where he kept his shotgun, grabbed his gun, and ran down the hill to his boat.

"Down at the dock, there was an old waterman bailing out his skiff.

"'Where you going in such a hurry there, Jake?' he asked.

"'I'm going to kill that Guineaman who's stealing my oysters,' he yelled.

"'Wait a minute, there, Jake,' he said as he climbed out the skiff and walked over to him. 'Let me tell you something about that Guineaman.'

"'What?' asked Jake.

"'More than likely, that Guineaman's got a mother in heaven and a father in hell, and he don't care which one he goes to see first. So, Jake, put that gun away and let the law take care of it.'"

Jake lived to see another day.

* A Guineaman is a man from Guinea Neck in Gloucester County, Virginia. Guinea is an area located between the mouth of the York and Severn Rivers. Over the years, it has produced some of the best watermen on the Bay.

A PINT OF WHISKY, A COLT REVOLVER, AND A BIBLE

In 1980, the late Billy LeCompte and I were sitting down on the dock at what was then Payne's Crab House in Urbanna. He told me a wonderful story of a legendary Virginia waterman who had outfoxed the Maryland Oyster Police up on the Potomac River.

Over the years, I've told this story many times in talks given around the Bay. In 1991, I told the story at the Calvert Museum at Solomons, Maryland. I was on stage with the renowned folklorist George G. Carey. After my talk, he grabbed my arm and said, "If you haven't written that one down, do it."

The story Billy told me was of a battle between the Maryland Oyster Police and several Virginia watermen who were illegally dredging for oysters at night on the Potomac River. It seems that these watermen had been making a habit of working these grounds and had successfully dodged the strong arm of the law for many nights.

On this particular night, however, their luck was about to change. It was a foggy, misty night, the type of night during which the Virginia watermen would least expect the Oyster Police to be patrolling. The police boat was armed with a Gatling gun on its bow as it moved slowly across the water with its lights out.

When the police came upon the watermen, they flashed a spotlight on the fleet and told them that they were under arrest. Exactly who fired the first shot is a matter of debate, but shots were fired, and when the smoke cleared, there were five vessels captured, one waterman killed, and several others wounded.

In the thick of the battle, one boat escaped and made it back to Harryhogan. The boat's captain had fought bravely but, seeing his chance to escape, had taken it. When he got back to the creek, he went to his mooring stake, untied his skiff, and tied it to the stern of his boat. His deadrise (V-bottomed) workboat was riddled with bullet holes, proof to anyone that he had been in the big battle.

He directed his boat to the deepest point in the creek, shut the engine down, and grabbed his gun and a picture of his wife that hung on the wall inside the pilothouse. He then loaded his double barrel and blasted holes into the bottom of his boat, sinking it on the spot.

He got in his skiff, rowed to shore, went home, and told his wife what had happened. He also told her that if anyone came looking for him, to tell the person he had been in bed all night, and that he had sold his boat the week before.

The next morning, Virginia and Maryland police came to Harryhogan looking for a boat riddled with bullet holes. They came to the house and asked his wife if her husband had been out on the water that night. She said that he had been in bed all night, and besides, he had sold his boat the week before. Naturally, the Virginia watermen who had been taken captive would not tell who it was who had made the big escape, and no charges were ever brought against the man.

The story of that misty, foggy night continued to be told and retold around the docks. The mystery man's legend grew. After some talking, I was able to pump Billy LeCompte as to just who this man was. I decided, on the spot, that I was going to Harryhogan and talk. Over thirty years had passed. Surely, he would be ready to talk about this now.

I called the waterman and told him I was a writer and would like to talk to him about his life as a waterman. He was very kind and invited me up. When I arrived at his home, I was met by an old man who was hard of hearing and whose sight was partially gone. We sat and talked for several hours about his life on the water, and after a while I saw the chance to ask him about that night.

"Tell me about that night when the Maryland Police came down on you boys with that Gatling gun?" I asked.

Suddenly, the mood of the conversation shifted, and there was silence. I knew that I had stepped onto forbidden turf.

"Are you the law?" he asked me.

I said no, but even if I were, so much time had passed that the statute of limitations would protect him.

The old man was sitting at a rolltop desk, and I sat very close to him so he could hear me clearly. He pulled open a drawer and reached down into it. He first pulled out a pint bottle full of what I assumed to be whiskey and set it on the desk top. He did not offer me a drink. Then, he reached into the drawer again and pulled out a 36-caliber Colt revolver that made me wonder what plans he might have for that. He placed the revolver next to the pint of whiskey, reached back into the drawer, and brought out a King James version of the Bible. He placed the Bible alongside the gun and pint of whiskey, put his hand on the Bible, and looked me straight in the eye.

He said, "As God is my witness, I wasn't there that night."

He then asked me to leave.

✳ *Over the years, I've done many stories on hand tonging for oysters. The scissor-like tongs have played a major role in the development of the once mighty Chesapeake Bay oyster industry, but with the decline of the oyster fishery has come the demise of the business of making shaft tongs.*

I feel very fortunate to have found George Williams, one of the last shaft tong makers in Virginia. George graciously agreed to share his knowledge of an American craft that goes back to the early 1700s.

14 : How to Make Shaft Tongs

TWENTY-FIVE years ago, George Williams of Naxera, Virginia, wanted shafts for a set of oyster tongs. There was only one shaft maker in the area, and he had such a backlog that George was placed on a waiting list. But George couldn't wait: he went home and made his own.

Since then, George has made hundreds of pairs of shafts and tong heads or baskets for Virginia and Maryland watermen, who use them in the same manner as their forebears. To work a set of tongs, Chesapeake Bay watermen stand on the washboards of their boats. They extend the tongs over the side and, with a scissoring motion, are able to gather oysters off the bottom.

Shaft tongs, one of the oldest gear forms in America, were first introduced to the Chesapeake in the early 1700s. Prior to this, oysters were so plentiful, American Indians and early settlers were able to walk out at low tide and pick up as much as they desired. But as the population began to grow, people quickly depleted the oysters that were close to shore. Hand tongs were introduced for harvesting oysters in deeper water.

Years back, almost every waterfront community had a village carpenter who would keep a good supply of shafts on hand. The shaft maker would shape the tong handles from either hickory or locust wood cut from the local forest. The heads on the very early oyster tongs were wooden; later, they were made of metal by the local blacksmith.

George Williams is one of the last builders of hand tong shafts in the Chesapeake Bay region. Using fir from the Pacific Northwest, he makes shafts up to thirty feet long.

The length of the shafts depended on the depth of the rivers and creeks that oystermen were working. Often, different lengths of tongs were carried for varying depths of water. For shallow water, a short-handled tong with a small head, called a nipper, was used. Generally eight to twelve feet long, these were especially good in creeks. Often children were sent out with a pair of nippers to catch a "mess" of oysters for the supper table. The long-handled tongs range from fourteen to thirty feet.

Several different types of tong heads were developed. One of the more interesting was the eel pot head. This particular style is used mostly in Maryland and was designed so that watermen would not have to open the basket to empty their catch. The eel pot head probably got its name because of its round shape, similar to a round eel pot. However, since oysters have a tendency to crib, or hang together, they seldom just slip freely out of the side of the eel pot head. After most good catches, the tong head has to be opened just like a pair of standard tongs.

For many years, George made standard flat/straight metal tong heads, such as this one, at his shop in Naxera, Virginia. For the past few years, though, he has concentrated on just making wooden shafts.

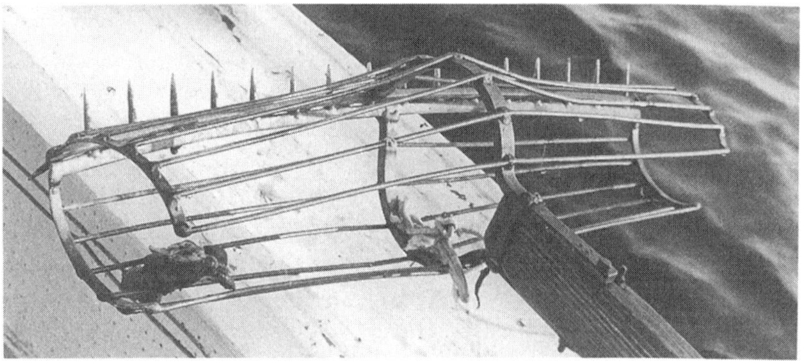

On occasion, George would make the rounded eel-pot heads. Maryland oystermen seemed to prefer this style of gear, designed to empty the catch from the side without the tongs opening.

GEORGE WILLIAMS, OYSTERMAN AND TONG MAKER

"That same year I went to get those shafts, there were 450 boats working in the James River," says George. "Otho Robinson was the only one around here making shafts, and he couldn't keep up with demand. When you have seven hundred to eight hundred oystermen needing shafts, one man can't keep up. Half the time, we would go there to get shafts, and he wouldn't have nothing.

"Back then, there were a lot of oysters around here. I had a forty-four-foot pound [fish] boat that I oystered from, and one day another man and I caught five hundred bushels of oysters on the Piankatank River. I oystered most of my life, and that was the biggest catch I ever had. Now, you are lucky to catch five bushels.

"I retired from working the water when I was sixty-two. Now I'm seventy. I figured if I could make enough to live off by making shaft tongs, I could give up the water. If the oystering business hadn't gone bad, I could have done it, too. God knows how many tongs I've made.

"I sold my boat and went to making shaft tongs full-time. I'm the youngest tong maker around, and I'm not young. When I was a boy, there were plenty of tong makers. Then, every little community had at least one. Now, I know of two others besides myself—one is eighty-seven, and the other is eighty-three years old. They've gotten too old to do much work now. All the rest have died out.

"I think it's the same way in Maryland. A few years ago, when the business was still good, I got as many calls from Maryland watermen as I did from Virginians.

"The reason I didn't go into full-time tong making sooner was because I loved working the water. When a bunch of us boys would get down there on the James River working, we had good times together. I loved the stories and the joking and the good food and good company. Working alone in my shop is not as much fun."

A GOOD STORY

"One day, we were all working close together on a good lump of oysters, and Bernard Sickal starting talking. He said one time during the depression his daddy took him to the stockyard to try and sell an old horse to get some money, but the man said the horse was too old and wa'n't worth buying.

"That night, Bernard's daddy sent him down to the store to buy some coal black shoe polish. They took a rag and they polished that old horse right up until his coat sparkled," says George.

"Next day, they took the old horse back to the stockyard, and the man said, 'Now, that's more like it. That's a good-looking horse,' and bought him on the spot." George laughs. "They were hard times in the depression."

MAKING SHAFTS

George sells each set of shafts for $3.50 a foot, unless it is over twenty feet and has to be spliced. Then, it costs more. "If I splice them, I have to charge more because it takes more time," he says. "I made a pair of twenty-eight-footers for a boy last year, and I had to splice it because I can't get good wood any longer than twenty feet anymore."

He recently suffered some vision problems and has stopped making the metal heads, but he can still shape a fine pair of shafts. George makes the shafts from clear straight-grain one-by-six-inch fir boards. The length is determined by the desired length of the shaft. If a waterman wants shafts over twenty feet long, George splices the wood together by using a V scarf joint. Otherwise, the shafts are made from a solid piece of wood.

George uses a rasp, or plane, or electric rotor to round the edges of the handles to give the shafts a comfortable feel.

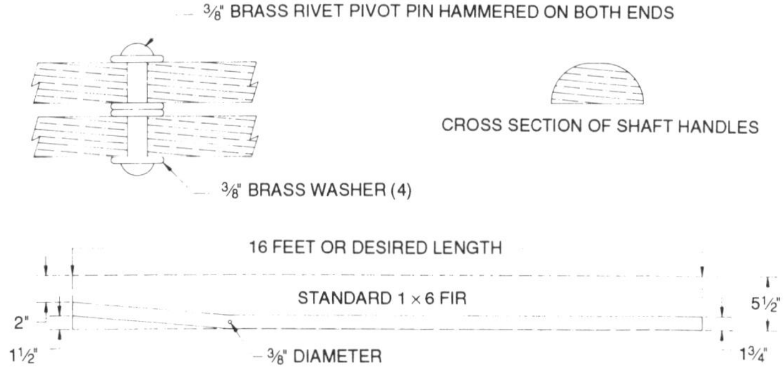

Drawing A
Drawing by Ray V. Rodgers, III

The shafts are laid out as in drawing A. The outer edges of the handles, from the pivot point to the end of both shafts, are smoothed as shown in a cross-section drawing of the shaft handle (drawing A). George does this by using a rasp or hand plane or electric rotor. The width of the handle varies to accommodate the size of the person's hand. "Some people want the handles big. Some people got little short fingers; they want little small ones. The widest I make are three inches, but if you don't have a big hand a three-inch handle will bust your fingers open," George says.

A 3/8-inch brass rivet pivot pin (drawing A) holds the tongs together and allows the shafts to move in a scissorlike motion. The balance point, where the rivet is set, is 4 feet from the base of 16-footers, 4½ feet on 18-footers, and 5 feet on 20-footers. On the outside of each shaft, George countersinks the rivet hole to the depth of a rove or washer. Four brass washers are used, two on the outsides with the furls, and two on the insides of the two shafts. Each end of the brass rivet is hammered flat so that an edge will hold the rove.

"Back there years ago, when we didn't have brass washers and rivets, I put many a wooden rivet in," says George. "I'd always keep plenty of hickory aboard the boat. I've put many a one on for the other boys working with me because they didn't know how. Hickory, oak, or locust was good. Something that was real hard. But old hickory was the best. That is, until brass came along."

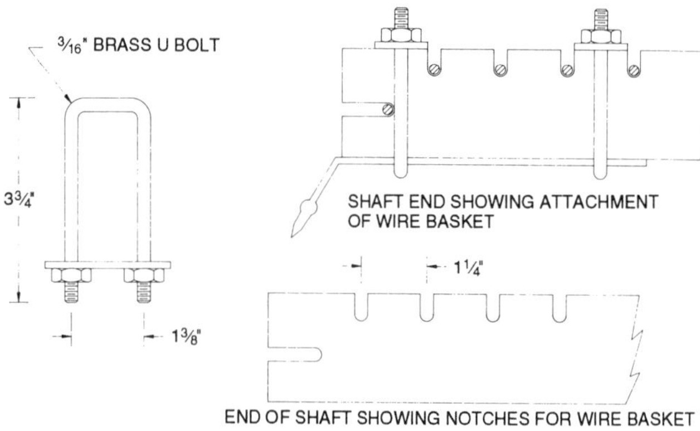

Drawing B
Drawing by Ray V. Rodgers, III

From the rivet down to where the basket is mounted, the shafts are tapered down to about a 2½ inches in width. The ends of the shafts are notched (drawing B). The notches on each shaft should be facing away from one another and are a mirror image of the other.

The fir wood comes from the West Coast and is hand-picked by George at a local lumber company that orders the wood especially for him. When it comes to finding good wood, George has faced some difficulties. "It's hard to find good stuff," he says. "There can't be a knot anywhere on the handle because it makes for a weak spot and will break."

CONSTRUCTING AND MOUNTING THE WIRE BASKET

For many years, George used a forge at his shop and other tools to make the wire baskets for his tongs. The gum of the basket (the part that holds the teeth) is made from ¾-by-¼-by-36-inch steel and hammered to a curved, tapered hook on both ends (drawing C).

The teeth are two inches long and made from quarter-inch rod. They are shaped to a point by heating and hammering. The teeth are welded to the front edge of the gum at a ninety-degree angle and are spaced two inches apart (drawing C & drawing D, right).

Next, the gum and tooth assembly is welded to a tongue or shank at an angle as in drawing D. The tongue is made of ¾-by-3/16-by-6½-inch steel and is attached to the gum off-center (drawing D, left) so that each basket will align with the wooden shafts.

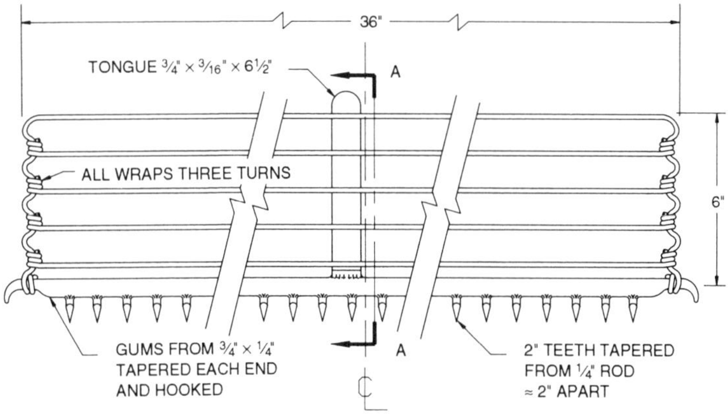

Drawing C

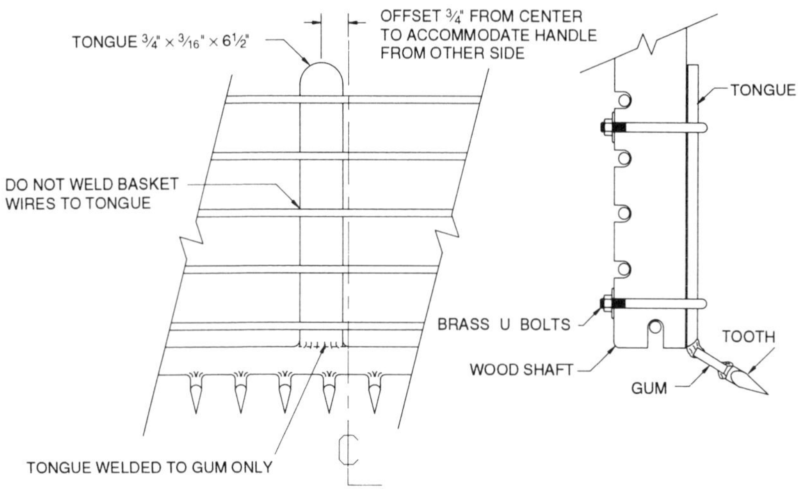

Drawing D

Drawings by Ray V. Rodgers, III

The wire basket is constructed of 3/16-inch wire. The outside rim of the basket must be crimped on both ends to accommodate the wraps from the middle wires, as in drawing C.

George designed and built his own homemade crimping tool to make his crimps (photo 1, drawings E and F). The wire is placed in the crimper as in drawing G. The crimp is shown in drawing H, left. The outer

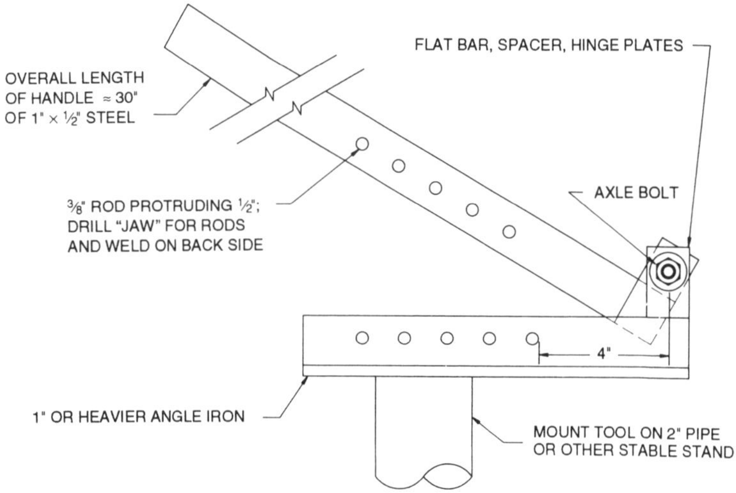

Drawing E

Drawing by Ray V. Rodgers, III

Photo 1

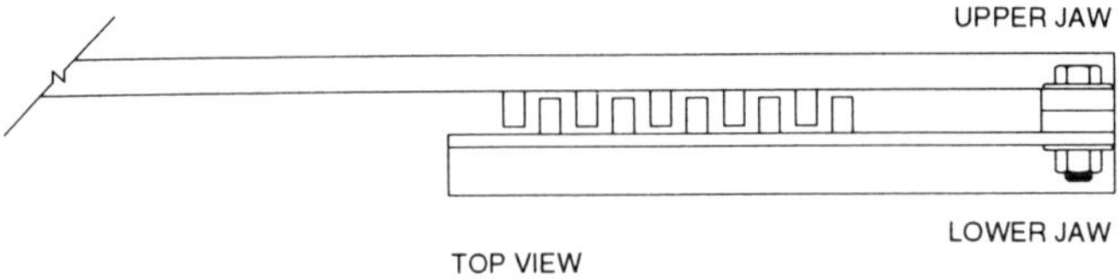

Drawing F

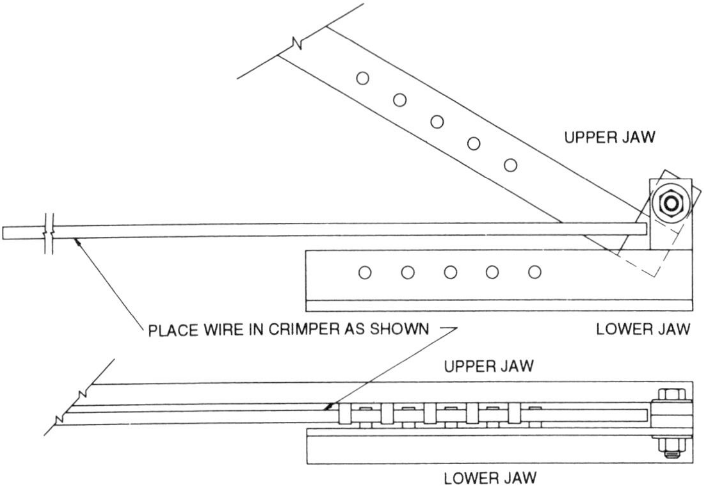

Drawing G

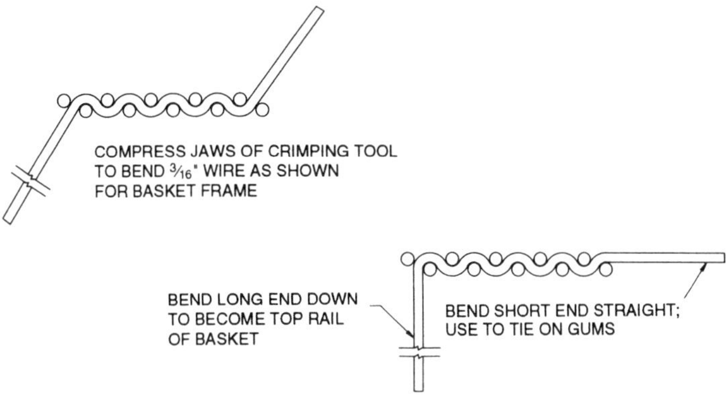

Drawing H

Drawings by Ray V. Rodgers, III

Photo 2

rim is completed by bending the top rail down and the short end straight (drawing H, right). The outer rail and the rest of the inside of the basket wires are attached as in drawing C.

The basket is attached to the shafts as shown in drawing D, right, with two brass U bolts. A U bolt is shown in drawing B, left, and photo 2. The tongue goes on the inside of the shaft, and basket wires go on the outside and fit in the slots cut into the wood. To protect the end of the shaft and to help hold down the basket wires, George makes an L-shaped guard strip (photo 2). This strip is made from copper tubing that is cut open and hammered flat. It fits on the outside edge of the shaft over the basket wires and is held in place by the U bolts and screws.

"I hope I can continue to work, but the oyster business down here has gone to pot," says George. "It's a shame, too. There is a type of freedom in working for yourself. If you get tired, you just quit. If you are working for somebody else, you work until he says it's time to quit.

"I really don't think it is much better in Maryland," says George. "I got a man up there who has been ordering shafts from me for right many years. He doesn't like fir. He prefers his shafts made from yellow pine. He didn't place an order this year because oystering was so bad up there. Before I started using fir, most all my shafts were made from yellow pine. Now you can hardly give them away. The fir feels so good on your hands when you are working.

"I used to sell right many nippers to Maryland watermen," says George. "Nipper tongs are different. The tong heads stay open. They are good for catching one or two oysters at a time. One man I sold a pair of nippers to in Maryland wrote me that he caught forty bushels in one day with my tongs.

"I know all this is about gone, but I hope the good Lord will help us bring the oyster back. It just doesn't seem right that there are so few oysters in the Chesapeake Bay. I know a lot of people don't think so, but I think they will come back in a big way one day. And maybe there will be a few oystermen left around that I can make shafts for."

✻ *Sometime in the mid-1980s, my longtime physician and friend, Dr. A. L. Van Name, Jr. gave me two photographs his mother, Ethel Coleman Van Name, had taken between 1900 and 1910. They were of Yankee skiffs being worked on Van Name oyster grounds on the York River.*

He suggested that I do an article on the history of these skiffs on the Chesapeake. Now I finally have the opportunity to write about these northern boats that were adopted in the Chesapeake.

15 : Yankee Skiffs

IN THE 1800s, northern oyster growers sailed south to the Chesapeake Bay to buy and harvest oysters. In those days, the northern oyster business was booming. Oyster growers (who raised oysters in natural waters by setting out young "seed" oysters) kept up with the ever-increasing demand for oysters in the big northern cities by sending schooners down to harvest the fertile grounds of the Chesapeake.

When northern boats arrived on the Bay, they created quite a stir, as the Yankee schooners were equipped with dredges, which were more efficient than the primitive hand tongs being used by Bay oystermen. In many areas, the northern oystermen raked the bottoms clean, and local watermen adamantly complained of the injustice of these men coming from the north and "stealing" their oysters.

Local watermen took their plight to state legislatures of both Maryland and Virginia, and laws were passed to prohibit the use of the dredge and the shipment of oysters out of state. Neither of these rulings amounted to much because there was no enforcement. However, some northern oystermen moved to the Bay, bought land, leased oyster grounds, and hired local tongers to harvest their grounds. They brought to the Chesapeake a new type of oyster skiff.

One area where the northern oyster business flourished was Prince's Bay, off Staten Island, New York. There, oystermen took vast areas of ocean bottom off Manhattan and planted skiff loads of seed oysters.

A type of skiff used there to harvest and plant oysters was the very stable Prince's Bay skiff, or Staten Island skiff, or as it became known down south, the Yankee skiff.

Staten Island skiffs were brought to the Chesapeake on schooners in the 1800s by northern oyster buyers, who were expanding their territory to keep up with the ever-increasing demand for oysters in the north. (Courtesy of Dr. A. L. Van Name, Jr.)

John Gardner, the longtime technical editor for *National Fisherman,* discussed the skiff in the July 1985 issue of the magazine:

> The origin of the Staten Island skiff can be traced back in direct line to the thousands of bateaux that were built for transporting troops and supplies . . . during the French and Indian Wars between 1750 and 1760.
>
> When the men of the Batoe Service, who built and used these boats during the war, returned home to the north Atlantic coast, they proceeded to construct small craft suited to local needs, but derived in part from the wartime bateaux.
>
> The boats they built included the various New England dories and wherries, the Sea Bright or Jersey Beach skiff and the Staten Island skiff. . . .

One of the first northern oystermen to bring Staten Island skiffs to the Chesapeake was Captain Dave Van Name, who, around 1870, bought a five-hundred-acre farm in Gloucester County, Virginia, on the York River, and named it Starvation.

Captain Dave hired hand tongers to harvest oysters from the fertile York River oyster grounds and to load his catch onto one of the Van Name schooners. He then hauled the catch "up the beach" to New York City.

Captain Dave and his sons, Peter, Jacob, and William H. Van Name had a flourishing oyster firm named Van Name Brothers of Staten Island. The firm retailed oysters at the docks in New York City from a large scow.

When the oyster industry was alive and well on the York River, the Yankee skiff was one of the main vessels used to harvest the beds. (Courtesy of Dr. A. L. Van Name, Jr.)

Doctor Arthur Van Name, Jr., is the great-great-grandson of Captain Dave. Although the Van Name oyster business was practically folded when he came along, Doctor Van, as he is affectionately called by many of his former patients, recalls with fondness Starvation Farm and the Yankee skiffs.

When Doctor Van was a boy, his father, Arthur Van Name, Sr., was still trying to make a go of the oyster business, and these skiffs were being used at Starvation on a regular basis.

"I remember the boats well," he says. "I rowed them myself. Yes sir, they were the best rowing boat in the world! I'm not a big man, but I'm fairly strong and pretty tough, and if the wind wasn't blowing against me, I could row a skiff full of oysters with ease.

"These boats were built for rowing, and it was intended for two men to row them. The oars were about eighteen feet long, and the skiffs were so balanced they would glide through the water.

"Pop [Arthur Van Name, Sr.] always called them Staten Island skiffs, but some people call them Yankee skiffs. I never heard the name Yankee skiffs until I was an adult.

"We had fifteen or twenty of them and they measured about twenty-two by six feet. They were lapstrake, or clinker built, and flat bottomed." Lapstrake is a type of construction in which each side plank is situated so that the edge of each plank overlaps the next plank. This is similar to clapboard construction on the side of a house.

"The first skiffs were brought here on schooners. I imagine Captain Dave [Van Name] brought many of them down. All they had to do was put them on deck, end to end, and bring them on down from Staten Island.

"We had two schooners, the *William H. Van Name* and the *David Carll,* which was later named the *Blackbird.* The *Van Name* and the *Carll* were both built by David Carll at City Island, New York. The *Van Name* was built in 1872 and considered one of the fastest-sailing schooners around.

"My family, along with a great many other people, had oyster grounds on Prince's Bay, and they used these skiffs. When they came to the York River, some of the best grounds were in creeks and on beds in the river in real shallow water.

"There were small boats down here, flat-bottomed and deadrise skiffs, but nothing the size of the Staten Island skiff that would row and carry a bunch of oysters like it would.

"Two big colored men would stand in the stern, back to back, tonging up oysters with hand tongs, [and] pile the oysters on a culling board in the middle of the skiff, while another man would cull the catch. There were two removable seats in the boat, which allowed them more space for catch. They had to save enough room for one seat so they could row back.

Dr. A. L. Van Name, Jr., holds a drawing he made of the *David Carll*, later known as the *Blackbird*. This vessel was used by the Van Name Brothers of Staten Island, New York, in the 1880s to haul Bay oysters "up the beach" and to bring Staten Island oyster skiffs to the Chesapeake Bay.

Each skiff was worked by two tongers and a culling man and was powered by oars. (Courtesy of Dr. A. L. Van Name, Jr.)

Judging from the photo, the skiffs could hold a pretty good load of oysters. (Courtesy of Dr. A. L. Van Name, Jr.)

"You'd look at those skiffs and think they wouldn't row to save your neck. But the oars were so balanced with the boat, that when you rowed it, the weight of the oar was all on the boat. You were just giving it a little pull, and you didn't have to row hard. You would give the oars a little heave, a rocking motion, and it would scoot right along.

"It had right much freeboard, though, so wind would play hell with you, but the tide not as much so. I don't mean you could go right along against the York River tide, but inshore you could get around pretty nicely.

The *Powhatan* was one of the few Staten Island skiffs that was converted to power, and it was probably renamed. It belonged to Captain Dick Coleman, the grandfather of Dr. A. L. Van Name, Jr., and was used for pleasure on the York River. (Courtesy of Dr. A. L. Van Name, Jr.)

"When internal-combustion engines came along, some oystermen put motors into them. My grandfather, Captain Dick Coleman, my mother's father, had a Staten Island skiff named *Powhatan* that he put power into, and it worked real good.

"I never saw them painted but two ways in my life. One was skiff green with yellow trimmings, and the other was white with a black stripe. On the skiff green ones, the outside was painted green and the inside yellow. Even today when I see that shade of green, I call it skiff green, and everyone in my family did, too. Sometimes the skiffs would have copper on the bottom. I never saw them painted any other way. It was a Van Name trait and, I guess, it was passed down to Pop from his father and his father before him.

"Each boat had a plug in the stern, which allowed water to be drained out when the boats were pulled up on shore.

"After we left Starvation, we did not sell the house or the property right away. I'm sure Pop had hopes of getting back there and doing that kind of work again. It was hard on him to give up the oyster business, but it went right down to nothing."

The Van Names moved to West Point, Virginia, which was not far from Starvation, in 1916.

"We'd go back down in the summer, and the skiffs would be pulled up under some cedar trees there on the shore. Pop would let some of the oystermen who used to work for us use the skiffs in the winter. He let them use them for two reasons: One, it was hard times and the skiffs were the only thing that could give them what little living they had, which wa'n't much. Also, if you don't turn over oyster grounds, they become nonproductive.

"The house was still standing then, and we had tenants in it. Pop would keep one room for us to spend the night and come and go. This allowed him to look over the property and skiffs when he wanted. He loved it at Starvation."

COMBATING OYSTER THIEVERY

"We had a trick to take care of oyster thieves. Of course, there were always thieves, and there were guardhouses built out on the oyster grounds, where a guy with a rifle would watch the beds at night.

"The guards would listen out, and on a quiet night, you could hear a whole lot on the water. If they heard somebody at night working the grounds, they didn't go right out and start shooting.

"The watchman would wait, and once the thieves had gotten all the oysters they wanted and were heading for home, he would follow them. You see, they couldn't take those oysters to an oyster house at night because the buyers would know damn well they were stolen. So, the guard would know they were not going to do anything with the oysters until the next day.

"The watchman would go and get two or three men, and they would go back and very quietly slip in and take the skiff full of oysters and row it to Starvation.

"If the thieves came for the boat, guess what? And if they didn't come for the boat, guess what? They didn't get the skiff back either way.

"Pop said it was a very effective way of breaking up thieving," says Dr. Van with a laugh.

LYNN PERRY

Lynn Perry grew up in West Point just upriver from Starvation and was a childhood friend of Dr. Van. Lynn first saw Staten Island skiffs at Starvation on weekend trips to the farm with the Van Names, but he got hands-on experience with the skiffs some years later.

When Arthur Van Name, Sr., decided to sell Starvation and his interest in the oyster business, oystermen Mike and Ed Scanlan of West

Point bought several of the Van Name skiffs. The Scanlan brothers leased oyster grounds near Purtan Bay on the York and would hire oystermen to work their beds from the skiffs.

In April, when the oyster season was over, Mike and Ed would gather their children and some of the kids in the neighborhood at West Point to ride down to Purtan Bay to pick up their skiffs and bring them back to West Point for a summer overhaul. Lynn was one of those kids who went along with the Scanlans.

"The Scanlans had an old log bugeye that was about fifty feet long. It had decks, one big hatch, and a right nice little fo'c'sle. They would sell their oysters to Marshall's Oyster House in West Point. They had about eight or ten skiffs, and the people who worked for them were colored men from Wood Cross Road [Gloucester County, Virginia]. The Scanlans would take oysters from out of the skiffs, load them onto the bugeye, and haul them to Marshall's in West Point.

"In April, after they got through oystering, they would pull these skiffs up on shore near their oyster grounds and let them dry out. The skiffs would sit there until a good warm day, and the two brothers would get their children and other kids around the neighborhood to go up to Purtan Bay to pick them up.

"We'd get on the bugeye at West Point, carry a picnic lunch, and have a good old time. The log bugeye had one sail—a foresail—and when they raised the foresail on her, if there was a good southeaster, she would sail right good. With the engine, it would make real good time.

"When we got there, they'd anchor the bugeye, and we'd all go ashore in a skiff. And each one of us would take a Staten Island skiff and row it out to the bugeye.

"We would hook all the skiffs to the stern of the big boat and tow them to West Point. There was a slip at the foot of Seventh Street in West Point where the Scanlans would roll the skiffs up onto the shore. They owned a big tin building close to the shore, and all the skiffs were hauled inside. From April to August, Mike and Ed would overhaul all the boats. Sometimes they would replace a frame or [do] whatever needed to be done. They would clean them up, paint, scrape them up, and I mean they were in perfect shape when the oyster season started in September.

"I was about fourteen years old, and this was in the late 1920s. I was just a teenager, but I remember I could row the skiff without any problem.

Lynn Perry recalls the last days of Yankee skiffs on the York River.

They were easy to row. We would carry a picnic lunch to make it a day, and the Scanlan children were always with us. We all went to West Point Grammar School together.

"After they got through overhauling the skiffs, they would put them overboard in September to let them swell up for a day or two, and then on Monday morning, they'd come down to the dock. Mike and Ed were real slow moving. You'd almost have to site them to make sure they were moving. And both of them chawed tobacco and smoked a pipe at the same time.

"After they would get their tobacco straight, Ed would loosen the lines on the skiffs and tie them to the bugeye, and they'd haul them back down to Purtan Bay for another oyster season.

"Mike told my daddy one time that the last good year oystering they had, they made twenty-five hundred dollars. Of course, that was split two ways, but they were living comfortably.

"Later on, Chesapeake Corporation [one of the largest pulp mills in Virginia] bought up most of the oyster grounds on the York River, and the Scanlans quit.

"Chesapeake used the skiffs to harvest oysters for a number of years, but the end was near for the Staten Island skiffs. Most of them ended up rotting in the marshes up and down the York River.

"I will tell you one thing, though, they were pretty little boats."

* *In 1985, I wrote a story on J. W. Hurley & Son, a seafood company founded in Urbanna just before the turn of this century. Hurley's was renowned for its "King of Them All" Rappahannock River oyster.*

When I decided to include a chapter on the history of the Bay's oyster packing industry, I remembered the story and Woodland Rowe's clear memory of day-to-day life at Hurley's oyster shucking house.

It just made good sense to go back to Woodland and talk to him some more.

16 : The Oyster Packing Business

EVEN THOUGH oysters were a staple food for many households in colonial times, the oyster industry in Virginia and Maryland did not grow significantly until the nineteenth century. Throughout the early years of English settlement in those colonies, most of the population lived close to the shores of the Chesapeake and its tributaries. This allowed easy access to the waterways where settlers could catch their own oysters, or send slaves out to "catch a mess," or barter or buy from a neighbor.

The Bay's first commercial shucking houses were small shanties either built along the shore or out in the backyard. There, an oysterman would shuck his day's catch and sell his oysters throughout the neighborhood from the back of a horse-drawn wagon or ox cart or to those customers who happened by.

Large packing houses did not evolve until the nation's population began to grow and large population centers were established inland, away from the waterways. With this growth, the oyster industry began to play an important role in the economy of cities such as Baltimore and Norfolk and in towns located close to plentiful oyster grounds.

The industry also received help from northern oystermen who came south to replenish an over-fished, exhausted northern oyster fishery. A very large and lucrative industry had been established in the northern states by the mid-1700s. But, by the early 1800s, Yankee oystermen had depleted their oyster stock and were looking to the Chesapeake to help supply the ever-increasing demand for oysters in big-city restaurants.

Many northern oyster firms set up shop along the shores of the Chesapeake. Northern oystermen came south, bringing with them new types of harvesting gear and knowledge of how to operate large shucking houses. Soon, oyster packing houses were established in Baltimore, Crisfield, and Norfolk; on the York and Rappahannock Rivers; and at other sites.

Richard H. Edmonds wrote of the packing industry in an 1879 report on the Maryland oyster industry:

> About 1834 or 1835 a small packing house was opened in Baltimore, but it soon passed out of existence, and no record of it can now be obtained. The first important enterprise in this line was the establishment of a packing house in 1836 by Mr. C. S. Maltby, a native of Connecticut. Mr. Maltby . . . confined his operations exclusively to the raw trade for a number of years. As his business increased he established a line of wagons from Baltimore to Pittsburgh; and was thus enabled to supply the West with fresh oysters long before the Baltimore and Ohio Railroad had stretched out its track to that then distant region. Mr. A. Field was the first to develop in Baltimore the steam trade. He began a few years after Mr. Maltby. His oysters were steamed and then hermetically sealed in small tin cans.

Virginia oyster shucking houses relied mostly on African-Americans to shuck oysters, whereas in Baltimore, European immigrants found shucking houses to be one of the first places they could find a job. (From George Brown Goode's *Fisheries and Fishery Industries of the United States*, published in 1887)

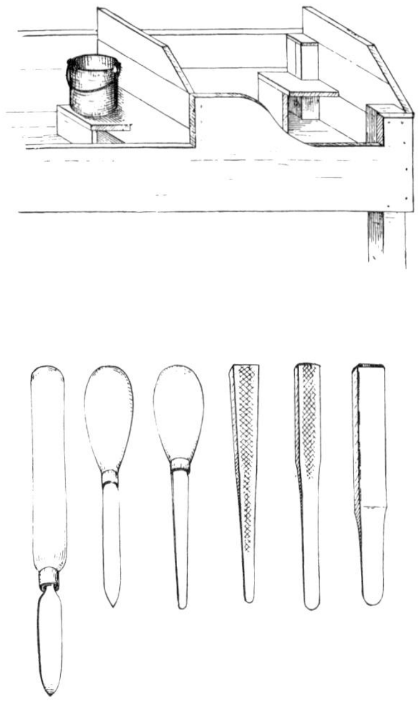

Although oyster-shucking troughs varied from oyster house to oyster house, this one was used in a Baltimore shucking house in the 1880s. The oyster knives are examples of types used in New England, New York, and the Chesapeake region. (From George Brown Goode's *Fisheries and Fishery Industries of the United States*, published in 1887)

After these first packing houses were established in Maryland, the city of Baltimore quickly grew into the world's largest oyster producer. Edmonds provided some specifics:

> Baltimore, the great oyster market of the United States, annually packs more oysters than any other city in the world. It is the great center of the packing trade, surpassing in that particular all other cities, and yearly handling more oysters than all the other packing points of Maryland and Virginia combined. During the season extending from September 1, 1879, to May 15, 1880, the number of vessels loaded with oysters arriving at Baltimore was 9,543 (or a daily average of 37 for the 257 days, bringing) 7,252,972 bushels, which would make the average cargo 760 bushels.

Although the industry started later in Virginia, it grew quickly after the Civil War. Edmonds described the Virginia oyster fishery:

> The packing trade of Virginia is of much later origin than that of Maryland. About the year 1859 a Captain Fitzgerald opened an oyster packing establishment in Norfolk, but [with] the war coming on, in a few years the business was greatly hampered and restricted, and it was not until 1865 that the trade gave any evidence of ever becoming very extensive. As the transportation facilities to cities increased, and the ill effects of the war began to die out, the oyster trade showed a very marked improvement, and during the last few years it has developed very rapidly. In Norfolk, as in Baltimore and other cities of Maryland, the trade is largely in the hands of northern men; one difference, however, being quite noticeable, and that is, that whereas in Maryland the packers are principally natives of Connecticut, in Norfolk they are nearly all either New York or Boston men. The enterprise and capital of these gentlemen has largely developed this business, which now forms one of the most important branches of Norfolk's trade.
>
> Although Baltimore is pre-eminently the great packing center of the bay, it is nevertheless true that, considering the amount of capital invested in the business, Norfolk handles proportionately a much larger trade than the former city. The number of shuckers employed and their wages are in about the same proportion in the two cities. In Norfolk the buildings are generally very plain, often mere frame structures, while in Baltimore many of the packing houses are among the finest buildings devoted to a trade in the city. The packing houses of Norfolk are not, as a general thing, used during summer for fruit packing, as is the case in Baltimore. The number of oysters packed at Norfolk during the season of 1879-80 was much larger than the combined totals of all packing points in Maryland, excluding Baltimore.

J. W. HURLEY & SON SEAFOOD

After the Civil War, the oyster industry began to spread to other areas on the Chesapeake besides Baltimore and Norfolk. In the 1880s, J. W. Hurley moved from the Eastern Shore of Maryland to Urbanna, Virginia, and opened J. W. Hurley & Son Seafood. Hurley's business flourished as the "King of Them All" Rappahannock River oyster provided an excellent product for his oyster house. The firm grew to be one of the largest packing houses on the Rappahannock and was typical of the oyster houses around the Bay.

WOODLAND ROWE

On July 3, 1925, Woodland Rowe of Guinea Neck in Gloucester County, Virginia, moved to Urbanna and went to work for Mr. Hurley and his

Woodland Rowe worked at J. W. Hurley & Son Seafood for thirty years. The oyster stall was made by Woodland. The bushel oyster basket, used to carry a bushel of oysters, came from the old shucking house.

son, Boyd. Over the next thirty years, Woodland, now eighty-three, worked in just about every area of the business. He recalls just how life was around the packing house.

"Papa and my brother Achilles had come over to the Rappahannock in the fall of 1924 to hand tong for oysters and to haul seine. They met Mr. Hurley, and he asked them if they wanted to work for him. Mr. Hurley also had a striker house where corn herring [salt herring] was processed. Papa had been a fishermen all his life, and Mr. Hurley sold as many fish in those days as he did oysters.

"The three of us came over to go to work for him on July third. I was just fifteen years old. We worked for Mr. Hurley for a month, and Papa liked it so much in Urbanna that he decided to move the entire family over. We came over in Papa's log canoe, but when we went back to get the family, he moved the rest of the family by car.

"He hired a jitney," recalls Woodland. "It was a Durant touring car with side curtains. Boy, we thought we were something riding in that thing. It was one bumpy ride. The closest paved road in those days was in Richmond."

WORKING FOR THE HURLEYS

Woodland did a little bit of everything for the Hurleys. "I was sort of a jack-of-all-trades. In the wintertime, I would dredge for oysters on Mr. Hurley's private grounds or buy oysters from tongers in the *Walter Boyd,* a fifty-five-foot buy boat."

"The *Walter Boyd* had been named the *J. Boyd*, but L. P. Price of Deltaville rebuilt her in 1924," says Woodland. "The old boat was in such bad shape that the only old part he could use was sixteen feet out of the keel. So, they decided to rename her. Boyd Hurley's wife, Virginia, was with child, and they waited for the baby to be born before naming the boat after him [Walter Boyd]," recalls Woodland.

"I was on her for thirty years. I loved that boat and the water she floated in," he says. "At first, she had a thirty-five-horsepower [gasoline] Palmer engine in her. Later on, Mr. Hurley put a diesel engine in her, which was the first diesel in our area. It was a forty-five-horsepower

Ben Wormeley unloads oysters at the Hurley packing house from the hold of the buy boat *Grace*. (Courtesy of Jonesey Payne)

Fairbanks Morse. In those days, we couldn't buy diesel fuel in town. I had to drive a tank truck to West Point [Virginia] once a week to have it filled with fuel."

Woodland bought market oysters for the Hurleys on the *Walter Boyd* from oystermen working the Rappahannock and seed oysters from James River oystermen in the spring. The seed oysters were hauled back to the Rappahannock and planted on the Hurleys' oyster grounds. He also dredged for oysters in the buy boat on the Hurleys' private oyster grounds.

"When I first started buying, there were still a few Tangiermen using sail power in their boats [log canoes], but by then, most everyone had installed engines," says Woodland. "Mr. Hurley remembered when there was nothing but sail. I've heard him say the buy boats would go over to Punch Bowl [near Water View, Virginia], and all the watermen were using sail and sculling paddles."

Woodland says he purchased oysters from watermen for as little as thirty-five cents a bushel, but that it averaged between fifty and seventy-five cents a bushel for good shucking stock.

"We had two men on the buy boat, and we could unload four boats at a time—two boats on each side. While unloading, we would number the boats to keep track of how many bushels and which boat it came off," says Woodland. "The first boat would be one and we would count, 'One [number-one boat] is a one [bushel], one is a two, one is a three,' etcetera. The second boat would be 'Two is a one, two is a two,' etcetera. We would jot it down on a piece of paper. This way we could keep track of who sold us what."

Woodland would usually buy between 300 and 400 bushels of shucking stock daily. The Hurleys had three other buy boats buying oysters elsewhere. In the spring, Woodland would go to the James River and buy seed, bringing home between 850 and 1,000 bushels of seed on the *Walter Boyd.*

SAIL POWER

"Mr. Hurley grew up in the days of sails, and he loved the old sailing vessels," says Woodland. "He owned the two-masted schooner *Man-a-Way*. She was lost in 1924. A fish steamer hit her in a thick fog off Windmill Point and cut her half in two. She was loaded down with canned tomatoes bound for Baltimore," he recalls. "Mr. Hurley had a tomato factory along with the shucking house.

The schooner *Man-a-way* was owned by J. W. Hurley & Son Seafood in Urbanna and was used to transport oysters and other supplies to and from Baltimore and Norfolk. The *Man-a-way* was lost in 1924 when a fish steamer hit her just off Windmill Point and cut her in half. The building out over the water with an American flag flying is the old Hurley oyster house. It was torn down in 1990 to make way for progress. (Courtesy of Edmond Ruark)

"He liked the old sailing canoes, too. I remember him saying to some oystermen that when everything was powered by sail, they'd go over to Morattico Bar and work all day, but when the motor came along, they wouldn't go out of sight of Urbanna Creek.

"One of Mr. Hurley's best friends was Harvey H. Conway of Cambridge, Maryland," says Woodland. "Mr. Conway was the patriarch of the noted family who owned the Conway fleet of sailing vessels.

"One of my jobs was to drive him around when he came to town. He would sail into Urbanna to buy oyster shells to sell to lime plants, and Mr. Hurley would get me to drive him around to the other packing houses in the area to buy shells.

"Captain Harvey told me this story: The schooner *Harvey H. Conway* was moored in the Patuxent River during a blinding snowstorm in the early 1930s. The skipper, Captain Harvey's son, Harvey H. Conway, Jr., had been anchored there for several days due to the bad weather.

"Captain Harvey was provoked with his son because the vessel was loaded down with oysters and should have been delivered to Baltimore, snowstorm or not," recalls Woodland. "So, Captain Harvey sailed across the Bay from Cambridge and found the schooner still moored in the Patuxent. He was mad. 'You can't sell a boatload of oysters sitting still,' he said.

"Captain Harvey took the vessel and sailed it to the docks in Baltimore in one of the worst snowstorms on record. When he got to the dock, several men were on the pier, and one asked him if he wasn't afraid of hitting a sandbar with the snow coming down so thick.

"Conway replied, 'If sometime or another, you've run into every sandbar on the Bay, then you know where they all are!'"

AROUND THE SHUCKING HOUSE

"When I came to the Hurleys there were about fifty or sixty shuckers working, but I was told that in the early days there were as many as a hundred," says Woodland. "Most of them were colored men, but later on we had more colored women. I remember the sounds of the shuckers. They would hum and sing as they worked. Some of them could really sing, too, boy.

A group of shuckers posed for this picture at the Hurley oyster house around 1900. (Courtesy of Walter Boyd Hurley)

Shuckers fill the stalls at the Hurley oyster house sometime in the 1930s. (Courtesy of Jonesey Payne)

"They would start work around 6:00 A.M. and leave at 5:00 P.M. During breakfast and lunch, they would gather near the pot-bellied wood stove and eat sandwiches [and] canned sardines and tell jokes on one another.

"There were also day men, or shell wheelers, hired to clean up and keep the shuckers in oysters. They were hired and paid for a day's work. Shuckers were paid by the number of gallons they could shuck. In the twenties and thirties, shuckers were paid between thirty and thirty-five cents a gallon.

"Shuckers would come from all over to work, and part of my job was to be a maintenance man. In those days, shuckers worked in wooden shucking stalls, and I made every one of them. We had a standard style, but I even made custom stalls. When Mason Carter got old, Mr. Hurley told me to make him a box with a seat in it. So, I made a stall he could step into, and a board would fit across for a seat.

"Oysters were handled in oak-splint or wicker bushel baskets that Mr. Hurley bought in Baltimore. Later, Boyd got wire baskets like they use today. I was told oak-splint bushel baskets were brought here by

Regular galvanized buckets were used to hold the shucked oysters. (Courtesy of Jonesey Payne)

Yankee oystermen. The oyster business was hard on baskets, and I was constantly repairing them.

"Wheelbarrows were another thing I had to always repair. I've made a boatload of handles in my life. In those days, the metal work was all made in town at Joe Pierce's blacksmith shop. The wood work was all made by me."

OYSTERING ON ICE

Woodland recalls one time when wheelbarrows actually took the place of boats. "It was during a big freeze in the 1930s when Boyd Hurley sent a group of men up to Turtle Point on Lagrange Creek near Remlik to harvest some oysters.

"We had a big order to fill but hadn't been able to buy any because the river had been frozen solid for days. Boyd had planted these oysters in four and five feet of water.

"We took axes to cut through the ice and used nippers and short-handled tongs to catch the oysters. Some of the men stood on the ice while others dragged a small skiff out on it, cut a hole big enough for it to fit,

A young J. Boyd Hurley stands in his father's oyster house around the turn of the twentieth century. (Courtesy of Jonesey Payne)

and tonged from the skiff. The oysters were loaded into wheelbarrows and pushed across the ice to a waiting truck. We caught enough to fill the order."

FIDO MAKES A MESS

"Hurleys' shucking house was built of wood, and the floors were made of wood, too, but Boyd wanted to make them concrete. So, in the off season, we tore out a wood floor in one of the rooms and started pouring concrete.

"Well, my brother Achilles had a dog named Fido. He was the ugliest damn thing in the world. He was gray and had white on his chin that looked like a goatee. One day when I was troweling, Fido walked in and started across the wet concrete. Josh, one of the men working with me, screamed, 'You gray son-of-bitch with a white goatee! Get out of here!'

"Fido took off across the concrete throwing it all over me as he ran," says Woodland with a laugh. "I said, 'Josh, if you hadn't said anything we would have been all right.' Lordy, we had fun working."

Shelton Lewis skims and packs oysters at J. W. Hurley & Son Seafood around 1932. (Courtesy of Jonesey Payne)

DELIVERY MAN

"Sometimes I helped with the packing and delivering of oysters. Most of Mr. Hurley's oysters went to O. E. Wentworth in Baltimore. They were shipped by steamboat.

"On Monday, Tuesday, Thursday, and Friday, oysters were shipped from Burtons Steamboat Wharf in Urbanna. On Wednesday, we had to go over to West Urbanna Wharf, which was about two miles outside of town on the [Rappahannock] river.

"Wednesday was the only day the side-wheeler [steamboat] *Middlesex* came in the river. It always went to West Urbanna Wharf because it was too big to turn around in the creek. At least that is what everyone thought. Captain Archie Long proved that wrong.

"On this Saturday, Captain Archie brought her in the creek and turned her right around. Everybody said he must have been half drunk to have even tried it, but he did it. That was the only time I ever heard of the *Middlesex* to come in the creek.

"To be hauled on the steamboat, shucked oysters were packed in five-, ten-, and fifteen-gallon cans and lowered down, three cans at a time, into a wooden ice chest. Crushed ice was spread all over the cans and down inside the chest before the lid was closed.

"The *Potomac, Calvert*, and *Middlesex* were the main steamboats we used to ship oysters on. On Saturday, though, I would drive Mr. Hurley's snub-nose International truck to West Point loaded with oysters. We would catch the boat on the York River because no boats ran on the Rappahannock.

"When steamboats stopped in the 1930s, I started driving to Baltimore. I'd go through Washington at midnight without a hitch and come back in the daytime and get lost every time," laughs Woodland.

STRIKER HOUSE

When the oyster season was over, Woodland would work in the Hurleys' striker house. During the spring herring run, fish were bought from local watermen and cured in salt brine.

"There were big wooden vats filled with brine. The fish would stay in [for] so many days. Then we would take them out and put them in thirty-gallon wooden barrels. The roe was cut out and packaged separately," he says.

FAVORITE RECIPES

"Mr. Hurley would put his favorite recipes on the back of his oyster cans," says Woodland as he picks up a one-pint oyster can used by the Hurleys in the 1930s. Embossed on the front of the green can is an eagle atop a sailboat's mast. Also embossed on the can are the words "King of Them All Famous Rappahannock Oysters; Direct to You from J. W. Hurley & Son, Oyster Grower & Packer, Urbanna, Virginia. On the back of the can are recipes for oyster cocktail and scalloped oysters:

Oyster Cocktail

36 oysters
lettuce
cocktail sauce
sliced lemon

Drain and dry oysters. Allow six for each serving and arrange in lettuce cups on individual salad plates. In the center of each plate, place a glass cup filled with cocktail sauce.

Scalloped Oysters

5 tablespoons butter
4 cups soft bread crumbs
1½ tablespoons salt
pepper
1 tablespoon lemon juice
1 pint of oysters

Melt the butter, add crumbs and seasonings, and mix well. Drain oysters and arrange in alternate layers with the buttered crumbs in a greased baking dish. Bake 20 minutes in a hot oven 450°F.

HARD WORK BUT GOOD PEOPLE

"There was a lot of hard work, but they were good people to work for," says Woodland. "Mr. Hurley [J. W. Hurley] was one of the neatest men I've ever known. If you saw him without a white shirt and necktie, it was some kind of hot! Mr. Hurley was something. He could chew tobacco so clean you never knew it was in his mouth.

"Mr. Hurley and Boyd couldn't be beat in my book," says Woodland.

Boyd kept the business open until the 1940s. After this, the building was used for a variety of different seafood endeavors, but in 1990, Southern States Cooperative tore the large white clapboard building down to extend a bulkhead so grain barges could tie up at its shore.

With the razing of the building, one of the last reminders of J. W. Hurley & Son Seafood and their famous "King of Them All" Rappahannock river oyster was gone.

✻ *When visiting George Williams's wood shop to do the chapter on oyster shaft-tong making, I noticed a clam rake propped up in a corner. George had made the rake.*

I was aware that rakes were used to catch hard clams in the Chesapeake region but had not considered a story on how they were made until then. George kindly agreed to help out.

17 : Clam Rakes

A SHELLFISH SPECIES treasured by Native Americans was the hard clam. American Indians caught clams up and down the East Coast and used them in a variety of ways. Their main method of catching clams was to wade out into the water, feel the buried clams with their toes, and nudge them out of the bottom. Treading for clams, as it is called today, is still a favorite method of some to find and catch clams.

In an 1887 report on the nation's clam fishery, Ernest Ingersoll wrote of the American Indians' love of the clam:

> How greatly the clam was prized . . . appears from the many mentions of it in early [1600s] writings. Not only the meat, but the shell was utilized by them [Indians] in making of various utensils and implements, such as arrow points, scrapers, paint-holders and spoons.
>
> It was from the purple eye and edge of the clam that the Indians fashioned their famous wampum, or dark shell beads with which they ornamented their clothing and furniture, adorned their hair and necks, or made their ceremonial peace and war belts and their insignias of authority.
>
> Wampum, combined with white beads made chiefly from the central column of the conch or periwinkles, also passed as money among Indians. . . . Shell money played an important part in the aboriginal economy.

Because they could be honed to great sharpness, clams were used by Native Americans for scraping and cutting in food preparation. They were also used in a more devious way. James J. McDonald wrote in *Life in Old Virginia* that the great chief Powhatan was cruel in his punishment of enemies. "Their joints were cut off with oyster and clam shells, and their skin scraped from their head and face, and their bodies ripped open and burned."

EARLY CLAM FISHERY ON THE CHESAPEAKE BAY

Although the early clam fishery did not have as much of an economic impact on Bay watermen as the oyster fishery did, a significant fishery had evolved in Virginia by the 1870s. Part of the reason the clam had a minimal economic impact was that, unlike the oyster, it was not found in great abundance up and down the Bay. Hard clams lived and grew in the saltier waters found in Virginia. Maryland's hard clam fishery has been relatively small because so few grow in that state's fresher waters.

Ingersoll discussed the clam fishery in Virginia in the 1880s:

> The Chesapeake Bay region is highly productive . . . The clamming ground extends from New Point [Virginia] north to Mobjack Bay on the western shore, to Oil Point on Hampton Roads. On the Eastern Shore, it extends from Pocomoke Sound southward.
>
> The principal markets are Baltimore, Norfolk and Yorktown. These clams are caught mostly by oyster tongers. When the summer close-season for the oyster-beds comes on, and the best market prices [for clams] are received in April and May, a whole army of oyster tongers are out there going after the clam.
>
> These clams are sold by the thousands and the general price ranges from $1.50 to $2.00, but $2.25 (per thousand) was paid in 1881. Estimates at hand of the present yield give to Baltimore about 3,500,000 yearly, to Norfolk 2,000,000 and to other markets (almost wholly to Yorktown) 2,000,000. These 7,500,000 clams will measure about 30,000 bushels and are worth at $1.75 a thousand $13,125.

METHODS USED TO CATCH CLAMS

As mentioned earlier, hard clams were caught by Native Americans by wading and feeling the clams on the bottom with their toes. Another way was by diving. Ingersoll wrote that this was the work of the "squaws and the older children, and was, of course, exceedingly laborious."

It wasn't until the settlement of New England and Virginia that tools were introduced as ways to catch clams. In the 1880s, Ingersoll wrote that oyster tongs, straight rakes, curved drag rakes, and dredges were used in the clam fishery.

On the Chesapeake, the oyster and clam tongs were probably the main gear used during this time. This would stand to reason, as watermen most certainly needed employment in warm-weather months, and rather than letting their oyster tongs sit idle, they could grab their hand tongs and go after hard clams.

Some fishermen, however, did have a special type of hand tong used just for clamming.

Ingersoll wrote: "The clam tongs of that day [1800s] differed from the oyster tongs, we are told, in having a wider head, 3½ feet being the average measurement. Quite opposed to this, we find that the tongs now in use in the Chesapeake Bay region differ from oyster tongs chiefly in having a narrower head, which measures only 1 or 1½ feet."

Hand tonging for clams declined as the crab fishery began to grow and expand in the late 1880s. Crabs provided a more steady and widespread warm-weather fishery for Maryland and Virginia watermen. Also, the patent tong, or deep-water tong, the gear most used today to harvest hard clams, was patented in 1887 by Charles L. Marsh of Solomons, Maryland. A very efficient tool, the patent tong allowed watermen to harvest clams and oysters in deeper water.

CLAM RAKES

Shallow-water clamming also provided income and food for families living near the Virginia clam beds. One of the most traditional means of

Treading for clams with feet is a method of clamming that goes back to Native Americans. (Courtesy of the Virginia Institute of Marine Science)

Digging clams at low tide is another method of clamming.
(Courtesy of the Virginia Institute of Marine Science)

harvesting shallow-water clams was with rakes. Clammers waded in the water or wielded the rakes from a small skiff.

Styles of rakes varied then and now throughout the East Coast region. Ingersoll described rakes used in the New England area in the 1880s:

> The rake employed at Wellfleet . . . is similar in form to an oyster rake, but made of steel instead of iron. In former days this instrument was of iron, the tips of the teeth only being of steel. An average rake has seventeen teeth and weighs about 12 pounds. The handle or tail is of wood and is about 23 feet long.
>
> The clam rake in use on the south shore of Long Island is much like a garden rake in shape but the teeth or tines are from 6 to 12 inches in length, and only an inch or so apart, while the head of the rake is from 2 to 3 feet across.
>
> Another form seen in Long Island Sound, New York Bay, etc., has its tines set very closely together and very much curved inward so that the operator can alternately push and pull with the rake in his swaying boat, and yet cause it to dig down into the sand underneath the clams. On the top of the strong pole-handle is a cross-piece to give a firm two-handed hold. The man who uses this rake generally goes alone in his small boat.

On the Chesapeake, rakes also varied in style and size. Clammers who worked from skiffs needed a long-handled rake, while those wading in the water at low tide used a short-handled rake. Also, some watermen

Styles of rakes used to harvest hard clams vary on the East and West Coasts and on the Chesapeake Bay. This one is pulled like a leaf rake. The ones made by George Williams are pulled by propping the handle on the shoulder and walking backward. (Courtesy of the Virginia Institute of Marine Science)

raked for clams with the handle under their arm, like raking a yard, while others put the rake handle on their shoulder and pulled and pushed to lift clams up from the bottom.

MAKING A CLAM RAKE

George Williams lives in Gloucester County, Virginia, near the areas mentioned by Ingersoll in his 1880s fish report as being prime grounds for harvesting hard clams.

George makes mostly shaft tongs for oystering, but requests for clam rakes from area recreational and commercial clammers encouraged him to go into the rake-making business. Most commercial clammers in Virginia use patent tongs, but a few diehards still rake the clams for market. The number of recreational clammers is also growing.

George's rake handles are made from a 1-by-1½-inch piece of wood. The length of the handle is made to the customer's specification. "Most of my handles range from six to ten feet," says George. "If you are real tall, then a ten-foot handle is what I recommend."

The type of wood is also the user's preference, but hardwood is preferred, says George, to withstand the pulling and prying while raking clams.

George makes clam rakes for both recreational and commercial clammers.

The end of the handle is notched to accommodate the wire basket, which is made from metal (drawing A). George prefers stainless steel, but mild steel may be used for the convenience of home welding.

The gum is made from ½-by-¾-inch metal and is between 16 and 18 inches long. The tines are made from ¼-inch round stock, 5 inches long, and are hammered flat on two sides (drawings A and B, photo 1).

The tines are welded along the entire length of the gum at 1-inch intervals (drawings A and B).

The tongue is made of 1-by-¼-by-5¾-inch flat stock (Drawing C) and is welded to the center of the gum (drawings A and C). (The gum is the rectangular stock material that holds the claws.) The basket is made of ¼-inch round stock bent and welded to the gum assembly (drawings A and C). George also welds side bars to the basket to keep clams from falling from the sides of the rake (drawing A).

The top wire on the basket passes in front of the tongue, and the remaining three wires pass to the rear of the tongue to shape a shallow belly in the basket for holding the clams when bringing them to the surface. The entire basket assembly is attached to the shaft by two sets of bolts/nuts/washers of appropriate size and length (¼- or 5⁄16-inch).

George's rakes are designed to be worked from the shoulder. Foam rubber is placed toward the end of the handle to give some cushion between the hard handle and the shoulder.

B

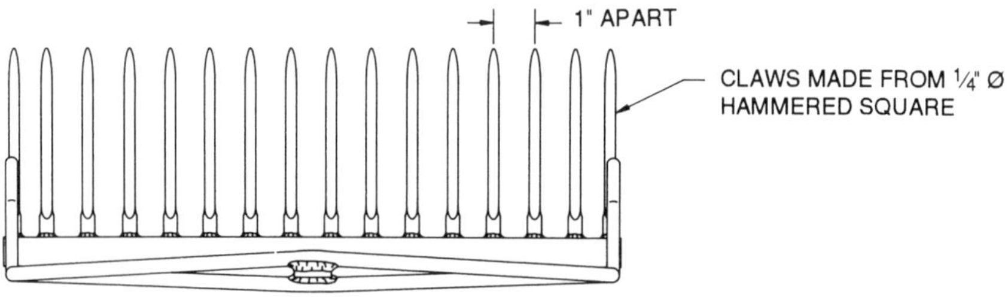

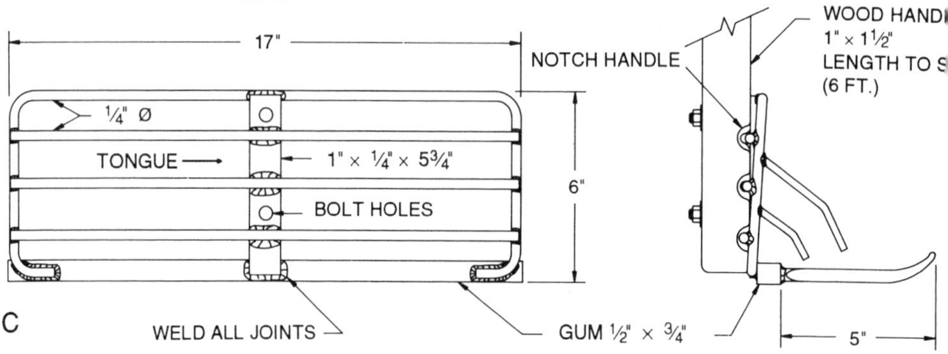

C

Drawings A, B, and C. (Drawings by Ray V. Rodgers, III)

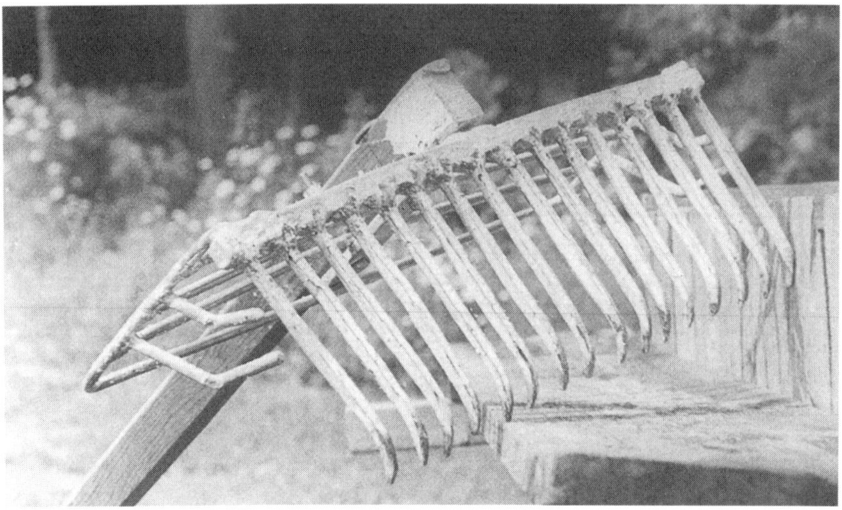

Photo 1

The clam rake maker demonstrates how it all works. "You put the handle on your shoulder, and you keep backing up until you hit a clam," he says. "Then you shove the rake down into the mud and dig him out. It's not hard to do when you know what you're doing."

A CLAM RAKE TALE

"Once, I sold rakes to two brothers," says George. "The older one wanted a ten-foot handle. The younger one wanted a six-foot handle because he was not as tall.

"One day, they were raking clams, and the older brother beat the younger brother bad and was teasing him about how he couldn't catch as many clams as he could.

"The younger brother turned to him and said, 'I reckon you ought to catch more clams; I ain't got but half-a-rake,'" George laughed.

THE FUTURE

"The old-timers who used to rake clams for a living around here are gone, but I still get some calls for rakes," says George. "Raking clams is fun, and there are people out there who do it just for fun. Anyone who is seriously clamming for a living is using patent tongs, but like I said, raking clams is fun. Recreational people want good rakes—the kind I make."

* *In 1987, I was assigned by an editor with* National Fisherman *to do a story on the summer conch season on Chesapeake Bay. I agreed and told him that I'd try to find a day that I could make a trip out on a conch boat. Little did I know that conches are nocturnal, so the day trip changed into a night trip. Leon King was kind enough to take me along into the darkness.*

18 : Dragging for Conch in the Dead of Night

ALTHOUGH THE Virginia Marine Resources Commission did not begin regulating the state's whelk (conch) fishery until 1980, conch have been eaten on the Bay since the 1600s.

In *The Historie of Travaile into Virginia Britannia,* William Strachey wrote in 1612 that "there is a kind of shellfish [conch] of the proportion of a cockle but far greater. It has a smooth shell, not ragged as our cockles; 'tis good meat though somewhat tough."

An article published in London in 1648 to encourage migration to the New World used conches and whelks as an enticement—even to the lazy: "He that is lazy and will not work needs not fear starving, but may live as an Indian, sometimes on oysters, cockles, whelks, clams, and scollons. Small fish in coves at low water will teach him to live idly," wrote Beauchamp Plantagenet.

Today, three species of *Busycon* whelk are harvested in Chesapeake Bay waters and off Virginia's Atlantic coast. The knobbed, or knobby, whelk is the predominant type; channel whelk and lightning whelk are the other two.

Knobby whelks make up nearly 100 percent of the summer conch catch and about 73 percent of the total Virginia catch. Lightning whelks are landed only as an incidental catch in the surf-clam fishery near the Virginia/North Carolina border between twenty and thirty miles off-shore and comprise 13 percent of the total Virginia landings. Channel whelks are caught in crab pots as an incidental catch and account for about 15 percent of the total Virginia catch. These conch are attracted by carrion, which explains their being fished with baited pots in New England. Most of Virginia's horseshoe crab landings are shipped north for use as conch bait.

GOING AFTER CONCH

Only an astute student of Chesapeake Bay fisheries might come close to guessing what Leon King and Billy Kellum are after as they slowly work their way along the Perrin River and head down the York River to the Bay—in the dead of night.

For King and his mate, Kellum, the answer is simple: conch. Over the past three years, when summer hard crabs slacked off during July and parts of August, King has turned to Virginia's small but growing summer conch fishery to help pay the bills. This year, however, crabbing has been so poor all season that King and his mate have slept their summer days away to conch six nights a week.

The summer conch fishery is actually an offshoot of the winter crab-dredging fishery (see *Harvesting the Chesapeake,* chapter 25), as conch are a by-product of that fishery. The same boats and gear used to catch crabs in the winter are also used to harvest conch in the summer. Of the fifteen licensed boats in Virginia's summer conch fishery, there are two types of vessel and gear configurations. King has a forty-two-foot deadrise workboat with two dredges mounted side by side on the stern. (A deadrise workboat is a classic bay vessel, which has a semi-V in the bow.)

The forty-two-foot dredge boat *Kelly Marie* is one of fifteen boats in Virginia's summer conch fishery. The boat is owned by Captain Leon King of Gloucester County, Virginia.

Larger buy boats, or deck boats, are traditional vessels in the state's crab-dredging fleet. Today, several are being used during the summer conch season. These deck boats fish one dredge from the starboard side and a second from the port side.

King's boat, the *Kelly Marie,* has Wagner dual hydraulic steering. One helm station is located inside the house, and another is on the starboard washboard nearly amidships so King can steer the vessel and work the hydraulically operated dredges at the same time. Powered by a 6-71 Detroit diesel, the vessel also has a Raytheon 1200 radar, a Morrow loran, a Si-tex DL-1 depth finder, two VHF radios, a CB, and a compass to help work in the darkness.

"All this takes a lot of guesswork out of it," says King. "If we make a good catch the night before, I can plug the location into the loran, and we can hit the same spot the next night. There is also a lot more traffic on the Bay than there used to be, and I like being able to see what's out there on the radar. It can get mighty dark out here."

On this hot July night, King and Kellum are bound for Area 4 near the high rise of the Chesapeake Bay Bridge-Tunnel, just above the 34th Island. Both men are from Guinea Neck in Gloucester County, Virginia, an area noted for producing some of the best Chesapeake Bay watermen. The region, situated between the mouths of the York and Severn Rivers, is ideally located near many of the Bay's most productive fishing grounds.

A PROUD HERITAGE

As King and Kellum begin the two-hour trek across the Bay to the conch grounds, they talk about conching and their heritage. Kellum has worked the water for nineteen years. His brother is skipper aboard a scallop boat that runs out of Hampton, Virginia. His father scalloped and trawled for forty-nine years before his death, and his grandfather fished and clammed the Bay for sixty-five years. "That's as far back as I know about," says Kellum.

"My father worked aboard scallop and trawl boats for forty-nine years. He'd seen a lot of rough water in his time. He'd been up as far as Nova Scotia trawling. His name was Stillman Kellum, Sr. Be sure to mention that because a lot of people knew Daddy. He could mend a net as good as anybody alive. I've had captains tell me that."

As King steers, Kellum stacks burlap bags on the washboards so they will be accessible when they begin working. The burlap coffee-bean bags come from Columbia, South America, and are given to the clammers by buyers. Each bag will be filled with a bushel of conch and, when full, will weigh approximately seventy pounds. King and Kellum are currently receiving eighteen cents per pound for conch. "It's been eighteen cents ever since I've been doing it," says King. "I heard that ten to twelve years ago, the price was twenty cents per pound. But now, you can catch a boatload or catch nothing, and it stays the same price."

DARK NIGHTS

The summer conch fleet fishes exclusively at night. Conch are nocturnal and feed at night on oysters and surf clams. Most often the darker the night, the better the catch. King and Kellum usually arrive at the grounds around 8:00 P.M. and fish until 4:30 A.M. "I don't know exactly how it got started [fishing conch at night], but I suspect someone decided to try it at night and probably loaded up with them," says King.

"One thing for sure—you do catch more at night than during the day, or I wouldn't be out here right now. This is one reason there are so few in the fishery, because a lot of the boys don't like fishing at night. I get home around 9:00 A.M., take a shower, go to sleep, get up at 5:00 P.M. and head out again. It's rough when the weather is nice and you want to be doing something around the house or with the family. All you feel like doing is sleeping," says King.

Besides the darkness, another factor that determines the catch is the weather. "We can't catch nothing on a northwest blow," says Kellum. "Southwester or northeaster is the best, and the darker the night the better."

On this particular night the moon is not bright, and the wind is from the northeast. "We ought to catch some conch tonight," says Kellum. "When things get too bad over here, we go down to Cape Henry at the mouth of the Bay and catch those big knobby conch."

DREDGING

Suddenly the engine idles down, and Kellum jumps up from the bucket he was sitting on. "I got to put the dredges over now," he says. As the chain clanks loudly in the stillness of the warm night air, he lowers the dredges into the water. The work deck is lit by two lights mounted on a wooden boom located just aft of the engine. A winch, referred to locally as a hoister, is mounted forward of the engine, and the chain runs around the hoister, up through the top of the boom, and down to the two dredges. The chain slides into the water over a roller mounted on the raised-stern work platform. The first tow yields less than a bushel of conch. "It will

Leon King, left, and Billy Kellum empty a tow of conch, or whelk, from the dredge on a hot summer night in July.

take us a little while to find the best spots," says Kellum, "but we'll do better than this."

Kellum has seen as many as eight bushels come up in one tow, but he admits this is not the norm. The best single dredge on this night is two bushels. It's been obvious from the start that the *Kelly Marie* is the only boat working. "There have been some deck boats working from out of Davis Creek this week," says King. "But when the catches are down, most don't come out."

A good night's harvest is between fifty and fifty-five bushels, says King, and during the past week, he has been catching between twenty-five and thirty-five bushels. "As long as the catch is like this, you don't see many boats, but later this month [July], it will pick up," he says. "Last year, we did good from the last of July right on up to the end of the season. There were twelve to fourteen boats out here working."

Besides conch, the dredges bring up horseshoe crabs, starfish, sand dollars, and an occasional flounder and blue crab. Everything other than conch is thrown back except the horseshoe crabs, which are sold for thirty cents apiece to local eelers who use them for bait. Last week, the dredge brought in a 13½-pound flounder, but it's against Virginia law for flounder or blue crabs caught at night to be sold.

Although the same gear is used for conching and crab dredging, there is one noticeable difference. Only two men work on the conch boats, whereas there are always three working on crab dredgers. King says there is less work to conching because the bottom where conch are harvested is not as muddy and trashy as areas worked by crab dredgers. Therefore, it only requires one man to sort through the catch. After each tow, Kellum culls the catch, bags it, and washes down the work deck while King goes inside the cabin to set up the next tow.

Throughout the night, Kellum works in the heat with a flotation vest around him. "Some people kid me because I wear this," he says. "I wear it, and I'm always going to wear it, because I can't swim a lick."

One of the more dangerous fisheries on the Bay is the winter crab-dredging season. "My cousin got drowned on December 4, 1986. He fell overboard while crab dredging, and he couldn't swim, either. One of these might have saved his life," says Kellum, pointing to his life vest. "It was the best nineteen dollars that I ever spent."

As the night passes into the early morning of the next day, green and orange lights on the bridge-tunnel that stretches across the Bay are the only sign of life. Conversations turn from working the water and

Once the dredge is empty, the catch is sorted. Billy Kellum gathers conches from the work platform and places them in a basket.

Conches are then transferred from the basket to burlap coffee bags.

conching to baseball. But every ten to twenty minutes, King and Kellum are back to business as usual, hauling up the dredges, lowering them, bagging the conch, and washing off the work deck.

MORNING

As the sun begins to rise over the Chesapeake, the men make their last tow. There are twenty-nine bushels of conch on the work deck when that tow is finished. Heading home, the waterways are noisy as a fish steamer makes a set on a school of menhaden, a half-dozen clammers work in the York River, and some pound netters head to their nets in the Bay.

The conch are delivered at the dock to York River Seafood Company in Hayes. They will be processed at a plant on the Eastern Shore where the meat is extracted and shipped to a canning factory in New Jersey.

At 8:30 A.M., King and Kellum arrive back at King's dock on the Perrin River. "Well, we made a dollar or two last night," says King. "Not the best night we've had, but not the worst, either. I've been on the job for fourteen hours. It's time to go to bed."

⁎ *The first I had ever heard of bottom lining for crabs was when I called Chris Hubbard about doing a story for* National Fisherman *on his new boat,* Defiance III. *Former* National Fisherman *senior editor Michael Crowley had assigned the story to me, and I owe him a debt of gratitude.*

19 : Bottom-Line Crab Potting

DON HUBBARD and his sons, Chris and Jeff, of Chase, Maryland, are a family of Chesapeake Bay watermen who come from traditional roots. However, their philosophy and method of catching and marketing the Bay's number-one money crop—the blue crab—are anything but traditional.

The most popular gear used to harvest crabs on the Chesapeake Bay, the crab pot, was designed and patented in 1928 by Benjamine F. Lewis of Harryhogan, Virginia. Mr. Lewis's invention is one of the most effective pieces of fishing gear to come out of this century. Today, crab pots are worked wherever blue crabs are found.

When Lewis started experimenting with pots, he rigged them by tying one end of a line to a pot and the other end to a stationary pole to mark and secure it. This worked fine when there were plenty of crabs in the vicinity, but watermen soon learned that they needed to easily move their pots to follow the migration of the blue crab up and down the Bay. They then changed from the pole, line, and pot to today's standard crab pot rig of buoy, line, and pot.

The Hubbards, however, have gone a step further and are fishing a bottom line which has twenty-five pots tied to it. The line is marked by two buoys—one at each end. Every seventy-five feet a pot is stationed. Each pot is tied to a six-foot snood line dangling from the main line. The gear is rigged similarly to trotline gear used by Bay watermen in the nineteenth and early twentieth centuries. Naturally, there were no pots, only bait tied to a six-inch snood line, and this short line was tied to the main one. Today, trotliners tie bait directly to the main line.

In addition, the Hubbards are not using the traditional Chesapeake Bay deadrise workboat. Chris, thirty, Don's eldest son, is captain of the

Chris (left) and Don Hubbard of Chase, Maryland, have been innovators in the development of bottom-line potting, a method of catching blue crab and eel in Maryland waters. The Hubbards and others have taken an old-style crabbing method of trotlining and adapted it to pots.

recently completed F/V *Defiance III.* The 42-by-14½-by-4½-foot fiberglass workboat built by Duffy and Duffy Boats of Brooklin, Maine, is one of the few Maine-built boats working the Bay. The Down East, semidisplacement lobster-boat style of hull of the Duffy 42 was unchanged for the Hubbards, while the wheelhouse, fish hold, deck layout, electronics, aluminum mast, and lighting were custom-built.

For generations, the classic wooden Chesapeake Bay deadrise work boat, with the V-bow, wide beam, and shallow-draft hull, has been the bread and butter of commercial watermen. The Hubbards raised some eyebrows when they went north to have a lobster boat built for catching blue crabs, but the reason for their unusual move lies in their harvesting methods and the waters they work.

Several years ago, Don and Chris began experimenting with bottom-line crab potting. Although there are now several other Bay crabbers and eelers using this method of fishing pots, they believe they were the first to use their design on the Chesapeake.

The *Defiance III* was launched in 1992 to be used for a new style of crabbing in Maryland waters. Bottom-line crab potting was developed in the 1980s as a more efficient way of harvesting crab and eel. The 42-by-14½-by-4½-foot fiberglass workboat was built by Duffy and Duffy Boats of Brooklin, Maine. (Courtesy of Duffy and Duffy Boats)

After seven years of experimenting with this rig and working from three different and distinct types of workboats, the Hubbards knew what they needed and wanted in a boat. The Duffy 42, with its sturdy construction, wide beam, deep draft, lightweight hull, and rounded bilge, was the answer.

Don started working the water in a Maryland-built wooden hull workboat but soon found that the maintenance and upkeep of a wooden boat were more than he could take. His next two boats were made of fiberglass: a New England-built Bruno & Stillman and a forty-five-footer built by the now defunct Glass Marine (of Glass, Virginia). Don had nothing but praise for both of these boats.

The forty-two-foot Bruno & Stillman, however, did not provide enough work and payload space, so the Hubbards sold it and had Glass Marine build them a forty-five-footer. That boat provided more on-deck space, but it was too heavy, costly to operate, and slow.

When the Hubbards first started experimenting with the bottom-line rig, they needed five crewmen using commercial reels to haul nearly one thousand pots a day. The overhead from working a five-man crew was eating up the profits from the boat. Today, they are using a heavy-duty crab-pot hauler and working fewer pots on a day-to-day basis.

The crabbers discovered they could catch just as many crabs because they had more time to study daily the trends of the crabs' movements and to move the lines accordingly. Although Glass Marine's boat was doing a good job, they realized that a smaller, more fuel-efficient boat would be more practical.

The Hubbards had looked around the Chesapeake for a fiberglass boatbuilder to build their new boat, but none of the builders they talked with could install the engine under the floor deck—a feature they were intent upon having. (Traditionally, power plants on Chesapeake boats are mounted on deck and covered with an engine box.) The Hubbards needed the deck space to accommodate a large work table, a four-man crew, and pot storage while the line was worked.

When a pot is fished, it is emptied, baited, and stored aft of the work table. When all twenty-five pots on a line are aboard, they are reset. One of the more interesting aspects of the way the Hubbards fish is the use of a tub trawl. Don took the idea right from the pages of early New England

With this innovative method of harvesting crabs, the Hubbards can fish about one hundred pots per hour. Menhaden (in basket) is used to bait the pots.

It was critical to the Hubbards that their new boat be able to store crabs below deck because of the amount of work space needed to fish twenty-five pots on a line at a time.

cod fishery. There, fishermen would row in a small dory skiff from a schooner out into the ocean to fish. In each skiff, they would carry a tub, which held long-line gear used to catch cod. It was a long baited line with hooks situated every so many feet. "When we first started thinking about this, we had a lot of line to contend with, so we came up with the idea of using a tub trawl," says Don.

As pots come aboard, line is fed into a barrel. There are loops in the main line (seventy-five feet apart) where each pot is attached. Each loop is placed over a pointed stick that is bolted to the barrel. When resetting the pot, the crew can easily determine when and where the next pot goes on the line by simply picking up the loop and attaching the pot to it.

The Hubbards' search for a new boat took them north. The New England–built Bruno & Stillman, with its relative deep draft, had worked fine on the Bay, and they realized that a shallow draft was not as important for them as for other local fishermen. The Hubbards moor their boat on a fairly deep creek (Seneca Creek) and can only work their pots in the Bay's deeper waters. (For conservation reasons, Maryland laws prohibit the use of crab pots on most of the state's shallower creeks and rivers.) Also, the Hubbards' entire livelihood is from crabs, while other watermen work in several fisheries—oyster, finfish, and crabs—and the latter's boats need a shallow draft to allow for versatility.

The Hubbards also wanted more under-deck storage space for crabs, which is what the Duffy 42 has. It holds seventy bushels of crabs under the work deck.

MARKETING THEIR CRABS

Seven years ago, Don realized that traditional methods of working the water would not support his wife, himself, and the families of his two sons. The problem was not in catching enough crabs to support them all. The problem was in the system itself. Selling crabs to a wholesale buyer, who in turn sells to a retailer, meant that too many hands were in the cookie jar. The waterman's being at the bottom just didn't seem right to Don.

Therefore, he established Don's Crabs Carryout Seafood, setting up his business on Joppa Road in Baltimore. Jeff took charge of the store; Chris, the boat; and Don and his wife, Joan, went about the task of managing the business. The plan worked well, and another store was opened several years later in another part of Baltimore. All their crabs are sold retail to a walk-in market.

A DAY ON THE WATER

At 4:00 A.M., down on Don's dock, there was a slight nip in the September air. Sylvester, a big, black cat with a white face, chest, and paws, lurks along the washboards of *Defiance III*, waiting for either Don or Chris to toss him a fish (menhaden) for breakfast.

Don and Joan live in a house they bought from Joan's parents in 1968 back in the days when waterfront property on the Bay was still affordable. The dock is located on Seneca Creek, a deep-water creek very close to the federally owned Aberdeen Proving Grounds.

The early morning darkness hides the rows of very closely situated docks along the shoreline. Don's home is in Baltimore County, a suburb of the city of Baltimore, a city best known for its baseball team, the Orioles, and its people's appetite for the Chesapeake Bay blue crab. This appetite has prompted reasonable men to pay as much as $120 for a bushel of number 1 jimmies (male hard crabs). Just about anywhere else on the Bay, a price like that would warrant a double take and remark like, "You've got to be kidding."

On the dock, Don is checking some peelers (A peeler crab is a blue crab in one of the three stages just prior to shedding) in floats built to his dock, while Chris and the crew load baskets of fresh menhaden from the dock onto the deck of *Defiance III.*

The Hubbards buy their bait from a seafood firm in Colonial Beach, Virginia. On occasion, razorback clams and catfish are also used for bait.

Catfish, however, have to be chopped in two to fit in the bait box, which takes time. When folded together, menhaden fit snugly in the bait box. At times, clams catch better in early spring, but generally, they are a better bait for crabbers working nearer the Chesapeake Bay Bridge. The Hubbards, however, spend most of their time near the headwaters. "We try a little of everything, but we'd just as soon use menhaden all the time," says Chris.

"Let's go, Dad," says Chris, and into the darkness *Defiance III* and crew head out into the Chesapeake toward the headwaters where the mighty Susquehanna, Northeast, and Elk Rivers all come together and empty into the Bay. It is the furthermost point where crab pots are allowed on the Chesapeake.

When Chris directs the boat past the mouth of the creek and past the Charles P. Payne Power Plant that is lit up like a Christmas tree, he pushes the throttle down. *Defiance III* begins to plane and cruises effortlessly at twenty-three knots.

"A lot of guys are afraid of big engines," says Chris. "The design of this hull makes going fast a dream. It just doesn't take much to push it. This was one of the things we wanted—a faster boat. It cuts out an hour of running time. And on weekends when people are lined up at our stores and want crabs—time means money."

The vessel is powered by a Merlin/Mack diesel that has been marinized up to seven hundred horsepower by Daytona Diesel Engine Corporation of Daytona, Florida, says Chris. The vessel is also more energy efficient than the larger forty-five footer they once used. "We burn fifty-five gallons of fuel a day, about 400 gallons a week," he adds. "The old boat burned between 490 and 525 gallons a week. It has cut our fuel cost by 25 percent and we are at least 30 percent faster." The Glass Marine boat weighed thirty-two thousand pounds, whereas *Defiance III* weighs in at twenty-two thousand. "When you are moving ten thousand more pounds through the water, it takes more fuel."

As the boat makes its way twenty-three miles to the headwaters of the Bay, floodlights provide excellent visibility. "We couldn't get out here without the lights," says Chris. "There are thousands of jugs [crab pot buoys] out here right now."

When they arrive on the fishing grounds, just a short distance from Turkey Point Lighthouse at the mouth of the Elk, the crew fishes its first line.

"Now watch this," says Don. "Chris is a real pro. He was crabbing in a wooden boat when he was thirteen years old and captained my Bruno when he was nineteen. Boy, I miss being on the water, but I learned that I had to look after the business."

Chris runs the boat up to one of two markers that mark the bottom line. A crew member picks it up and puts the line in the hauler. By foot peddle, Chris operates a Hydroslave pot hauler and pulls in the two-thousand-foot line as the crew empties crabs onto a work table near the middle of the boat and baits and stacks the pots. When all the pots are emptied, Chris lets the line back out, and the pots are clamped onto loops positioned every seventy-five feet in the line. The first and last pots are anchor pots. They have heavier frames than the ones in between to help keep the line straight and to keep it from being shifted around by tidal currents.

The advantage to bottom-line potting is that pots are seldom lost. With the thousands of single pots up and down the Bay, crabbers lose many pots when other boats cut their lines off. "We don't ever lose a pot. If our lines are cut off, we have the location plugged into a loran and can pick it up with a grapple hook," says Don.

The main disadvantage is that four men are needed to operate a bottom-line rig, whether "you are catching a bushel a day or a hundred bushels," says Don "It's a trade-off. I'm paying out in labor what I used to lose in pots, but this is a much more efficient way of catching crabs. We can fish more pots in a day."

The other disadvantage is that bottom lines do not work well around other pots. "We can't work in shallow water where there are a lot of pots, so we sail off into deeper water where it is less crowded," says Don (and on this day, there are more crabs, also).

Some pots Don and Chris are fishing are eight years old. Most Virginia watermen are lucky to get three years out of a pot. The Hubbards use vinyl-coated two-by-two-inch square-mesh wire with no sacrificial anode. Most Bay watermen use galvanized hexagon mesh wire with a sacrificial anode, or zinc bar, to help slow corrosion of the pot wire caused by salt water.

The headwaters of the Bay are brackish—more fresh than salt. There is thus very little electrolytic action on the wire. Also, the main disadvantage of coated vinyl wire throughout most of the Bay is that it gets dirty quicker than standard galvanized wire. Many watermen feel that the labor and time required to keep it clean is not worth it. The Hubbards, however, work in an area where there are strong tidal currents coming out of the Susquehanna and other rivers. "It keeps our pots real clean,"

Between hauls, crew members pass the time by resting on the washboards and talking about the day's catch.

says Chris. "Sometimes, grass floats out of the rivers and catches on the pot, but we can pull it right off."

Throughout the day, the work table is loaded with large and medium-sized crabs. It takes about 10 minutes to fish the twenty-five pots and, once fished, about 2½ minutes to set the pots. The crew could fish about a hundred pots an hour.

About eight hours later, the fish hold of the *Defiance III* is loaded down with seventy bushels of crabs, and the deck holds another thirty-one bushels. It is one of the best days the Hubbards have had in the seven years they have been working a bottom line.

"The first year we did this, a lot of people questioned us," says Don. "They said it would never work."

When *Defiance III* arrives back at Don's dock, the crew rushes the crabs from the boat into a refrigerated truck bound for Don's crab stores. Don jumps into the truck and leaves with his truckload of crabs.

Chris and the crew scrub down *Defiance III* until washboards and work deck look like a cat had licked them. With the job done, everyone walks toward his truck or car. "See you in the morning, boys," says Chris.

✻ *Shortly after* Harvesting the Chesapeake: Tools and Traditions *was first published, I went to Marshall's Drugstore in Urbanna to pick up a prescription.*

Mary Crockett, formerly of Tangier Island, was behind the counter and took my order. "I sent a copy of your book to my brother on Tangier," she said. "He loved it, but he said you left us out."

Even though there were chapters in the book that related to Tangier Island and its people's strong ties to the water, I realized that Mary's brother had a point. I decided then, if I ever did another book, it would include a chapter on Tangier Island.

20 : The Boatbuilders of Tangier Island

THE CHESAPEAKE BAY region is one of the last strongholds of wooden boatbuilding in North America. As fishermen throughout the rest of the country have turned to steel, aluminum, and fiberglass for their workboats, many Bay watermen have held true to their heritage and continue to work the water in wooden boats.

The traditional wooden Chesapeake Bay deadrise-style workboat evolved over the centuries to meet the fishing needs of those hardy souls who worked from them. Joseph F. Gregory, the foremost designer of deadrise boats, wrote in *Deadrise Is from Here . . . to Yonder*, "My general summation of workboat characteristics is that every feature, designed or built in by early builders, evolved from a definite need. There were no frills or goodies on the early Chesapeake workboats. Every item served the purpose of making a living from the Bay."

The Chesapeake is a relatively shallow body of water, and as the wind and tide work against the bottom, a choppy wave action is created. The V-style deadrise hull evolved from the need to cut through this chop and to provide a shallow draft so watermen could work their boats in these shoal waters.

One of the most asked questions around the Bay is, what does "deadrise" mean? Gregory defined it: "The word 'dead' means straight, direct, among other things, therefore: a straight rise of a bottom from keel rabbet to the chine."

The Bay deadrise workboats also have a relatively wide beam that provides a stable working platform. Working the Chesapeake can be risky business. Storms often come from nowhere, with such force that a stable vessel is paramount. The wide platform on the Chesapeake Bay deadrise evolved out of fishermen's having to weather these storms and to provide adequate space for payload.

Since early Bay fishermen did not need to venture far from home to catch enough for supper, the early log canoes and plank boats were generally open boats. But as the commercial fisheries began to grow, watermen needed to travel a good distance from home. Then, they began installing trunk cabins on their boats and later pilothouses atop the cabins for storage and on-board living accommodations. Windows were installed around the pilothouses to provide visibility. These boats took on the look of what is now the classic Chesapeake deadrise workboat.

The Chesapeake Bay deadrise workboat is still king on Tangier Island, Virginia. The island is one of the inhabited islands of the Chesapeake, which are some of the last traditional fishing villages left on the Bay.

A VISIT TO THE BOATBUILDERS OF TANGIER

Tangier Island lies in Chesapeake Bay about midway between Tidewater Virginia and Virginia's Eastern Shore and about ten miles below the

For over three hundred years, this small Chesapeake Bay island of Tangier, Virginia, has produced successful watermen and traditional wooden boats.

Main street, Tangier Island, is like stepping back in time. With such narrow streets, walking, golf carts, bicycles, and small pickup trucks are the main means of transportation onshore. Wooden boats are the main transportation on the Bay.

Maryland state line. Since its settlement in 1686 by John Crockett and his eight sons, Tangiermen have harvested seafood from the Bay, gaining renown for their skills as watermen.

Today, the island is one of just a few traditional fishing communities on the Chesapeake. Although modernization is creeping in—electric lights, paved (one-lane) roads, a brand new firehouse, and a satellite dish—the water is still the cornerstone of the lives of the eight hundred or so people who dwell along the marshes and shores of Tangier.

There are but two ways to get to the island: via a twenty-minute commercial flight from Topping, Virginia, or by boat. No bridges connect Tangier with the rest of the world. Cruise boats from Crisfield, Maryland, and Reedville, Virginia, bring tourists over by the hundreds during warm-weather months. They wonder what breed of people has survived so long on this tiny island in the middle of Chesapeake Bay.

The answer to that question is written across the faces of the men and women who inhabit Tangier. "It takes a hardy one to live here," says Micky Parks, whose home is just a short distance from the airstrip on the island.

YOUNG BUILDER

Parks, at thirty, is one of Tangier's three boatbuilders. He is also one of the youngest workboat builders on the Bay. "My granddaddy [Charles

Micky Parks was one of the last backyard commercial boatbuilders on the Bay to build under the sky. Most builders have a shed to build in, but traditionally, commercial boats were built out "yonder" in the yard and were worked on by boatbuilders on good-weather days.

This deadrise workboat was being built outside by Micky Parks on Tangier Island in 1988. There are no large trees on the island to keep the rain off when the weather is bad.

Roland Parks] built little sail-rigged bateaux, back before they got power," says Parks in the English accent that is still prevalent among natives. "They were little skiffs used to scrape for peeler crabs. I guess I inherited a little of his talents. There have always been boatbuilders on Tangier. Everybody works on the water, and they got to have boats to do that."

"Things have changed, though, since my granddaddy built boats here," Parks continues. "The boys are fishing three hundred and four hundred crab pots out in the middle of the Bay, so they need a big boat."

Before starting his own boatbuilding business several years ago in his backyard, Parks apprenticed with his brother-in-law Jerry Pruitt, who owns and operates a maintenance yard and is another of the three builders on the island.

"I guess everybody started this way," says Parks of his outdoor boat shop. "I've seen pictures of them building log canoes right out under the trees on the western shore. I'd like to have a roof over my head one of

Deadrise workboats like the *Valerie Faith* are still built on Tangier Island and are the boats of choice for most Tangiermen. Micky Parks built this workboat with cedar topsides, pine crossplanking in the bottom, and a twelve-by-twelve-inch keel.

these days. You take a day like today, when it's raining a little—it's hard to say whether or not we'll get a full day of work in."

Since he started, Parks, with one helper, has delivered five deadrise workboats. He now has a forty-six-by-fourteen-foot deadrise under way for local crab potter Clyde Pruitt. Two of his completed boats went to watermen in Onancock on the Eastern Shore of Virginia, and the others were built for Tangiermen.

He recently delivered a Maryland-style Hooper Island design to Tangier crab potter John Charnock. The 39 by 10½ foot *Valerie Faith* has more flare in the hull than the typical Virginia-built boat, but unlike the Maryland deadrise, she has a fairly high stem to counter the rough seas found in the lower Bay. Charnock works 360 pots in an area called the Coral Bed, which is about eighteen nautical miles from the island.

Typical of the boats built by Parks, the *Valerie Faith* has cedar topsides, pine cross-planking in the bottom, a twelve-by-twelve-inch fir keel, and a horn timber fashioned from a single piece of fir.

Parks knows firsthand what a crabber needs in a boat. Like most Tangier boys, he started crabbing at a very early age and, after graduating from the island's high school, went to work with his father, dredging crabs in the winter and potting in the summer.

"When my daddy had the *Irene and Pearl* [deck boat], I worked for him, dredging crabs in the winter until I was twenty-five years old," says Parks. "She was a buy boat and was the sister ship to the *Iva W.*" (For a description of *Iva W.*, see *Harvesting the Chesapeake,* chapter 25, pp. 229-240.)

"Daddy sold her year before last [1987], down to the Bahamas," he says. "It's a shame, but them kind of boats are obsolete: they're just in the way. He's using a box stern [classic Bay deadrise] now, like everyone else."

Up until the mid-1970s, buy boats, or deck boats, were virtually the only style of vessel in Virginia's winter crab-dredging fleet. Yet sometime in the 1970s, watermen began using the smaller deadrise boats with two dredges mounted on the stern. This has contributed to a boom in the state's crab-dredging fleet but also left the larger, more-expensive-to-operate buy boats with less work.

This change in crab-dredging style has also meant that builders up and down the Bay are seeing more demand for deadrise boats in the forty-four- to fifty-foot range. Traditionally, watermen requested vessels of forty to forty-two feet, but lower fuel costs, reasonable interest rates, and the demise of the Bay's oyster industry have made many watermen consider ways to improve their winter dredging operations. The larger hulls work better in this fishery, where a lot of space is taken up with gear.

The classic forty-two-foot deadrise has been popular with watermen for years because it performs better than the larger hulls in the patent tong oyster fishery and is more adaptable to other fisheries, such as crab potting. However, with the Bay's widespread epidemic of MSX and dermo, two deadly oyster diseases that have killed off the oysters, many watermen have turned to crab dredging. Currently, there is concern over the health of the crab fishery, and both Maryland and Virginia are looking at tougher regulations to help conserve this most important resource.

Another reason the forty-two-footer was so popular is that Bay watermen and builders preferred full-length side planks. Some builders are now having to piece these planks together because they are unable to get stock planking over forty-two feet on a regular basis.

Besides his boatbuilding business, Micky runs the island's bottled propane gas business. "Nope, I ain't got no big trucks to haul my gas around like they do on the mainland," he says. He points to a white golf cart he uses to make bottled gas deliveries. "That's all I need right there."

Golf carts are not an unusual sight along the narrow roads of Tangier. Carts, bicycles, motorbikes, and small trucks and cars are the most common motor vehicles on the island, but most people seem to prefer to walk.

BOBBY CROCKETT

On the other side of the island is the boatbuilding shop of Bobby Crockett. The road leading to it travels across a narrow bridge into the heart of the Tangier community, where houses are just a few feet apart. Wooden picket and wire fences separate the homes and yards, most of which are so neat and clean they look "as if a cat just licked them." Graveyards are scattered over the island in the yards of many homes. The island's nautical heritage is chiseled in stone; many of the tombstones are embossed with a boat with raised sails catching a fair breeze.

Boats are at the heart of this community. Every gut and channel is filled with some style of a boat, some dying and others in their prime.

"We've got plenty of boats over here," says Bobby, standing beside a deadrise hull with the bottom nearly complete. "This can be an awful one-handed place for building boats. You take that keel over there; it's twelve-by-twelve-inch fir nearly fifty feet long. We can't bring it in here

Bobby Crockett runs a railway and builds boats on the island. He learned what he knows about boatbuilding from Grover Lee Owens of Deltaville, Virginia, a community that was once a center of deadrise boatbuilding on the Bay.

on a tractor trailer like they do at Deltaville [Virginia]. We get them to haul it to Reedville [Virginia], and we float it across—drag it behind a boat. Nobody wants to put that on his boat, it's too big and heavy.

"Some of my other wood comes from a yard in Snow Hill [Maryland], where they load it onto a truck with a forklift and take it to Crisfield, where I've got to unload each piece by hand and haul it across on a boat. It's a hard place to do this kind of work."

Bobby, fifty-three, started building deadrise workboats about fifteen years ago. He had been crab potting in the summer and working on a dredge boat in the winter when he decided he'd rather try his hand at boatbuilding. Realizing he needed some help to get started, he called Grover Lee Owens of Deltaville, a former cabinet maker and a highly regarded deadrise boatbuilder.

"I called Grover Lee and asked him if I could come over and learn from him," recalls Bobby. "He said that it would be fine, and I worked with him for a week or so. He taught me as much in a week as it would have taken me to learn in a year by myself."

Owens obviously left a mark on Bobby, whose boats have "that finished touch"—a trademark of Grover Lee, as everyone calls him on the lower Bay.

Shaping the deadrise in the hull by eye, Bobby cuts the V-bow from the large fir keel with hatchet and chain saw. His boats are a typical Virginia style, with a high stem, plenty of deadrise to cut through rough seas, a wide beam to carry plenty of payload and to give added stability, and a standard Bay-style pilothouse and trunk cabin configuration.

Bobby builds about two boats a year and runs his railway, which keeps him quite busy. His most recent forty-two-by-twelve-foot deadrise went to a Smith Island, Maryland, waterman, but most stay right on Tangier. "A man's boat is important to him over here," says Bobby. "Men take pride and joy in their boats, and they want them to look nice."

This is evident from just walking around the docks, where there are probably as many deadrise workboats as anywhere else on the Bay. In fact, during the off-tourist season, you would be hard-pressed to find any other style of boat there. Most Bay communities today have more yachts and sailboats around the shoreline.

Most of the workboats on Tangier are spit-shined from top to bottom. Their mahogany sterns are finished off with about seven coats of clear varnish. This detail is a trademark of Tangier watermen and one that has spread to other Virginia fishermen.

For those who live on the island, working the water is about the only livelihood. This has caused many young people to choose not to live there, says Bobby. More and more are going to the mainland to get an education, and that means they do not come back to the island. "There's not much here for an educated person. We have our school, but there aren't many teaching positions available. I've seen the population drop over the years. When I was a boy, there were over a thousand people living here. Now, I'll bet there are less than eight hundred."

The cost of living is high on the island, too, says Bobby. "We don't have chain food markets here, and everything you buy has the cost of freight tacked on to it. Whether it's a piece of lumber or a loaf of bread, you've got to bring it over here by boat, and I understand that cost has to be added on.

"A lot of people don't think we know how to drive a car over here because most of us either ride bicycles or motorbikes, but I've owned a car and kept it in Crisfield [Maryland] for twenty years. Most all the families have a car somewhere so they can travel on the mainland."

ISLAND TOUR

Up until several years ago, the roads on Tangier were too narrow for even a Volkswagon Bug, but they were recently widened enough for small vehicles to go one way and for motorbikes and bicycles to go both ways. Bobby drives a small pickup truck on the island, and he offers a short tour of the fishing village.

The first stop is Lorraine's Diner for lunch, a small diner that is a reminder that there are other places to eat in this world besides a fast food joint. It's one of the few places left anywhere where hamburgers actually taste as if they were cooked at home and do not need a pound of ketchup to hide the flavor. Inside, the locals chat about the weather and fishing. The only obvious outsiders are myself and a doctor who flies over from White Stone, Virginia, to administer to the medical needs of the island's people.

Inside Lorraine's, the weather is an ongoing topic of discussion, and for good reason. It has often been an enemy to the people of Tangier. One of the most disastrous floods came during the famous August storm of 1933. Then there was the Great Freeze of 1917–18, which left the community stranded for fifty-two days; no one came to or left the island. Today, one of the main concerns is the Bay's constant chipping away of the island's fragile soil, to the tune of about twenty-five feet per year. Over the years, erosion has been a constant threat to the people of the island. When he was mayor of the island, Bobby was instrumental in obtaining federal and state funds to place a jetty near the airport to keep the sea from taking the shore away.

The doctor is very interested in this project. Bobby explains that the new jetty will cost five million dollars, with state and federal aid taking care of all but two hundred thousand dollars. "We had to raise taxes 400 percent to get the money, but no one complained much. I mean, what choice do we have?" he says.

Crockett's tour then takes us from Lorraine's to the crab dock, where several deadrise workboats are pulling up with some freshly caught blue crabs. Across the way, on pilings, are crab shedding houses, waiting for the big run of soft crabs that would come near the end of May. On a building next to the crab house is a reminder that Tangier is a place unto itself. Although the paint is nearly worn away, a sign reads, "Swim Suits Prohibited on Streets."

As we move from the dock down the main street, tiny stores are everywhere, most sustained by the summer tourists. A short jaunt toward the heart of the island is Swain's Memorial United Methodist Church, the center of most island activity, second only to the waterfront.

A little farther is a state historic sign explaining that Capt. John Smith explored Tangier in 1608, just one year after the founding of Jamestown. Although the origin of the island's name is in question, the most popular tale holds that Smith called it Tangier after the city in Morocco where he once was held captive, says Bobby.

We pass one of the most renowned seafood restaurants on the entire Bay, Hilda Crockett's Chesapeake House. The sign outside depicts an island with sea gulls soaring overhead. On a scroll the menu for today reads: "The very best home style cooked meals—Prepared by the island's finest cooks."

The last stop on the tour is the island's new firehouse. With an air of pride, Bobby walks through the building, pointing out this and that. The International (regular size) fire truck is the pride and joy of the islanders.

Bobby makes the turn across a little bridge over Big Gut Canal, which leads to the boat shop of Jerry Pruitt. "Well, you've got just enough time to go talk to Jerry before you catch the plane home," he says.

JERRY PRUITT

Jerry's yard is just north of the airport. There, the forty-three-year-old boatbuilder builds two deadrise workboats a year in a World War II Quonset hut. Several years ago, Jerry was building more boats, but his maintenance work has grown so that he can only turn out a limited number of new vessels, he says.

Jerry comes from a long line of boatbuilders—both his grandfather and great-grandfather built boats on Tangier. As a boy, Jerry received his first schooling in the trade from his grandfather Willie Frank Pruitt, who built flat-bottomed and deadrise skiffs. "He showed me how to make the bends, and after a while, I just picked it up from him," says Jerry.

His great-grandfather Raymond Thomas Pruitt built traditional Tangier Island barcats, which are small skipjacks, usually twenty-six to twenty-eight feet long, with a catboat-style sailing rig. Before the advent of marine engines, barcats were used mostly to scrape for peelers (molting crabs) in the shallow flats along the shores of the island. "I've been told he built some of the fastest sailboats around," Jerry says. "Those little barcats could solid fly."

Jerry also learned about boatbuilding from Leonard Marsh, a renowned skipjack builder on Smith Island, Maryland. "He is a very kind

Jerry Pruitt has the largest boat yard and boatbuilding business on Tangier. On a given day in Pruitt's repair yard, such seldom-seen boats as drake tails, round sterns, and diamond-stern workboats can be found.

man," says Jerry, "and years back, he and his father were well known for their skipjacks. He's as good a builder as anyone on the Chesapeake."

Jerry has been turning out deadrise workboats for twenty-three years. Many have stayed on Tangier, while just as many have gone to the Eastern Shore of Virginia and to Deal Island, Maryland. His deadrise style varies only slightly from those of Bobby's and Micky's. One difference is Jerry's use of spruce pine in the keel.

"If I can get a piece of pine for the keel, I'd rather have it because it doesn't split like fir," Jerry says. Finding a twelve-by-twelve-inch piece of pine over forty feet long isn't always easy, though. "There's a place up in Westover, Maryland, where I've been able to get pine for the keel, but it isn't always available."

Most of Jerry's boats are thirty-eight to forty-five feet long and have either fir or cedar for side planking and yellow pine in their bottoms. His boats are used for crab potting in the spring and summer, and for crab dredging and oystering in the winter months.

Throughout the Chesapeake and the rest of the country, there's been a decline in wooden boatbuilding. But on Tangier Island, wooden boats are still preferred. "I've been real lucky. There's always plenty of work," says Jerry.

The sound of the shuttle plane back from Hummel Airfield in Topping, Virginia, could be heard off in the distance. "There's your plane," says Pruitt. "You'd best go catch her, or you'll have to swim home!"

Over the years, Tangier has been home to some of the Bay's most successful watermen. From the look of things, that tradition is going to last a while longer. As long as it does, there will always be a place for boatbuilding on the island.

I first wrote a story about the sterns on deadrise workboats for National Fisherman *in 1985. I thought then, as I do now, that it was a good story idea because the different types of sterns help show how frame-built workboats evolved into today's deadrise commercial fishing boats, the favorite working platform of Bay watermen.*

Part of the history and lore of Chesapeake Bay watermen is their boats. And there is one thing Bay fishermen do love on a wooden boat—and that's a pretty stern.

21 : Sterns on Bay Workboats

THE CLASSIC Chesapeake Bay deadrise* workboat is indisputably the most popular vessel with Virginia and Maryland watermen. The boats feature a V-bottomed hull that flattens out in the run aft. Different styles vary only slightly—until one looks at the sterns.

Among the Bay boats still plying the waters of the Chesapeake, there are several distinct types of sterns, including the Hooper Island drake tail, Pot Pie or tuck sterns, logged and staved round sterns, Poquoson or diamond, and square versions. These different shapes evolved over the years in an attempt to develop a workboat comparable to the Chesapeake Bay log canoe, the forerunner of today's deadrise frame-built boats.

Before the advent of the internal-combustion engine, the sail-powered log canoe was the vessel most used by Chesapeake Bay watermen. In 1880 U.S. Census Bureau investigators revealed in a Fish Commission Report that 6,300 canoes were in use on the Bay, and that about 175 new vessels were turned out annually. The sharp bow and stern of the log canoe allowed it to push the chop away when running and made it possible to maintain a stable platform while anchored stern to sea.

Construction of the log canoe slowed down when logs large enough to be used in the boat's building became scarce. The growing acceptance of gasoline engines played a significant role in this decline as well. But the watermen were soon to take advantage of this technological break-

* Deadrise is the name of a V-bottomed vessel on the Chesapeake Bay. The name came from the word "dead," which means straight or direct; therefore a deadrise bow is the straight rise of a bottom from keel rabbet to the chine. This creates a semi-V in the bow, which helps to push chop away from the vessel when it is under way.

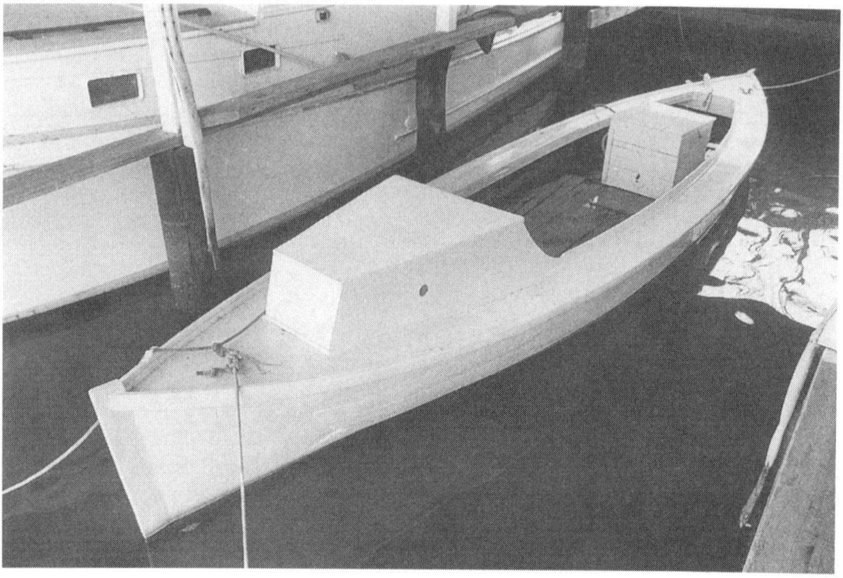

This Chesapeake Bay log canoe was the precursor of the modern-day deadrise workboat. Some attributes of log canoes were built into frame-built deadrise boats. Early on, boatbuilders copied the V-stern from the log canoe in an attempt to match the sea-keeping qualities of the double-ended log canoe. The V-stern worked well in sea conditions where there was a strong following sea.

through and were quick to modify their log canoes. When the early one- and two-cylinder engines first arrived on the Bay, the watermen cut the masts off their canoes, filled in the centerboard slot, bored a shaft hole, and installed the motors.

This worked fairly well until the fishermen decided to add a small house. Even with engines set as far aft as possible and the house as far forward, there was too little space in some of the smaller canoes for payload and gear. Most of the canoes were quite narrow, and as the engines got larger, the sterns had a tendency to squat in the water. Technology was shoving the log canoe toward obsolescence. As the canoes began to wear out, the watermen needed a comparable vessel with the canoe's sea-keeping qualities that could accommodate the larger motors.

DRAKE TAIL

In response to these demands, Maryland boatbuilders came up with the Hooper Island drake tail more than seventy years ago. The original

The Hooper Island drake tail was taken from racing boats of the early 1900s and adapted to workboats.

Hooper Island craft had a long, narrow, lightweight hull of shallow draft. The boat sported a rounded fantail stern with a reverse rake, as well as a chine that followed the waterline throughout the length of the boat.

Built predominantly at Hooper Island, Maryland, these boats were modeled after early racing launches and torpedo boats. Many of the early drake tails were easily driven up to ten knots with the five to fifteen-horsepower engines available before the 1930s.

Drake tails are seldom built on the Bay today, but there are some still being worked in Maryland and Virginia waters. Early versions were generally very narrow, with the beam at the waterline less than one-sixth the length of the vessel. As the engine became larger, so did the beam.

POT PIE, OR TUCK STERN

The Pot Pie stern was another Maryland style that arrived shortly after the canoe began to disappear. This model was probably taken from the so-called schooner stern, where the deck line extends farther aft than the waterline. Examples of Pot Pie boats can still be found in Maryland waters today.

"Pot Pie" is the name of an area in Talbot County, Maryland, near Wittman. It was there that this style of vessel was probably first constructed, and thus the name "Pot Pie stern" was coined.

The early Pot Pie boats also had a narrow beam and, therefore, suffered the same problems as the Hooper Island drake tails. To counteract the boat's tendency to settle aft when under way, watermen built a squat board, or settling board, or planing board, and attached it to the stern, extending the waterline and giving buoyancy to that area. This problem with squatting was not exclusive to Maryland-built tuck-stern boats, however. In Virginia, numerous round-stern workboats still use squat, or planing, boards.

ROUND STERNS

The round-stern vessels can still be seen on the Bay—from small thirty-eight to forty-two-footers to buy boats measuring sixty feet or more. The larger buy boats are used for a variety of tasks, including planting seed oysters, dredging crabs in the winter, and trawling offshore in the ocean. Fewer and fewer of these vessels can be found now, because the decline of the Bay's fisheries has taken away much of their work. Also, Bay watermen now use smaller deadrise workboats in areas where buy boats were once used exclusively. Virginia's crab-dredging fishery is an example. Several years ago, watermen began experimenting with stern dredging. They perfected a way to haul two dredges from the stern on the smaller deadrise workboats just as effectively as pulling side dredges from the larger buy boats. This worked so well, that most everyone has converted over because of the lower expense involved in operating the smaller boats. Lack of work has just about choked the buy boats out of existence.

The round stern has been very popular among Bay watermen. Just thirty years ago, boatbuilders in Deltaville, Virginia (once a center for the building of wooden deadrise boats) had more calls for round-stern vessels than for anything else.

Willard Norris, a noted Deltaville builder of deadrise vessels, says there are two methods of construction used on the Bay for building a round stern, the logged and the staved styles.

"The logged stern was more popular," says Norris. "We would shape the pieces from large timbers. It takes five pieces for the bottom rim. The second layer was set on top of that rim and lapped over the butts. Each piece was then bolted down." This was continued until the stern reached the desired height. The transverse layers were then all bolted down.

The staved style was started like the logged stern, using the bottom and top rims, but each was rabbeted out. Planks were then fastened

The Pot Pie, or tuck-stern, boat was modeled after the so-called schooner stern, where the deck line extends farther aft than the waterline. This style was probably first developed on Maryland's Eastern Shore near Pot Pie, in Talbot County, Maryland.

Round-stern boats were built on smaller deadrise crab and oyster boats and also on the larger Bay buy boats (sixty feet or longer).

vertically to the two rims to fill in the stern. This method was not used much on the Bay but can be found on a few boats, Norris says.

POQUOSON, OR DIAMOND, STERN

The diamond stern, or V-stern, is another style used by Chesapeake Bay watermen. It is not clear exactly where it originated, but the pronounced V in the stern would appear to have evolved directly from the sharp-sterned log canoe.

This style is also called a Poquoson stern by some watermen, which suggests it may have come from the Poquoson area, a center of log canoe building in Virginia during the late nineteenth and early twentieth century. Poquoson canoes were top-of-the-line workboats when canoes were the main style of vessel used by fishermen.

The diamond stern, or V-stern, appears to have evolved right from the log canoe. This style is also called Poquoson stern, which suggests it may have first come from the Poquoson area of Virginia, once a center of log canoe building.

William Rollins, builder of deadrise workboats in Poquoson, says he thinks the stern was built for haul seiners and clammers. "The V makes it easy to bring in a net over the stern. It also works well for clammers, who often have to work stern to sea."

Although the diamond-stern boat is seldom built on the Bay today, numerous boats with diamond-sterns (as well as round, Pot Pie, and drake tail sterns) are still being worked around the Chesapeake.

THE NEW STANDARD

The square, or box, stern has become the standard for workboats in recent years. The main difference between Maryland and Virginia box-stern vessels is below the waterline. Virginia builders install a "guinea" horn timber. In wooden boat construction, the horn timber ties the keel and transom together, with the propeller shaft running down through the timber from the reverse gear. In the typical deadrise, a reverse curve in the horn timber gives the boat a concave bottom at the stern.

This type of horn timber is made from a solid piece of twelve-by-twelve-inch Douglas fir. Before the solid-piece horn timber was developed, Virginia deadrise boats had a reputation for leaking around the stern. This was because the forerunner of the solid-piece reversed-horn timber was made from five different pieces, resulting in leak-prone joints where the shaft log was drilled through the structure.

Norris says the solid horn timber led to the decline of round-stern vessels on the Bay. Since the logged and staved round sterns were

The square, or box, stern is the standard used by most Chesapeake watermen today.

structurally weaker than the box stern, the raised square-stern vessels resulted in a very efficient style, he believes. "The watermen don't even consider a round-sterned boat anymore," he says. "But before the solid-piece horn timber, I was building round sterners all the time."

When watermen look at a deadrise workboat, the first thing they notice is the stern. The sterns on the Bay boats have evolved from the sea conditions associated with the Chesapeake and from the methods of harvesting seafood while working in these conditions.

But there's another reason: Watermen just plain like a pretty stern.

✻ In 1990, I did a story on traditional railways. I realized then, these small railways that serve mostly working watermen were being replaced by high-dollar marinas with travel lifts and a preference for fiberglass boats.

The old railways played a vital part in the livelihood of fishing communities throughout the Bay. The railway man was a friend of the working watermen.

I want to thank Willis Wilson of Deltaville for directing me to Winegar's Marine Railway in Ocran, Virginia. I probably would not have found Cathy Davenport and Joe Winegar if it were not for him.

22 : Winegar's Marine Railway

YEARS BACK, log canoes and small frame-built boats were the main working platform of commercial watermen. These boats were small and sturdy enough so that several strong men could pull them up on shore, flip them over, and do the repair work.

As watermen began using larger frame-built deadrise vessels, they needed a railway close by to haul their boats and a talented jack-of-all-trades railway man to help with repairs.

In those days, wood was the only material boats were constructed of, and little railways, often situated on narrow strips of land leading down to the water, bordered almost every creek up and down the Chesapeake Bay.

Just a few of those railways remain. They are the last haven for many working watermen who find it hard to accept modern-day changes that accompany the modern-day marinas.

One such place is Winegar's Marine Railway in Ocran, Virginia, on the Northern Neck. Winegar's is one of those places where time seems to have stood still and where a workboat can get the tender loving care needed to begin another season of fishing.

THE HISTORY OF WINEGAR'S

Shortly after the Civil War, five Winegar brothers moved south to Virginia from New Jersey. Following the war, the economy of Virginia and the Northern Neck was at rock bottom. Many northerners came down after the war with greenbacks and were able to purchase large tracts of land. The Winegars purchased several hundred acres on Dymer Creek.

The Winegars were talented artisans of German descent. When they first arrived, the brothers built a large barn to work from and to live in until homes could be built.

One of the brothers was John Chrysler Winegar, the great-grandfather of Cathy Davenport and her brother, Joe Winegar. Cathy runs Winegar's Marine Railway, and Joe is a fish spotter for one of the menhaden firms on the Northern Neck.

As a wheelwright, John Chrysler built items such as wagon wheels, wheelbarrow handles, and coffins. Another brother was a blacksmith, and another was a carpenter. Two of the five brothers eventually went back to New Jersey. In the 1880s, the brothers started a menhaden plant, buying fish from small snapper rigs (independent fishermen). Some years later, the fish factory was sold to Raymond Humphreys from the Eastern Shore. Humphreys and his family were to become the owners of

The railway at Winegar's is one of the few remaining all-wooden cradle railways on the Chesapeake.

The oak cradle rolls on a metal track that extends down into the water. Winegar's specializes in hauling deadrise workboats like the one in the background.

one of the largest menhaden firms in the country, known as Standard Products. The firm has since been sold, however, and is known today as Ampro Fisheries of Reedville, Virginia.

John Chrysler had a son, John Joseph Winegar, who was manager of the fish plant for many years. In 1911, he decided to start a small railway just a short distance down the road from his home. This railway became known as Winegar's Marine Railway. John Joseph's son, Joseph David, took over the railway in 1939 when his father died. Cathy (Winegar) Davenport took over the management in 1982 when her father died.

Cathy and Joe have fond memories of life around the railway and the old Winegar fish plant. They graciously agreed to share some of their memories.

FAMILY AND NEIGHBORS REMEMBERED

Cathy: "Our children are the fifth generation of Winegars to live here and the railway has played a big part in our lives. My grandfather started it in 1911. He ran it until he died in 1939. My father operated it until 1982,

Started in 1911, Winegar's Marine Railway is still in the family. John Joseph Winegar started the railway and passed it on to his son, Joseph David. On Joseph's death, Cathy (Winegar) Davenport, his daughter, took over the business. Cathy and her brother Joe stand beside the hand- or horse-operated windlass that their grandfather used to haul boats.

when he died, and now I've got it. It has been in continuous operation since it was started.

"We don't know too much about our grandfather because he died before we were around. We know that my grandfather lived with his father when he first got married in the big red house. The red house was the first house they built here. It is gone now. Before the red house was built, they lived in a large barn for several years.

"Later, my grandfather built the house Joe is living in now. It was built between 1900 and 1904. Granddaddy went to Baltimore and bought all the lumber for the house and had it shipped down here on the steamboat.

"My father had four older sisters. One was born in the red house and two twin aunts [sisters] and Daddy and another sister were born in Granddaddy's new house.

"My daddy wasn't named after his father, because they had about given up on having a boy. When the fourth sister came along, they named her John Anna, after my grandfather. When Daddy came along, they named him Joseph David."

Joe: "I remember Daddy talking about when the aunts would come down and turn the windlass to haul the boats. [The Winegars still have the windlass hand winch used to haul boats before motor power was installed.] You see, most of the boats were small back in the early days. They hauled mostly small bugeyes. They weren't big and heavy like boats with engines are today. Most were little sailboats, but they had horses, too. If they needed to haul a big boat, they could hook those horses to the windlass.

"After the windlass, we got a one-cylinder make-and-break Lathrop and hooked it up to a belt system to haul the boats, and then we went to the Model A Ford engine. Believe it or not, we are still using that Model A engine today."

Cathy: "We never have hauled many big boats. The biggest Daddy ever hauled was the *Virginia Dare.* She was a seventy-five-foot deck boat. The

Most railways use chain or wire rope to haul boats up on shore. At Winegar's rope is used. This old-time sprocket winch is operated by a Model A Ford engine. In 1911, boats at Winegar's were hauled by manpower or by horses. Later, they used a Lathrop one-cylinder engine. Their next engine was the Model A Ford still in use today.

This round stern deck boat was hauled at Winegar's in the 1940s. The boat is from Crisfield, Maryland and was probably used in the pound net fishery, judging from the pound skiff atop the stern. (Courtesy of Cathy Davenport)

story goes that Daddy was hauling the *Virginia Dare* when Papa John was on his deathbed. Someone came up and told Granddaddy, and he sat right up in the bed [and said], 'He can't do that! It's too big!'

"He [lay] back down and died shortly thereafter.

"When Daddy had the place, he could fix up anything, and people would say, 'David, why don't you get a new this or that?' He would say, 'Why? It will last my lifetime.'

"When he died, the very next week, I hauled a boat, and when I put it over the cradle, everything went to pot. I had divers come in, and they found that the track was worn completely out twenty feet on each side. There was nothing there. The car [cradle] was going out on mud.

"The first year Daddy was gone, everything that could go wrong did. The dock caught on fire, and we had to completely rebuild the small cradle. Every time I'd haul a boat it would blow fifteen or twenty [miles per hour].

"When Daddy would get mad or fed up with something around the railway, he used to say, 'When I catch my jet to heaven, I'm going to fly over this place and spit all over it," she laughed. "He was awful."

"When things were going real bad, I looked up in the sky and said, 'Daddy, quit spitting all over us.'

"He'd always talk bad about the railway, but the last thing he asked me to do before he died was to 'please scatter my ashes in the creek by the railway.'

"We put some roses in with his ashes, and I dumped them in the water. They floated right up to the railway."

There was silence for a moment.

Joe: "Daddy was a good railway man, but he had a soft heart for the watermen. I know one man who had a bill here for three years, and he got hauled every year.

The *Leolyn* was hauled on the railway at Winegar's in the 1920s. This style of yacht was common around the Chesapeake during that period. (Courtesy of Cathy Davenport)

"There were a lot who would give him five dollars here and ten dollars there and there were those who would say, 'David, I just don't have the money. Will you haul me and carry me for a while? Daddy never turned a waterman down. No sir!

"I remember when this one guy Daddy had carried for three years struck it rich. He was a haul seiner, and for three weeks he hit it big. This was in the mid-1960s, and he made fifty thousand dollars. He came in here the first week and paid off the whole bill and gave Daddy an extra hundred dollars for carrying him so long.

"I'll never forget what Daddy did. He gave him the hundred dollars back and said, 'I only want what you owe me, put that hundred dollars away for your family.

"Daddy carried a lot of people, but that's how people got along back then. He wasn't the only one who did that. It's an old way of thinking, and I know business people today would say he was foolish, but he would do it the same way today. I know he would."

Cathy: "He had people who would pay him in fish and crabs. If they had something in the garden, they would bring it to him. Deer hunters would bring him venison, and wives of watermen would bring him pies and cakes. He knew who could afford to pay and who couldn't. All he ever asked was for them to try, and most of them did.

"The biggest problem I have now, and it's my own fault, is that I don't charge for every hour I work. Every January, my New Year's resolution is 'Everybody is going to pay me for every hour I work.' My husband tells me every year, 'Cathy, I don't want to hear it.'

"When you work on a man's boat and you buy fish from him, too, you know his situation. He's out there beating himself to death trying to make a living. He's got a family to feed, and I know he's not making it. I can't charge him for every hour. I just can't do it." [Cathy also has a fish house on the property where she buys and sells fish.]

Joe: "To make money, you need to work on fiberglass pleasure boats. Daddy used to take care of a lot of pleasure boats from Windmill Point, but sailboats are the big thing now, and they are better off on a strap travel lift than on a railway."

Cathy: "Sailboats require a whole different set of blocking, and a sailboat person is not like a Chesapeake Bay waterman. Every sailboat I've ever hauled, I've had that man looking over my shoulder, trying to save a dollar. I've seen them walk in the water with a fifty-dollar pair of Topsiders on their feet to put a zinc on the boat to save themselves five dollars. They would ruin a pair of fifty-dollar shoes to save five dollars. Now, you tell me, does that make sense?"

Joe: "The people coming from the city to the country don't understand where we have come from. We had a fellow who had been working here since the 1950s. He got sick three years ago and doesn't work now, but he used to come down in the morning before work and soft-shell crab along the shore. A couple had just moved in across the way, and they saw him out there and came running. The man screamed, 'What are you digging up off my bottom?'

"My goodness, you could have heard him all the way to Kilmarnock. He was mad for three days. All he was trying to do was catch a soft-shell crab.

"Some people who own waterfront think they own as far as they can see."

Cathy: "We have good neighbors around here. They are not picky, picky, picky but they complain about the workboats starting up at 3:00 A.M. There is a different attitude now towards Bay watermen than it was in the 1950s. Because it's not a 9-to-5 job, people think of it as not being a real job."

Joe: "I was real fortunate coming along. A lot of boys had to go to gas stations to get a job, but I started going to the [fish] factory with Daddy when I was nine years old. We'd work all day at the railway, and he would work at the factory in the evenings. He would repair machinery and do other odd jobs. We'd ride over in his 1954 Ford, and he and Woody [his father's friend] would work until 2:00 or 3:00 A.M. I'd help for a while, and then I'd go to sleep on grass [fish scrap] sacks by the engine rooms. It was warm there.

"Woody was Daddy's best friend. He worked at the railway, too, and they would fight all the time. It was play fighting. They'd play tricks on each other. It was fun to work with them; there was no tension.

"Sometimes we would eat at the cook shed at the factory. In those days, people worked for a pittance, but they got fed during the day when they worked.

"A man could feed thirty-five head for three hundred dollars a week. I'm talking about good food now—homemade bread and biscuits, apple pies, cherry pies, pumpkin pies, chocolate pies, ice tea in five-gallon buckets. We'd go over there and sit right down and eat until we couldn't eat no more.

"It took a lot of people in those days to run a factory. The scrap shed alone took a bunch of people. Men and women were lined up sewing the scrap bags together.

"There were shanties where the colored workers would live during the week. Whites would drive to the plant. I can hear that old lunch bell now. Sometimes I'd run over from the railway to get something to eat and I'd take a baseball with me. After I'd eat, all the white and colored boys would be sitting around, waiting for the next shift, smoking cigarettes, and letting the shade from the old trees take them. Nobody was in a hurry. I'd start tossing my ball up in the air, and they'd all start playing. They were big-time ball players, too. After an hour or so, the oil, steam, and press rooms men would go on inside the plant. Then, a little while later, you would hear the boats coming loaded with fish, and everybody went to work.

"It started fading out in 1962, and by 1968, the plant closed down, and Standard Products moved everything to Reedville. Before it closed, it was one busy place, I'll tell you that."

Cathy: "Daddy had watermen come to the railway from all over the Bay, and we had a lot to come from Tangier Island. I remember William [Bill] Pruitt's father [Bill Pruitt is the director of the Virginia Marine Resources Commission] would come over here, and Joe and my sister would go over there and stay at his home.

"He had a workboat named the *Yamacraw.* I asked him one time, Where did he get a name like that?

"He said, 'I was stolen by the Indians when I was a little boy, and I learned Indian language.'" Cathy shook her head and smiled. "He was crazy, but I believed him then.

"He was a nice man. When my daddy was real sick, he had just got home from the hospital, and William brought the *Yamacraw* over just before he sold her. He said he wanted to haul her out one more time. We hauled her up, painted her, and away he went. I knew it was the last time I would see her. It was real sad. He and Daddy both died the same year."

Joe: "Tangiermen are nice people. There was old Duck Egg [Carroll Bradshaw] and Sherman Pruitt. Sherman stopped in here not too long ago, just to say hello. I miss that type of thing. People had more time for people years back."

Cathy: "Things have changed. The old-time railway men are just about gone. There are very few good boat carpenters out there anymore. There is a house carpenter and a boat carpenter, and it is not the same thing. It is absolutely different. The mind-set is different. With a house you are looking for squares—nothing is square on a boat. You are looking at multicurves and multibevels. You can't just say you are going to cut that piece of side out. You've got to cut a bevel here, here, and here."

Joe: "It's a dying art. I'd say in the next fifteen to twenty years you are going to be able to count all the good boat carpenters on one hand. A railway man had to be a good boat carpenter, machinist, and painter. That kind of knowledge is gone from the railways today. One man could run the whole thing. Daddy could do the lathing, carpentry, and welding."

Cathy: "People are going to fiberglass and aluminum [boats]."

FUTURE OF WATERMEN

Joe: "The whole Bay is dying. It can't support what's happening to it now."

Cathy: "Until people realize it's pollution that's doing more damage to the Bay than the watermen, I don't think it's going to get any better."

Joe: "I doubt my child will work the water. Cathy's son is in the water business, but I doubt mine will be. I'm not going to discourage it, but I'm not going to push him in it, either."

Cathy: "My son is a waterman. It's not by my choice. It was not what I wanted him to do; it was something he wanted to do."

Joe: "If mine goes into it, I won't stop him. After I get him out of high school, he can do anything he wants. I don't want him to stay around the water because his grandfather did it, though. It's not a growing industry."

FATHER REMEMBERED

Joe: "When I was eighteen years old, Daddy and I built a skiff one winter. We always had a skiff going in the winter when things were slow. If we couldn't sell it right away, I would use it to catch oysters from. We built boats in a small boatbuilding shed. The shed wasn't very tight. I can remember coming down in the early morning and having to sweep snow off the boat.

"When we finished the skiff, I went out that winter, and I was catching forty bushels a day. Daddy had a twelve-stall shucking house on the end of the dock, and he owned two patent [oyster] tong rigs. We had to do a lot of different things to make a living back then. Now, I couldn't catch an oyster to save my life." [The Virginia oyster industry is at an all-time low. MSX and dermo (two oyster diseases), pollution and, overharvesting have destroyed the industry.]

Cathy: "Daddy worked hard and he did things his own way. One time, somebody wanted him to build a wheelhouse on a boat, and he proceeded to tell Daddy the type he wanted.

"Daddy paused and then said, 'I ain't building no damn Guinea Neck wheelhouse on any boat. I'll build it my way, and if you don't like it, build it yourself.'"

Joe: "Railway men had their own styles. The way they built a wheelhouse was the way they built it. If you don't like their style, you better go somewhere else. I used to go with Daddy to a lot of railways. Those old-timers acted rough, but if they liked you, they were all right."

Cathy: "From the time we were little kids, Daddy stayed right with Joe and me. We started coming to the railway as soon as we could walk and he would stop working to watch us. We learned how to swim so if we fell overboard we could get to shore.

"When we would come down, he would stop and make us a little boat."

Joe, laughing: "Those boats weren't nothing fancy, but he shaped the hulls, drilled a hole for the mast, and put a mast in her. They would float, all right. I can see him now, looking around the corner watching us sail those boats."

Cathy: "I didn't forget that when our own children would come down, either. I enjoyed so much making the little boats for them. They deserved that. Daddy taught us what life was all about."

Joe: "Yeah, he did!

"When I was a little boy, I had a go-cart that was hard to start. I'd ride it all over the place. I got in trouble with the school bus driver one day, and I said something to her I shouldn't have.

"She talked to my Mamma, and Mamma told Daddy. The next day when I got home, Mamma told me Daddy wanted to see me at the railway. I knew I was in trouble.

"He was working on the bottom of a boat. He said, 'I heard what you said to the bus driver. Go in there and pull your pants down.'

"He came in and tore me up with his belt. I ran out crying and pulled that go-cart, and she started the first time. I got home and ran to my room.

"A little while later, I heard Daddy downstairs. He came up and picked me up and hugged me. 'Daddy didn't want to spank you, but you didn't do right, and you've got to go apologize to the bus driver. You know your Daddy loves you.' He hugged me and hugged me.

"Lord, I loved him so much. He was a good daddy!"

Cathy: "We have a lot to be thankful for. Sometimes I feel like [our] Daddy used to feel about this place: 'When I catch my jet, I'm coming back and spit all over the place.'"

Cathy pauses and then says, "There are too many good memories for that, though."

✻ *It occurred to me while writing the chapter on Winegar's Marine Railway that the story of a long-time railway man would be equally interesting.*

I had interviewed Morton Clarke for an article in 1990. Recalling what a good conversation we had had, I decided then that a short chapter on his life as a railway man would make a colorful addition to this volume.

23 : A Longtime Railway Man

MORTON CLARKE, eighty-two, started his railway business at Regent, Virginia, over fifty years ago. The railway, located on Locklies Creek just off the Rappahannock River, has two small railways situated in front of two slightly crooked buildings that Morton moved there from his grandfather's farm across the road. One had been a corn crib, and the other, half of a chicken house. The other half of the chicken house sits up the hill next to Morton's 1948 Dodge pickup truck. The smell of chickens has long since been replaced with a musty odor that comes from the marine products now stored there. Besides Clarke, a friendly, wide-eyed beagle named Spot watches over the place.

"No sir, it ain't many railways left . . . not these kind, anyway," says Morton. "Years back, every creek had one or two little railways. You got to understand, though, that right many years ago, there wa'n't no need for railways.

"When I was a small fellow in the 1920s, everybody in the neighborhood had [log] canoes. There wasn't any need for a railway because they'd get a bunch of boys and skid the canoes up on shore, flip them over, and leave them there for the summer. You see, a lot of the boys didn't use the canoes for anything but oystering. They'd farm or do something else in the warm-weather months. The boats weren't very big, either. Canoes would run twenty, twenty-two feet, and the biggest was about twenty-five feet long.

"I'll tell you something else. Most of the canoes in our neighborhood didn't have sails or even a mast in them. The boys around home would scull out to the oyster beds. The beds were close to home so they didn't need a sail. Other neighborhoods were different because they had to go far off to catch a mess of oysters.

Morton Clarke

"I tried oystering one time but I didn't like it. I went out one day with Grayson Dunlevy and helped him cull for a little bit. I told him at the end of the day, 'This ain't for me.'"

REGENT STORE

Morton's father, Morton Emory Clarke, Sr., ran a little neighborhood general merchandise store overlooking the creek. Their property extended down to the creek, which was where Morton eventually placed his railway.

"Daddy started the store before I was born. My grandfather, John C. Clarke, was a farmer and he lived up at Waterview Farm [a large Victorian-style farmhouse that is still in the Clarke family]. At one time, all this land was part of that farm."

The store got its name in 1894 when the U.S. Postal Service decided to open a post office there. They wrote to Mr. Clarke and asked what they should call the post office. Morton says that his father looked on a shelf in the store and saw the name "Regent" on a box of white starched men's collars (the kind that buttoned onto shirts). "Daddy liked the name so he called the store Regent," says Morton. The post office was discontinued in 1950.

As a boy, Morton played around the store and the waterfront that he would one day make into a railway. "Back then, everybody stayed around the neighborhood. The store was the best place around to shop. A lot of people had to walk to the store. They didn't have cars, and some rode horses and mules or came by water in their canoes.

"I remember when Mr. Walter Baker would bring eggs to Daddy and trade for groceries," says Morton. "Daddy carried a lot of tick [credit] too. He didn't let nobody go hungry.

"I have fond memories of coming home from school and playing on the hillside behind the store. Charles Miller [a childhood friend] and I would go in the store, and I'd fill my pockets with cakes and candy. Daddy would say, 'Boy, you better get out of that candy. You are going to ruin your teeth.'"

THE NEIGHBORHOOD

"When I was a boy, there wa'n't railways like this, but there were individuals around who would work on boats. When the motor came along, my uncle, Charlie Lawson, who lived across the creek, would overhaul the old engines. He had a little shanty where he worked on Palmer and Lathrop engines.

"When the canoes began to go, Mr. Lawrence Parker began building round-stern canoes [frame-built deadrise boats]," he says. There are some areas in Virginia where round-stern workboats are still referred to as canoes. The pronunciation is more like "kay-noo." This is a holdover from the days when log canoes were the best and most used style of workboat on the Chesapeake.

"Mr. Parker lived up the road there, and he would build boats back in the woods," recalls Morton. "He built them by a wide stream that ran through a swamp. When he had a boat just about completed, he would wait for a real high tide and float it out into the creek. He did everything by hand. He didn't have no electricity. He built mostly round-stern boats, and I've hauled a many a one that he made."

MORTON CLARKE'S RAILWAY

"I started the railway in the early 1940s," says Morton. "My brother had started one over by the store, and I came over here and started mine. It looked like it was a good idea, because there were a lot of workboats around then. There were still a few log canoes, but by that time the round-stern canoe had taken over. We also began seeing Maryland-built boats. There were several Hooper Island drake tails on the creek.

"The round-stern canoes and drake tails were bigger and wider than the old canoes. There was also a prop sticking out [from] the stern that they didn't want damaged. The days of dragging boats up on shore and flipping them over were gone. So, I decided to try my hand at the railway business, and I've been doing it ever since.

"I never have hauled big boats [deck boats]. It's always been small workboats and now small pleasure boats. My favorite boat is the round-stern canoe. There ain't nothing any prettier in this world, but nowadays, all they build are square-stern workboats. That's because the round stern takes heavier timber and is more expensive to build. It also takes longer. But, you know, most good things do take longer to do.

"That's one of the main differences in the way it was and the way it is now. A man took the time to do it right, no matter how long it took. Nowadays, everybody wants things quick. Years back, people didn't have much, so they had to look after what they had. Nowadays, if something gets broken, people throw it away and get another one.

"The price of things has skyrocketed, too. I used to haul boats for five dollars. I'm still cheap compared to those yacht marinas. I've had watermen who were tight, but none to complain like those yachtsmen. I hauled a boat for a Richmond man once. I painted the sides, and I don't know what all I did. The bill came to less than thirty dollars. He raised the dickens.

"Some watermen grumbled, too, but they didn't have much money. Things were tight for people in the neighborhood, and we all knew that. We tried to help one another.

"I haven't always charged enough money for my work. I've been lenient on it, and that's why I haven't made a lot of money. You've got to understand, though, times were different. We're in a different world.

High [cost-of-living] prices are hard on old people. We didn't know everything was going to cost a fortune. But, even if I had charged a fortune, nobody could have paid it.

"Back in those days, things were tight in the water business, but the boys did not have the same type of expenses. There wa'n't an electric bill or a phone bill coming every month. There wa'n't no insurance, and taxes were practically nothing."

LUNCHTIME

Suddenly Morton looked up from the rolltop desk that had been his father's. Well! It's twelve noon. I've got to go to lunch. My wife's expecting me. Ever since I started this place, I eat at twelve noon no matter what."

Morton stood up and headed out the door. As we walked toward my car, he said, "I don't know much, but I hope I've helped you some."

"I'll bring you something to eat," he yelled to Spot who was barking.

"Ain't nothing like an old dog," he said to me, and then he went up the hill for lunch.

✻ *Several years ago, the Urbanna Oyster Festival Foundation honored Willis Cannon as captain of its annual festival. The committee chose people who had either worked the water or made their living at sea. Willis had spent a lifetime at sea and was a natural for the honor.*

I was sent by the editor of the Southside Sentinel *to do a story on Willis and to photograph him. I suggested we go down to the shore on Urbanna Creek and shoot the photo with him standing on a dock with his boat in the background. When we arrived at the dock, Willis jumped down into a skiff that had a beautifully braided bow fender covering the bow.*

"Where did you get that fender?" I asked.

"Oh, I just whipped it up," he said.

24 : How to Make a Rope Bow Fender

YEARS AGO, when wood was the only material used in the construction of boats, rope fenders were used to protect the hulls of Chesapeake Bay boats. Watermen and yachtsmen alike could braid the decorative and useful fenders. They either dangled from the sides of the vessels or covered the bow.

Rope fenders are still used on pound net skiffs today to protect the small craft when it beats up against pound poles during rough seas. Years back, rope fenders were used on wooden menhaden purse boats, steamers, tugboats, and recreational yachts. Few old-timers around today still know how to whip up a rope fender. Captain Willis Cannon, eighty years old, is one of those old-timers. He can still make the old-style fenders, and he was kind enough to share his knowledge.

Willis grew up in Urbanna, Virginia, on the Rappahannock River. He started his seafaring career at an early age working aboard sail-driven schooners. From the schooners, he progressed to the merchant marines and worked aboard tugboats and oil tankers that traveled up and down the East Coast and on the Mississippi River.

He doesn't recall when he made his first rope fender, but he knows it had to have been made some sixty years ago. "I don't know who taught me to braid a rope fender, I sailed with so many guys. It was something

Willis Cannon has been making rope fenders for boats for years. In fact, he has made so many he can't remember the first one he ever made. Here, Willis holds one of his skiff fenders all ready to be attached to a bow.

Willis makes his fenders from strands of discarded rope. He also uses a pointed splicing fid to open the strands of rope as he knits.

"Ain't nothing prettier than a pretty skiff with a pretty bow fender," according to Willis Cannon.

we did when the weather was good and we were on watch. You know, just to kill time. If I was on watch from 6:00 A.M. to noon and it was a nice day, I would sit around on deck and work on a fender."

"Nobody does this much any more," says Captain Willis. "This is the best system of fendering that you can get. We found out on the tugs that rubber is good when sides of the ship and fenders are dry, but if either get wet, rubber fenders will slip." Most tugboat companies have adopted rubber bow fenders for their tugs. These fenders are less expensive than rope fenders and easier and quicker to obtain.

"Rope will grab and hold, but when rubber is wet, it will slip like a dance floor," says Willis with a chuckle.

"The biggest fender I ever helped make was twenty-three feet wide and thirty-six inches in diameter. It covered eleven and a half feet around each side of the tug. We used chain for the chore because there was so much pressure on the side of a tug when it was coming ahead and beating up against a pier.

"Rope fendering not only works good on tugboats, they are great on small craft, too," says Willis. "I've got one on the bow of my skiff, and

Once the center core of the fender is made, Willis begins knitting the outer layer with the help of a splicing fid.

Although Willis does not whisker, or beard, his smaller fenders, here he shows how a whisker is attached to a fender. When he was making fenders for tugboats, he added whiskers to help protect the knitted portion of the fender. When the whiskers wore out, they were replaced.

years back, many crabbers, fishermen, and oystermen used either bow or side fenders made of rope.

"On the large tugboats, we made the fender with a bend in the middle to wrap it around the bow, but on a skiff, the fender is small enough it will bend right around. As it wears and as rain hits it, the rope will stretch on out. There ain't nothing any prettier than a pretty skiff with a pretty bow fender," he says.

On the larger rope fenders, Willis used an old technique called whiskering or bearding to give the braided fender even more protection. Whiskers are simply strands of rope tied to the half hitches and allowed to tangle down over the fender.

"We made whiskers on the big ones to protect the braided part of the fender," he explains. "When the boat rubs up against a pier, the whiskers take the brunt of the motion and will wear out first. When they wear out, all you have to do is put on new whiskers. If you keep whiskers on it, a fender will last for years."

Willis started his seafaring career working on the sail-driven schooner the *Kate Tilghman* and later went to work for Exxon and worked aboard such tugs as the *New Jersey, Maryland, Maine, Long Island, Virginia, Massachusetts*, and *Vermont.* Most of these tugs were used to tow oil barges.

"I know that there are few people around now who can make a rope fender, but they [the fenders] sure look a lot prettier than an automobile tire, and it's a heck of lot better way of fendering," says Willis.

STARTING TO MAKE A BOW FENDER

The bow fender on Willis's skiff is made from a piece of ¾-inch rope about five feet long. The center of the fender is shaped from a series of half hitches woven over a core that is made from old rope bundled into the shape of a slender football.

WHIPPING THE ENDS

The first step is to unstring the ends and whip each strand of the five-foot-long line to keep it from unraveling. Using a piece of common string a foot or so long, line it up along the strand end, and whip it (drawing A).

Starting at the end of the strand, wind the string around, working back along the rope to cover the string end as you go. Continue for five or six turns (drawing B).

Now make a loop as shown in drawing C. Make it large enough so it contains sufficient string to wind around the rope three or more times.

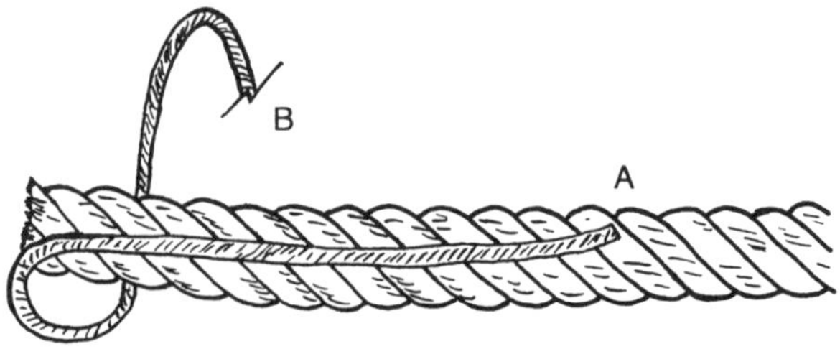

Drawing A

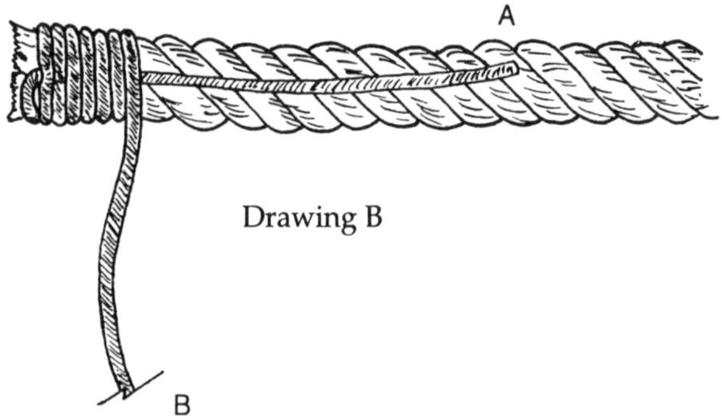

Drawing B

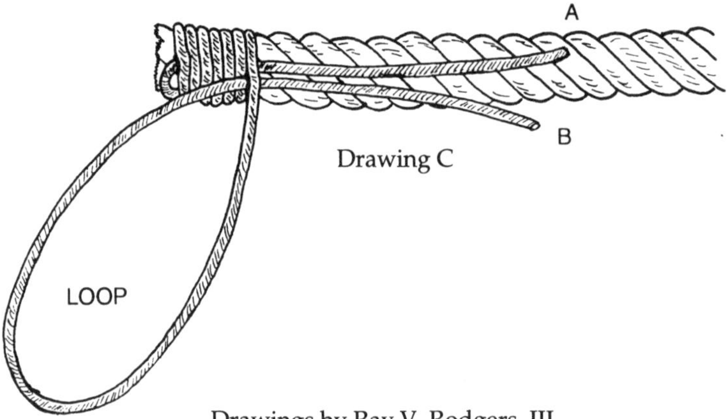

Drawing C

Drawings by Ray V. Rodgers, III

Using the string in the loop, wind several more turns around the rope, covering both ends of the string as you go. The loop continues to get smaller as you go. When this step is completed, it should look like drawing D.

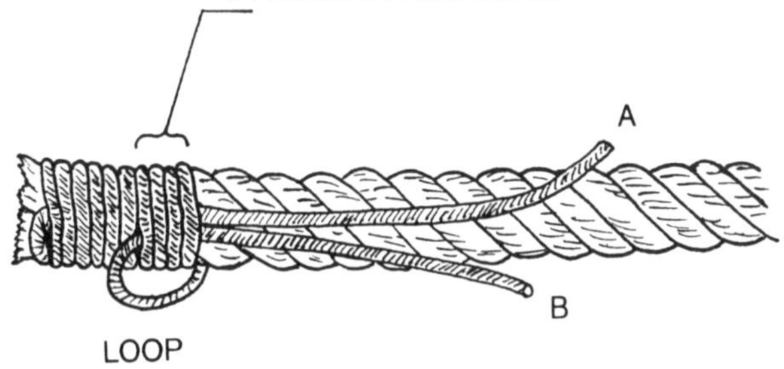

Drawing D

Drawing E
Drawings by Ray V. Rodgers, III

Finally, pull ends A and B snug, and trim them (drawing E). Whipping the strands is optional, but Captain Willis says it makes the rope easier to work with.

SPLICING THE LOOPS

Once the strands are whipped, loops are shaped on the ends. These loops are used to secure the fender to the bow of the skiff (see photo on page 219).

To make a loop, unwind about 6 or 8 inches of each strand from the end of the rope. The length of the strand depends on the size of rope used, but 8 inches is good for ½- and ¾-inch rope. Bend a loop in the rope of the desired size (drawing F).

Starting the splice is the hardest part. Where the rope is unwound is called the ends. There are three ends. Where the rope is still twisted is called the turns. There are also three turns. Pick a point on the rope that will make the loop the desired size, and take one of the ends and pass it under one of the turns as in drawing G, where end 1 is passed under turn

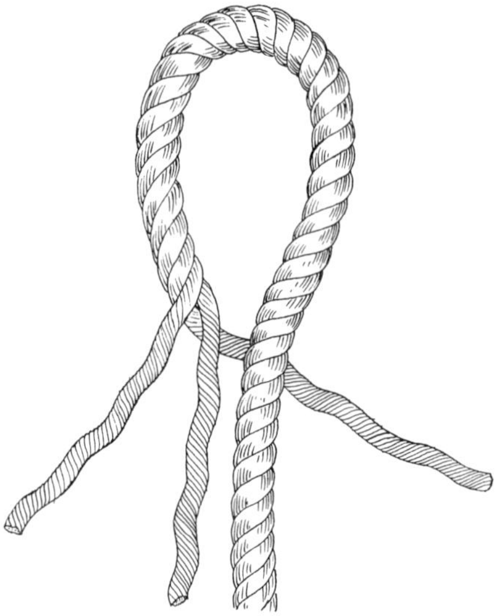

Drawing F

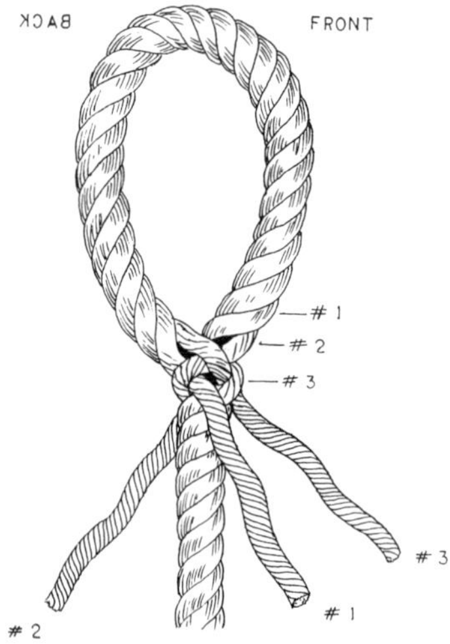

Drawing G

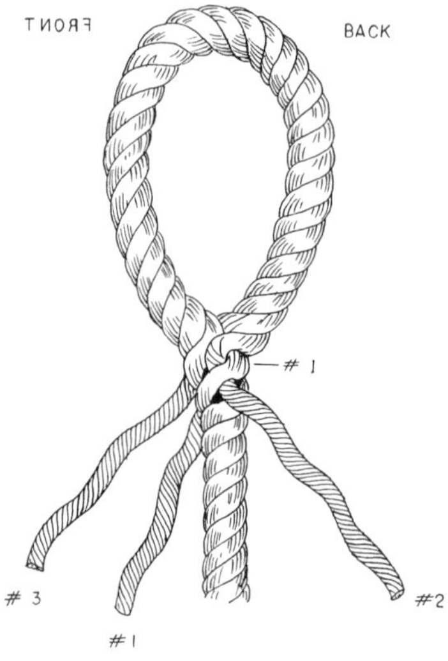

Drawing H

Drawing I

Drawings by Ray V. Rodgers, III

Drawing J
Drawing by Ray V. Rodgers, III

2. It makes no difference which end goes under which turn to start. Just make sure that each end goes under a different turn (i.e., no two ends go under the same turn.) Drawings G and H illustrate how the start should look, both front and back. In these illustrations end 1 went under turn 2 (end 3 went under turn 3), and in the back view, end 2 went under turn 1.

For the rest of the splice, take each end, one at a time, and go over the next turn and under the next. Do not work one end to its conclusion. Work all three ends along together. Drawing I shows the splice after two rounds of "over-under" have been made.

Continue to work all three ends over and under down the rope. You will notice a basket-weave effect start to take shape. The finished splice is shown in Drawing J.

The loose ends may be left out as shown or tucked inside the rope for a neater look.

MAKING THE CENTER CORE

Once loops are spliced in both ends of the rope (drawing K), the center core must be made. The length of the fender is determined by the size of the skiff and how big the person wants the fender to be.

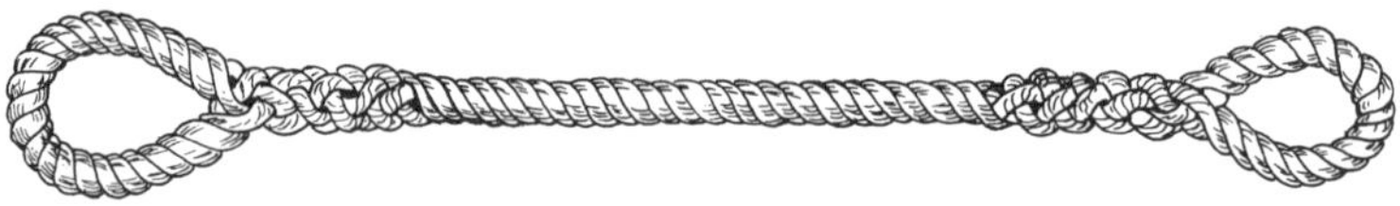

Drawing K

Drawing L

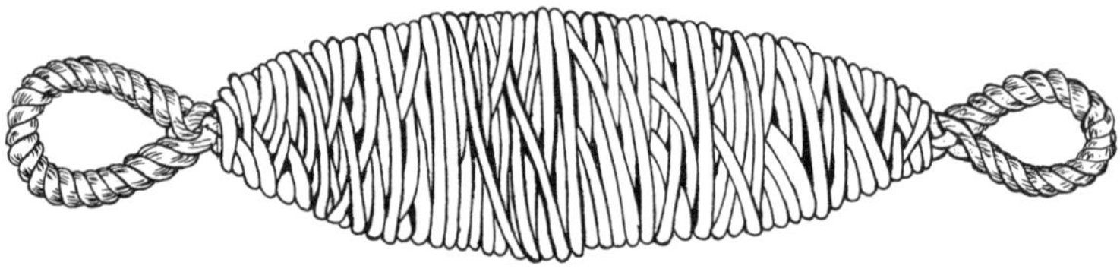

Drawing M

Drawings by Ray V. Rodgers, III

To make the center core, take lengths of rope and unwind them into three separate cords. Take one end of one cord and tuck it under a turn near the center of the main rope. Wrap the cord around the rope snugly and tuck the other end under a turn in the rope (drawing L).

Continue to add cords of rope, building up the core of the fender to the desired thickness. The shape of the finished core should resemble a long, slender football (drawing M). As you build up the core, the ends may be tucked in anywhere it is convenient.

STARTING THE FENDER COVER

Take more rope and untwist it into three separate cords. Whip both ends of each cord. Put the end of a cord through the splice loop at one end of the core. Make a figure eight through the loop (drawing N). Take the other end of the cord and pass it through an eye made in the end of the cord. This eye is made by separating the strands of the cord (drawing N).

Using the cord that passed through the eye, proceed around to the back of the fender and make a half hitch around the lower part of the figure eight. You have now generated loop 1 (drawing O).

Proceed around to the front and make another half hitch (loop 2), around the lower cord of the figure eight (drawing P).

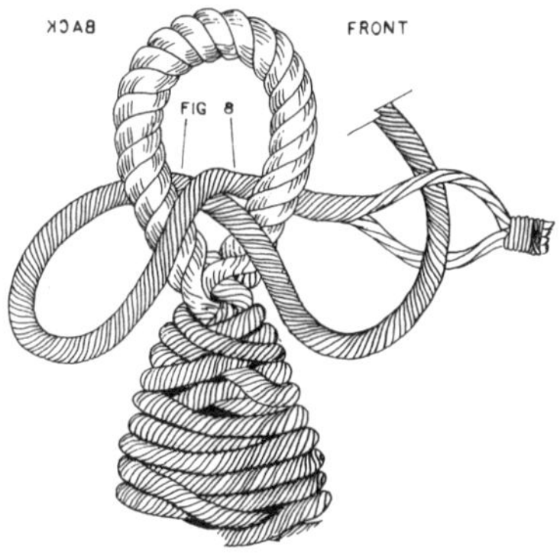

Drawing N

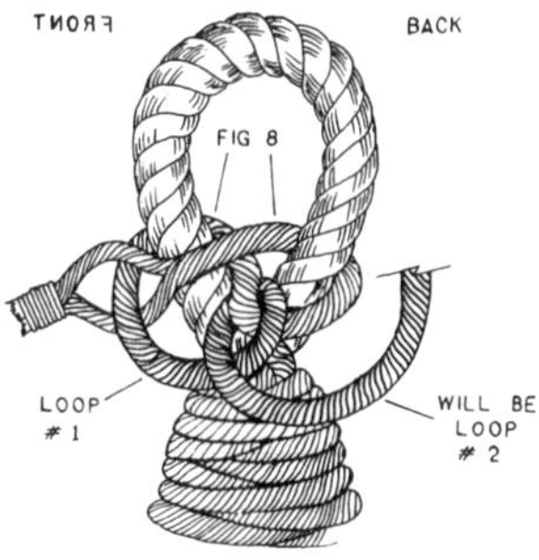

Drawing O

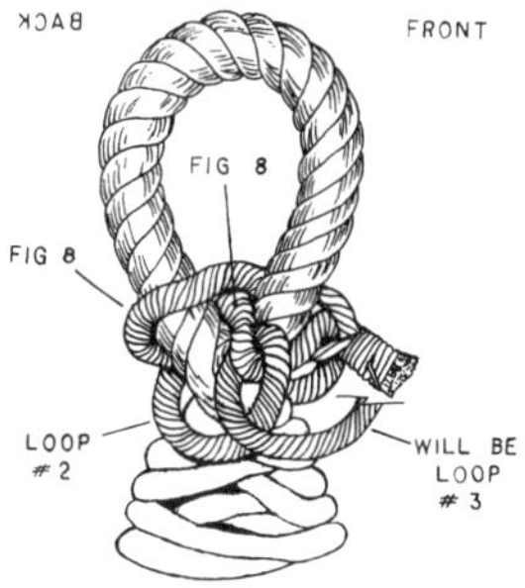

Drawing P

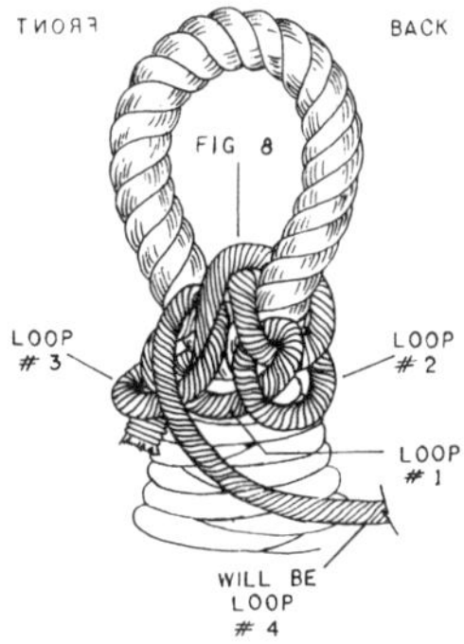

Drawing Q

Drawings by Ray V. Rodgers, III

Continue to work around the fender to the back and make loop 3 with a half hitch around the top cord of the figure eight (drawing Q).

Continue to make half hitch loops to cover the entire bumper. Start by making loop 4 around your original loop 1. Then loop 5 is around loop 2, and 6 is around 3, and so on. The pattern of stitches is shown in drawing R. These loops should not be as loose as the ones shown in the drawing, which are shown loose for clarity. However, the loops should not be too tight, as you will have to pass the rope through them on successive rows of loops. How snug to tie them will be quickly determined by experience. If you find your previous loops are too tight to work through, or too loose so as to unravel too much of the core, do not hesitate to untie and redo.

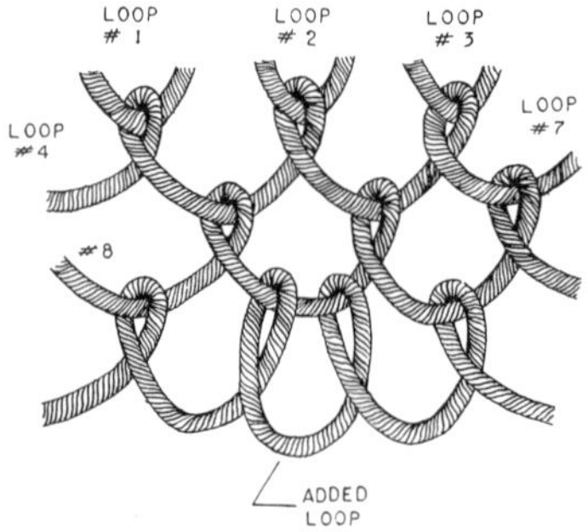

Drawing R

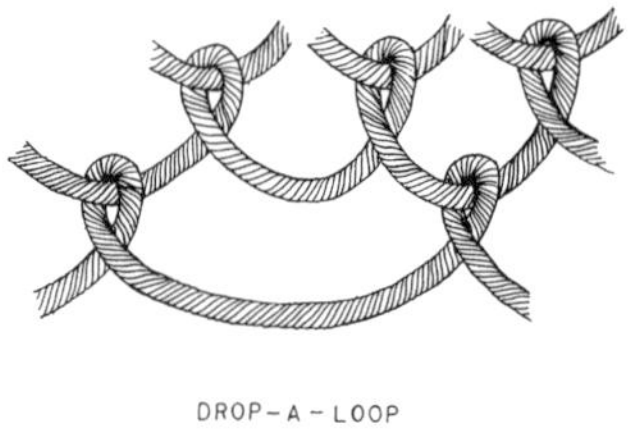

Drawing S

Drawing T
Drawings by Ray V. Rodgers, III

Because of the football shape of the core, as you work down, the core begins to get too big for the number of loops that have to go around it. At this point, usually as early as the second or third row, you must "add a loop" by hanging two half hitches on one loop (drawing R). When you get to the other end of the fender where the core size decreases, you will have to decide when to "drop a loop." This is done by simply skipping a loop as you tie half hitches (drawing S). More than one loop, on more than one row, will have to be added and later dropped. Just look for a smooth and even appearance.

As you work, you will undoubtedly run out of cord. When this happens, use a splice as shown in drawing T. Separate the strands at the end of a whipped cord and pass the cord to be spliced through.

When you get to the end of the fender, you should have reduced the number of loops to three. The work should resemble drawing U.

To finish it off, pass the end of the cord through the spliced eye at the bottom of the fender from the back side. Then pass the cord through two of your last three loops on the fender cover. Return the cord end back through the spliced eye. You are now making another figure eight on this end of the fender (drawing V).

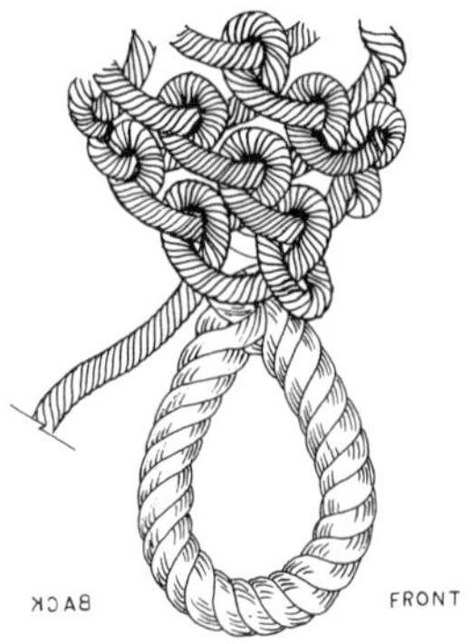

Drawing U

Drawing V

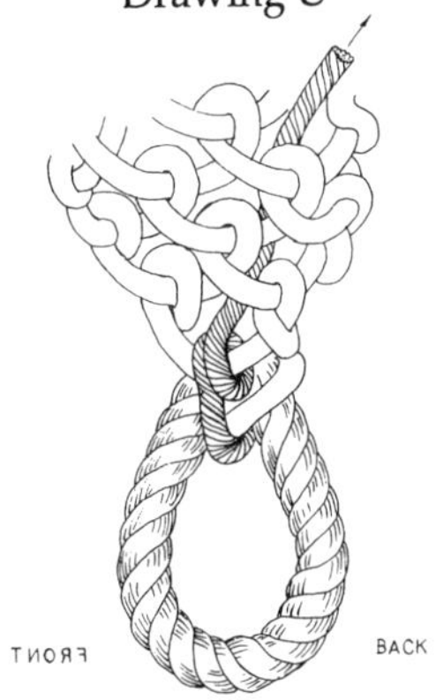

Drawing W

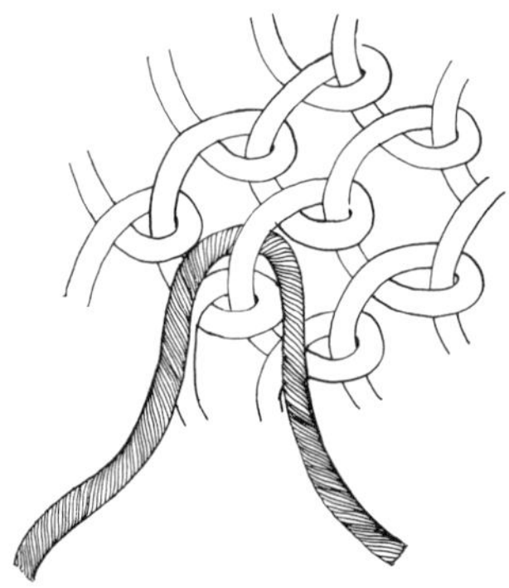

Drawing X

Drawings by Ray V. Rodgers, III

The cord comes through the spliced eye from the front to the back and then half-hitches around the last of the three loops on the fender cover. Now tuck the cord end under the cover for a distance sufficient to hold it secure. The direction or method of securing the end is not absolute. Just be sure it is secure (drawing W).

Next, lay the fender on the floor and roll it back and forth with your foot applying pressure. This action smooths the fender.

One of the last details is whiskering, or bearding. This is done by unwinding three-strand rope as before. Using a cord about fourteen to sixteen inches long (longer or shorter as desired), pass the cord through one of the loops on the fender cover (drawing X).

Separate the strands of the cord. Pick out one strand and take the ends to opposite sides (drawing Y).

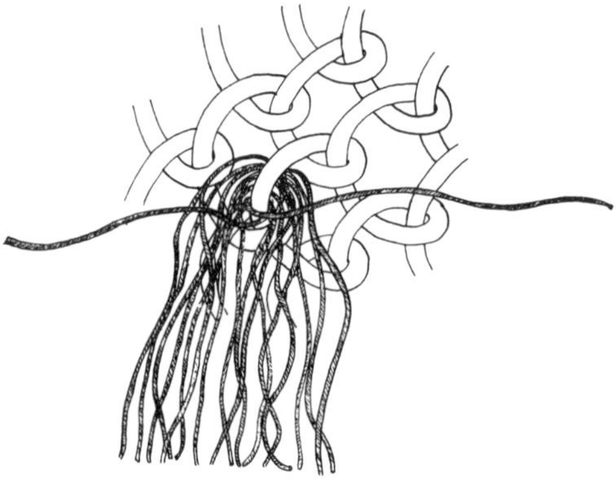

Drawing Y

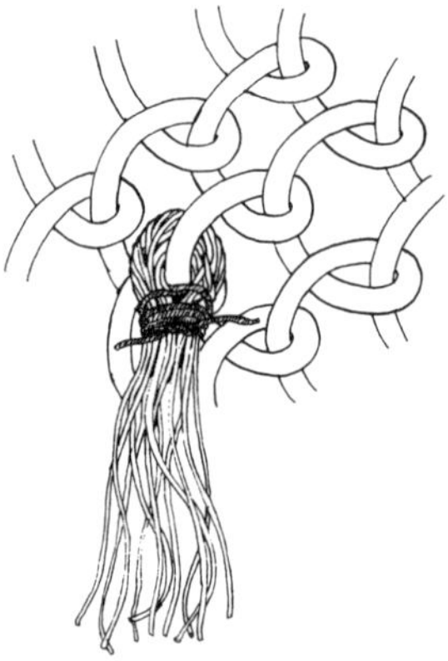

Drawing Z
Drawings by Ray V. Rodgers, III

Wrap the whisker with the two ends from the step above. Use two or three turns and tie off with a square knot (drawing Z). Finally, tie whiskers on every other loop of the fender cover. Whiskering may be replaced as it wears out. Also, whiskering is optional. Captain Willis does not use whiskers on his small fenders, but he recommends it to give added protection.

Once the fender is made, it is attached to the skiff. Captain Willis screws an eye on each side of the boat and uses copper wire to attach the loops to the eyes.

Captain Willis Cannon has related a craft that has practically died out on the Bay. "I don't know anyone left that can do this," says Willis. "All the old boys are gone."

✻ *In 1992, publisher and editor Fred Gaskins of the* Southside Sentinel *was asking around for story ideas for what was then a spring publication called "Summer Lifestyle." I suggested we do a series of stories on cruises offered throughout the area. I also asked for first choice of a cruise.*

I had been to Tangier and Smith Islands and had just visited St. Mary's, Maryland, a few weeks before. Even though the Rappahannock River was in my own backyard, I had never been above Tappahannock by water.

For my story, I chose the cruise on the Captain Thomas *and a visit to Saunders Wharf. My trip there led to the idea for this chapter .*

25 : Steamboats and Seafood

THE SEAFOOD industry got a shot in the arm in the 1800s when steamboat lines linked small waterfront villages up and down the Chesapeake to major cities. These cities—Baltimore, Norfolk, Washington, and others—had the population to support a strong and steady demand for Chesapeake Bay seafood.

Before the steamboat, watermen living in rural Maryland and Virginia sold most of their catch to local markets. The steamboat helped to expand those markets.

Along with the steamboat came steamboat wharfs. These wharfs became the social and economic lifeline of rural communities along the Bay. Just about everything imaginable came and went by steamboat, and a trip to Baltimore to shop, visit relatives, and the like, was an annual event for many households.

The little country store down the road was stocked with goods from the big stores in the city, all delivered by steamboat. The furniture in the homes, the dishes in the kitchen, the tongue and groove boards on the walls, and, yes, even the chamber pot (or johnny bucket, as it was commonly known) which was kept under the bed for a late-night emergency, came by steamboat.

The steamboat also carried goods from the country to the city. Chickens, cows, bulls, fish, crabs, oysters, vegetables, and furs were just some of the commodities delivered by steamboat to buyers in the city.

Historically, the steamboat stands alongside good roads, refrigeration, crab pots, pound nets, and other innovations for making a significant contribution to the seafood industry. Steamboats allowed watermen to expand their markets and helped the industry grow to national levels.

SAUNDERS WHARF

Saunders Wharf on the Rappahannock River is perhaps the last steamboat dock still standing in its original state on the Chesapeake. The wharf is located on the shores of Wheatland, an 1810 plantation in Essex County. Wheatland was built by John Saunders, for whom the wharf was named.

In 1828 the steamboat *Patuxent* made an experimental run up to Fredericksburg. Two years later, the Baltimore and Rappahannock Steam Packet Company built the steamboat *Rappahannock* for a regular run up the river.

Saunders Wharf on the Rappahannock River is the last remaining steamboat dock in the Chesapeake region. Started by John Saunders in the 1830s, Saunders Wharf is now owned by Fielding Dickinson, a great-grandson of Saunders. The wharf is one of just a few that survived the devastating August storm of 1933 and perhaps the only one that lasted through the demise of the steamboat. Today, visitors can catch a cruise boat from Tappahannock, Virginia, and ride upriver to the dock where Fielding and his friend, the Reverend Joe Gardner, meet their visitors and spin their tales of the way life used to be when Saunders Wharf was a hub of activity.

Wheatland was built in 1810 by John Saunders. Legend has it that when the Yankees came upon Wheatland during the Civil War, a northern commander issued an order to burn it to the ground. The northern officer commanded Saunders to get everyone out of the house. Instead, he called everyone—slaves, children, and adults—to the house and ordered them to the front porch steps where the Yankees could see them clearly. Saunders then hollered, "If you are going to take Wheatland, then you will have to take us all!" The Yankees then turned their guns on a nearby barn and blew it to pieces, leaving Wheatland and its stubborn owner safe and sound.

The original wharf sign.

This desk was used by John Saunders at the dock. When the steamboat dock and the post office at Saunders closed in the 1930s, the desk was moved to a new post office at Loretto on the main road. When the Loretto post office closed several years ago, the desk was brought back to the dock.

Shortly after this, Saunders built a dock down by the river. It remained open until the last steamboat came in 1937. During the steamboat era, Saunders Wharf was a busy place. Passengers caught the steamboat to Baltimore, and local farmers and fishermen brought their goods to be shipped to buyers in the cities.

FIELDING DICKINSON

John Saunders was Fielding Lewis Dickinson's great-grandfather. Fielding lives at Wheatland today and still maintains the wharf as a public museum.

Fielding was too young to remember much about the dock in its heyday, but he recalls a lot of what his grandfather and father told him about those days so long ago. They were both wharf masters at Saunders Wharf.

"We don't know for sure when the first dock was put here, but we know it was in the 1830s," says Fielding. "The dock you see now was built in 1915, and it's exactly the way it was when my grandfather had it built.

My father was a young man then, and he and Alex Johnson used a pair of oxen to snake the timbers out of the woods. They brought them down here and built the dock.

"My grandfather and father used to talk a lot about the wharf. You see, we had a big lumber yard on the other side of the pier and a dock for the schooner and bugeyes to tie up, too. The lumber was hauled by sailboats but most everything else went by steamboat.

"Every kind of thing came to the dock. I've heard my father say the market hunters up this way would sell their wild ducks by the barrel. They would be shipped to Baltimore, and later on, my father would get letters back from the buyers saying those boys had stuck an old crane [great blue heron] down in it to help fill up their barrel. Nobody wanted a crane for anything. Later, they passed laws to stop the commercial killing of ducks."

BLACK BULL

"Another story Daddy told me was about a black bull they tried to load on the steamboat. The boat would leave Fredericksburg right after lunch and get here about seven or eight o'clock at night.

Fielding Dickinson (left) and the Reverend Joe Gardner recall the days when the steamboat plied the waters of the Chesapeake. Today, they greet visitors who come to see the last steamboat wharf on the Bay.

"Once a month, a group of men in a poker club would get on the boat at Fredericksburg and ride down to Leedstown. They played poker and drank whisky and ate supper. Before they would get to Leedstown, they would stop at our dock. A carriage would meet them at Leedstown and take them back to Fredericksburg.

"A farmer had sold a black bull to a slaughterhouse in Baltimore and brought him to our wharf. The deckhands loaded him on the boat, but the bull went wild, broke out of his pen, went up through the saloon, jumped right down in the middle of that poker table, and went through the window and ran off.

"The next morning the bull came back to the dock, and he was loaded back on."

THE WHARF AND SEAFOOD

"There were all kinds of people coming to the dock then. I remember one old fellow who would come in there in a modified bugeye. We called him Skipper. He had taken the aft mast off and put a cabin and engine in her.

"I've seen that boat come to the dock with its hold full of salt herring. It was cured in the hold. He had a layer of salt and a layer of fish, layer of salt, layer of fish, all the way up to the top deck.

"When people heard he was coming, everybody came running to buy enough salt herring to last the winter. Henry Young ran a sawmill, and he had to feed his men. He'd come down here with three or four great big barrels, buy the fish from Skipper, and pack them right on the dock.

"He'd stay until everybody bought what they wanted and then move on to another dock."

FROG PONDERS

"We are above the saltwater line here so we don't have oysters and crabs. I shouldn't say we don't have any; we do get some crabs but not enough to support a commercial fishery. So, the only things we shipped from our wharf were fish and eels.

"There were a group of fishermen who we called Frog Ponders. They lived up on Frog Pond right on the line of Westmoreland and King George Counties.

"They shipped all their fish fresh and iced down. They'd cut their own ice in the winter off the river or an ice pond and store it in an icehouse. Come spring, they'd pull out some ice and ice their fish down in barrels and ship it to Baltimore.

Barrels like this one were used to store grain and to carry iced-down fish by steamboat to fish buyers in Baltimore. The oak barrel was made at Wheatland.

"These Frog Ponders would bring barrels full of fish covered in ice to the dock. One day, the wind went northwest and caught four or five of them at the dock, and they couldn't get home. They were in small skiffs and the wind was blowing up a storm, so they spent the night in the passenger room at the wharf.

"We had a great big potbellied stove in there, and my father had a stack of lumber on the shore ready to be shipped to Baltimore. The next morning, my father walked down to the dock, and he couldn't believe his eyes. The stack of lumber was gone. The Frog Ponders had burned the whole thing up to keep warm. He said they must have had it a hundred degrees in there to burn the whole pile up."

ICEHOUSE

"The icehouse we have here on Wheatland is a deep hole with brick walls from the bottom to the top. It is about fifteen feet deep and has a fifteen-foot diameter, with an A-frame shed to cover it.

"Every winter, we would cut the ice with a handsaw from the pond and haul it up to the icehouse on a horse-drawn wagon. I was just a kid, but I would help put the ice up. We would put it down in the hole and cover it with straw and sawdust, and I've seen it keep all summer long.

"My grandmother would keep her milk and cream fresh by lowering it down into the ice hole with a rope. The rope was tied to the rafters of the A-frame so milk and cream cans could be pulled up when she wanted it."

STRINGING FISH ON OAK REEDS

"We caught fish, too, and we packed all our fish in barrels, but most places used wooden boxes. Since we were above the salt line, we caught mostly catfish, perch, rockfish, and shad and herring in the spring.

"When those big schools of shad would come in the spring, women would come down to the dock and string fish. They would string them through the gills with an oak reed. I can remember when the dock was full of women. They would string fish and ice them down in the barrel. They were paid to do it, but I don't know how much they got.

"They would pick a big oak tree and split it up and pull the splits off to make the reeds. It was the same type of oak split used to make baskets or to make seats in chairs.

"I can remember Uncle Al [an African-American who worked at Wheatland] bringing in a boatload of fish from his haul seine. He would bring them up to the dock, and all the women would be sitting around stringing fish.

"One time a man shipped a barrel of fish to Baltimore. Whoever got them wrote back that the price of the fish would not pay for the freight, so he didn't send him anything.

"He wrote at the bottom of the letter: 'P.S. If you want I can send you some fish.'

"Now, they were tight times when a fish buyer wasn't getting enough to pay the freight on a barrel of fish. I remember a many a time the boys would get a dollar for a barrel of fish, and they were darn lucky at that."

WHISKEY HOLE

Inside the storage room on the wharf is a hole in the floor as big around as a fifty-cent piece.

"Let me tell you the story about this hole," says Fielding. "Time ago, we would get whisky in the barrel and store it right there in that corner.

"One dark night, someone came up in a skiff under the wharf and drilled a hole right through the floor and the whiskey barrel. The next day when they went to load it on the steamer, she was plumb empty," Fielding laughs. "Somebody had to get good and drunk from drinking all that whiskey."

BARREL OF MOLASSES

"Daddy told me about another time when a deckhand was unloading a barrel of molasses on a cart. He tripped and the molasses went all over the deck.

"The captain told one of the men to go to the galley and get as much bread as he could. The deckhand brought up the bread and captain gave some to everyone. They sopped up all the molasses in a hurry and they had a damn good meal.

"That was one way to clean it up," Fielding laughs again.

THE REVEREND JOE GARDNER

The Reverend Joseph Gardner, eighty-two, is a Baptist minister in Essex County. As a minister, he followed in his father's footsteps. The Uncle Al referred to earlier in this story was Joe's father. He was a "great" preacher, and Reverend Joe has the same reputation.

Reverend Joe grew up on a farm next door to Fielding and worked for Fielding's grandfather, who called him Tom Thumb. Later, Joe worked as a deckhand at Saunders Wharf and was a cook aboard the steamboat *Middlesex.* He too recalls how life was when the steamboat stopped at Saunders Wharf.

"I remember when this wharf was rebuilt in 1915," says Reverend Joe. "I was five years old. I was crawling around here when they were building it, and they would say to me, 'Boy, get out of the way so we can build this wharf.'"

Sitting in the old waiting room at the wharf, Reverend Joe continues, "I can remember them unloading the tongue-and-groove wood that is on the walls of this room. It came by steamboat from Fredericksburg from Master's Lumber Company.

"In its heyday, this place was as busy as Fifth Avenue, New York—traffic coming and going, people catching the steamboat, people getting off, people bringing things to be shipped. People would come down that little [dirt] lane in horse and buggy, and if it wa'n't a horse it was a mule.

"I remember all the steamboats that came up here in my lifetime. There was the *Dorchester, Lancaster, Calvert, Three Rivers, Talbot, Middlesex*

The *Talbot* was one of several steamboats that cruised up the Rappahannock all the way to Fredericksburg. One of its stops was Saunders Wharf. (Courtesy of Buddy Davis)

. . . The *Calvert* was the first to come with a propeller in the back. Before that, they were all side-wheelers.

"I worked on those boats as a deckhand. I liked the *Calvert* because that smooth-bottomed deck made her easy to load and unload freight. Side-wheelers had that old high shaft that we had to go over. It was always in the way. I didn't like to see a side-wheeler coming."

LOVE STORY

"The boat would always leave the dock in the evening, but sometimes the captain would have to wait around for his crew to come aboard. You see, there would be plenty of local girls coming down to meet the deck-hands.

"Those deckhands would get over in the bushes with those gals, and captain would start blowing the whistle and shining the light along the shore trying to get them back on the boat.

"They were behind wood piles and anywhere else they could find cover. Those gals would have most of their [deckhands'] money before they left.

"Boy, when Captain shined that light on shore you could see some of the darnedest sights you've ever seen in your life," laughs Joe.

JOE'S PAY AND DUTIES

"When I was a cook and deckhand on the old *Middlesex,* I learned to burn water," he says. "I also worked on the dock loading calves, chickens, and whatever else needed to be loaded. The steamboat would carry just about everything—sardines, bags of sugar, tobacco, jelly, nails, bails of hay, et cetera.

"The boats would bring supplies to stock the country stores. In those days, a five-hundred-pound bag of sugar from Baltimore cost a store-keeper seventy cents, a fifty-pound bag of coffee cost twenty-two cents, a fifty-pound box of peaches cost eighteen cents, and a seventy-pound case of candy cost twenty-five cents.

"When I worked on the boats, I didn't make much money. I got eight dollars a month working on the *Middlesex,* but I got all the food I could eat for free. That eight dollars went a long ways because the prices of things were so low."

THE LAST TRIP

"I later left the steamboat business and went up north, but I was here in 1937 when Captain John Davis brought the *Anne Arundel* down for the last time. I stood right here on this wharf and cried like a baby when she pulled away.

"You couldn't find a dry eye anywhere. Even the captain was crying. He turned his head, but I know he was crying. Captain Davis had a long history in the steamboat business. His father had been a steamboat captain on the *Lancaster.*

"When it ended, Captain Davis captained a supply ship in World War II. Later on, he got a little cabin cruiser and stayed in Urbanna during the summer and at Saunders Wharf in the winter. He ran fishing parties in Urbanna, and Fielding's family kept him fed in the winter. He was a rough old cob, but he had a good heart.

"I miss the old steamboats, but I enjoy coming down here with Fielding and just talking to people about those days. It's hard to believe, but there are more people alive now who have never heard a steamboat whistle blow than there are who have.

"It was a glorious time. I'm glad I had a chance to see it."

✳ When I was a little boy, I heard the stories of the steamboats coming to Urbanna. My great-great-grandfather, Alfred Palmer, was dock master and owner of what was known then as Palmers Steamboat Wharf in Urbanna. My great-uncle, Charlie Palmer, would reminisce about Alfred's favorite steamboat, the Matilda, *that visited Urbanna regularly.*

My maternal grandmother, Minnie Heath Blake, grew up just a shell's throw from West Urbanna Wharf. She, too, loved the steamboats, and one of the following stories shows her girlhood devotion to them.

For those who lived through that golden era on the Chesapeake, the steamboats have a way of bringing back fond memories, memories well worth recording.

26 : Steamboat Recollections

EMILY CHOWNING: "IT COST A NICKEL"

AT THE TURN of the twentieth century, Oleathia and Minnie Heath, two sisters, grew up just outside of Urbanna, Virginia, next door to West Urbanna Wharf on the south side of the Rappahannock River.

This story was passed down by them to Minnie's daughter (my mother), Emily Chowning. My mother and I seldom talk about the old days, but one summer night as we were sharing a meal, she told me this little story about her mother and aunt. Minnie died in 1970, and Oleathia is ninety-four-years-old and living in a nursing home.

"When Mamma and Aunt Leaf were little girls, their mamma would let them ride the steamboat every Saturday to Burtons Wharf in Urbanna. It was their favorite thing to do on Saturday, and they would get their chores done early to make sure they would not miss the boat.

"Mamma and Aunt Leaf would ride the steamboat over and walk back home. Urbanna was about a two-mile walk from West Urbanna Wharf, but they could take a shortcut over a footbridge on Perkins Creek and it shortened the walk by about a mile.

"On this morning, they got up early, made their beds, fed the chickens, gathered the eggs, and when they finished they ran down to the steamboat dock. As they were just about ready to board the boat, the

The steamboat era was a glorious time on the Chesapeake. This scene was an every-week occurrence for many waterfront communities on the Bay from 1813 until the late 1930s, when the steamboat era came to an end on the Chesapeake. (Courtesy of Emily Chowning)

Emily Chowning

captain came over to them. [He said,] 'Girls, I know you have been riding the boat for a long time for free, but I've got to charge you a nickel apiece from now on.'

"Mamma and Aunt Leaf didn't have a dime for both of them to ride—in fact they didn't have a nickel for one of them to ride. As they moved aside and let others pass, the captain realized they were not coming aboard.

"'All right, girls, come on aboard, but next Saturday you've got to have a nickel each.'

"Mamma said she and Aunt Leaf couldn't enjoy the ride, knowing it would probably be their last. During their walk home, they cried all the way. There was no way they could afford a dime a week for the two of them to ride the steamboat to Urbanna."

DOROTHY (NORTON) NORRIS: AN ICY TRIP TO NORFOLK

Dorothy Norris of Deltaville, Virginia, tells this story about her sister, brother-in-law, and niece who made this trip on the steamboat *Potomac.* The trip was made during the Great Freeze of 1917-18, when the entire Chesapeake Bay was frozen solid for fifty-two days.

"Mildred Barnes, my niece, was nine years old when her parents moved from Deltaville to Norfolk. Her father got a job there at the shipyard," recalls Dorothy. "They would come home on holidays to visit all the Norton family here in Deltaville.

"It was during World War I, and the year was 1917. I remember it well because it was the year of the big freeze on the Bay. They had come home to Deltaville to celebrate Christmas with all of us. My father, Hervey Norton, was in the oyster business, and he had an oyster shucking house on Jackson Creek. He shipped most of his oysters to Norfolk and Baltimore by steamboat.

"They spent Christmas in Deltaville but had to get back to Norfolk the next week. We knew things were iced up bad, but we heard the *Potomac* was going to try and make a trip. So, all of us went down to North End Wharf [on the Rappahannock River] and saw them off on the *Potomac* bound for Norfolk. They left on a Wednesday, expecting to get there early Thursday morning. But they ran into trouble.

"As they went towards Norfolk, the boat had trouble breaking through the ice. The *Potomac* would move ahead a little to break the ice, but it was so thick that it would stop and have to build up steam to move forward again. Finally, the engine ran hot and a fire broke out in the engine room.

"I remember Mildred saying, 'I guess we were in real danger but I didn't realize it. I thought it was great watching them put out the fire.' She was just a little girl, and I guess it was a real adventure for her.

"The crew was able to get the fire out, but the *Potomac* continued to have trouble moving. About halfway home they came across a stranded motorboat, so they stopped, which was easy enough to do.

"Mildred's father and some other men walked across the ice and helped a lady and a man get out of the boat and cross the ice to the *Potomac.* Their boat had been frozen in the ice for a couple days.

"Mildred's family finally made it to Norfolk late on Friday, but not before the crew of the steamboat had to open some of my father's prized oysters to help feed the passengers and crew.

"Those oysters saved the day, because they were running short on food," she recalls. "My father had some of the best oysters in the world."

COURTNEY "CODY" NEALE DOWELL: SLEEPING SOUNDLY

Around 1915, Cody, her sister, Kitty, and their mother left Bowlers Steamboat Wharf on the Rappahannock River aboard the steamboat *Middlesex,* bound for Baltimore. About halfway there, Cody, then six years old, decided she would take a nap in a top berth. It was a nap that would get her into a heap of trouble.

"Every fall and every spring, Mamma would take us on the steamboat to Baltimore to go shopping," she recalls. "There weren't many good highways back then, so the steamboat was the fastest and best way to get to a city. We did go to Richmond some, but we would have to go to Lester Manor [King William County] in horse and buggy and catch a train. It was quicker and certainly more comfortable to go to Baltimore on the steamboat.

"We'd spent a night on the boat, and then we would stay up there for a while at my aunt's house. My father, Robert G. Neale, owned Bowlers Wharf, and he had a store, a [tomato] canning factory, a hotel on the shore, and an oyster shucking house at the end of the pier.

"When I was growing up, Bowlers Wharf was booming. Everyone came to meet the boats and to sell their produce, calves, chickens—anything like that. They had a cart on the pier that ran on a rail all the way to the end, and they would strap those animals onto the cart, and half the

Cody Dowell

time they would break loose and jump overboard. It was a real exciting time. You'd hear that old whistle blow, and everybody would head to the pier.

"The old *Middlesex* was my favorite boat. The food was so good on board, and the captain would let us eat at his table and afterwards take my sister and I up into the pilothouse, and I just loved to go up there. We used to know all the captains.

"On this one trip, we were going to Baltimore on the *Middlesex* to do some shopping, and I was dying to sleep in the upper berth, because my mother always let my sister sleep up there. She was older than I was, and I guess she thought it was safer for her. She figured I might fall out.

"I was determined, though, to get in that upper berth. Some way—I don't know how I did it because I was so young—I got the key to the berth out of my mother's pocketbook and went in, crawled up in it, locked myself in, and went fast asleep.

"In the meantime, Mamma missed me. She looked but she couldn't find me. She and my sister ran and found Captain Hart; he was the captain on the *Middlesex*. He stopped the boat right in the middle of the Chesapeake Bay and had all the crew looking for me.

"They searched and searched, but couldn't find me. Everybody was frightened. Finally, my sister, Kitty, thought where I might be. She knew I wanted to sleep in that top berth. She said to Mamma, 'I bet she has crawled up in that berth.'

"There was lattice on the top of the berth that you could look down and see through. Kitty crawled up on a chair and saw me in there asleep.

"When we got to Baltimore, Mamma went out in my aunt's backyard and got one of those thin switches that would hurt real bad and switched my legs good.

"That will always be vivid in my memory!"

SHERMAN HOLMES: REVIVAL TIME

"I've always been a member of Calvary Baptist Church at Christ Church [Virginia]," recalls Sherman Holmes, "and one of my fond memories of the steamboat was our trips by car down to North End Wharf to see all the people from Philadelphia and Baltimore who were coming to our week-long revival.

"We always had our revivals in August, and it always began on the third Sunday—that was Homecoming Sunday. It was a time of celebration, picnics, gospel singing, and some fiery preachin'. Lord, boy, some of the best eating in the world was at those revivals.

"All the people who had moved to the cities to get jobs would come home for some of that good old down-home cookin' and religion and it

Sherman Holmes

was great fun. It was a joyous time—a time to see kinfolk and friends again. It was during the depression, and times were hard for city folk and country folk, too. Revivals brought us all together and took our minds off those hard times.

"The revival lasted throughout the week, and they were in the daytime. We didn't have them at nights then. On Mondays and Tuesdays, we had preachin' in the afternoons. On Wednesdays, Thursdays, and Fridays it was held all day. On those days, we had preachin' all morning, dinner on the grounds at midday, and we would go back in for more preachin' in the afternoon.

"I remember three of the names of the steamboats that came regularly. There was the *Potomac, Calvert,* and the *Anne Arundel.* What would tickle me was the way they pronounced *'Anne Arundel.'* Most of the folks would say, 'Annearunel,'" he laughs.

"On that Saturday night before revival, lots of people in the church would meet at North End Wharf to see who was coming to the revival. There were cars lined up along the side of the road for miles waiting for the boat.

"You see, that was the first wharf on the *Middlesex* side [south side of the Rappahannock River] that the boat stopped. The steamboat got there around eleven-thirty or twelve o'clock at night. Everyone met there because it took much longer to get to the other docks. The boat would zigzag to the steamboat docks on both sides of the river. North End was the first wharf and where everyone got off.

"We would all stand on the end of the dock, waiting. When they would get off the boat, I can see the people now, screaming and crying, and hugging and kissing for joy. You know, there is nothing like a homecoming."

BURHANS WHARF: PLENTY OF SEA OATS AND MARL

"When I was a boy, we lived very close to Burhans Steamboat Wharf on the Rappahannock River near Locust Hill, Virginia," recalls Sherman. "My father was a farmer and an oysterman.

"I can remember when sea grass was growing several feet deep close to the shore around Burhans. We called it sea oats. The grass is all gone now, but back then, things were better. The water was cleaner and clearer, and the grass would grow and grow.

"Every year in the spring and fall, we would go down there to get loads of sea oats. Daddy and I and the other boys would get the horse and wagon and go down to the shore, load the wagon full of grass, put it on the land, and plow it in for fertilizer. There was so much grass that that's what everybody around home did. It was great organic fertilizer.

"It would wash up on shore in piles. You could drive the wagon along that broad shore, pick the grass up with a pitchfork, and throw it on. We would spread it on the land like we did manure.

"For lime, now, you see, we didn't buy lime; we got oyster shells and had a lime kiln where we would burn the shells. Also, there was a marl bank at Burhans, and we would go down and dig the marl out of the bank and use it to lime the fields. [A marl bank is an area where shells have been in a bank for centuries. As the shells have broken down into the earth, a chalk-colored soil, full of lime, is left.]

"We would be down there and the steamboat would come in, and all of us would stop and watch the people get off the boat. I hear people talk about going to shopping malls now, just to watch the people. It was the same type of thing. We'd be sitting up in the wagon wondering where all those people lived and got enough money to buy all those fancy clothes. Burhans was a busy place in those days."

✳ *Much has been written about Chesapeake Bay watermen and life around the Bay, but not as much has been said of the wives and daughters of the men who worked the water.*

Their stories, though, are just as important, and their role just as significant. They managed the household, kept the home fires burning, raised the children, and often waited weeks and months for their men to come home from distant waters.

27 : The Woman's Perspective

MARY THOMAS

MARY THOMAS, sixty-four, was born in Norfolk, Virginia. By the time she was nine years old, Mary had lost a father and a stepfather to the sea.

Her natural father, who was from Holland, died when she was nine months old. He fell between a tugboat and barge and was crushed. When she was nine years old, Mary's stepfather fell off a barge and drowned on Christmas Eve. Her stepfather's death would eventually leave the family in a state of poverty.

Mary's mother remarried for a third time, but this marriage was more tragic than the first two. The new stepfather turned out to be an alcoholic and was abusive. When Mary was fourteen, she married a Chesapeake Bay waterman, more to get away from a bad situation than out of love, she says.

She and her husband moved to her father-in-law's home on Dyer Creek near New Point, Virginia, in Mathews County, where they lived in an attic of a two-hundred-year-old home.

"There were nine of us living in the two-bedroom, two-story clapboard house," says Mary. "Me and my husband slept up in the attic. It wasn't finished off—just enough floor to put a bed and a dresser.

"In the wintertime, when it would snow and the wind would blow, snow would seep in and get all around our bed. We kept warm, though, because we had the feather mattress and a whole lot of quilts.

"My husband worked with pound net fishermen around home at first, and then he started working on a fish trawler. The man who used to run Sandbank Wharf bought a trawl boat, and my husband went to work on it. They would fish in the ocean and be gone for a week to ten days at a time.

"When he was gone, I stayed around the house with my mother-in-law and father-in-law and their children. My mother-in-law and father-in-law were good people, and they treated me good. I had to work hard, but I didn't mind working. My father-in-law's name was Johnny ("Boy") Pugh. He weighed over three hundred pounds, and when he died the preacher said he was a legend for his strength.

"When I first got there, my mother-in-law did all the cooking on a wood stove and would cut all the wood. I took over all the wood cutting because I felt like I was in her way in the kitchen. I would cut up all the wood to heat the house and to burn in the wood cookstove.

"When a storm would come and pull up the pound [net] poles out of the mud, my father-in-law would get in his skiff and scull down to New

Mary Thomas was just fourteen years old when she married a Chesapeake Bay waterman and moved from Norfolk, Virginia, to this two-hundred-year-old house on Dyer Creek near New Point, Virginia.

Point Beach. He would raft the poles and pull them to the house for me to cut up. Most of our wood came from pound poles, and I chopped every bit of it up. I think that's why I've got such big arms today.

"I'd go out after breakfast and cut wood until dinner. I'd go in the house, eat dinner, and go back out and cut until supper. We didn't have a woodshed then to keep the wood dry. I'd pile a washboard full and tote it to the house by myself and put it on the porch. I did that most every day. Sometimes it was cold enough to kill you on that creek.

"When it rained and the wood got wet, my mother-in-law would put the wet wood in the wood stove oven to dry out before burning it. She knew a lot about things."

COUNTRY LIVING

"We lived a real country type of life. We had a big garden and plenty of hogs. We killed hogs the first of October, but later on, the winters started getting warmer, and we had to wait until November and, sometimes, December. I remember one year we were concerned we wouldn't have a ham for Christmas. We would put up thirty-five hundred pounds of hog meat every fall in the smokehouse.

"Mother-in-law and me would take white feed bags, the type poultry feed came in, wash them up real good, and cut and sew them into small sausage bags. We used to stay up all night long grinding sausage with a little hand grinder. Then we would stuff the sausage in the bags and pour hot wax over the outside of the bag to keep mildew and mold from getting to it.

"If we didn't get enough meat from our own hogs, we would buy hog meat. One year we bought fatback from Harry Owens. I'll never forget it. The fatback was seven inches thick, and I saw the hog. It was a big red one. One of the biggest I ever saw.

"Every year, we had plenty of salt fish. In September, the men would set gill nets to catch fish for salting. I've stayed up all night long, cleaning fish by lantern down by the shore. The gnats would near about eat you alive. Spot, herring, and trout was what we salted. We had a big wooden barrel with staves around it in the smokehouse, and we would fill it up with fish. We would also fill up two or three stone crocks and lard tins. Spot was my favorite.

"When I was young, I didn't like fish, but when I got to Mathews we had them so fresh all the time. They fished the pound net every day, and they'd bring a bucketful home. My mother-in-law would cook them in corn bread. Lord, boy, was that good.

"You take a good-sized spot, a fresh tomato, and an ear of sweet corn right out the garden, you've got a good meal. Yes sir! There was a lot of things I didn't have when I was at New Point, but I never went hungry.

"When my husband would come home, he would bring us ocean fish—flounder and sturgeon. My favorite was sturgeon. It's just like fried chicken. The only bone is right down the back. We would skin it and steak it like you do swordfish. It was real good.

"Like I said, we had a big garden, and we would grow kale and butter beans. We'd take pound poles my father-in-law would bring up from the Bay and put them in rows in the garden. Then we'd run wire between the poles and grow the best butter beans in the world on them. I'd pick butter beans until November. If you leave butter beans on the vine until after the first frost, they turn real sweet.

"We also grew kale. We had a great big, long, wide bed of kale. In the spring, I'd go out and save the seed. I would take a washtub, take my arms and pull and shake the seed into the bucket. Then, we would leave it outside and let the wind blow the husk away.

"My father-in-law had two acres of oyster ground right on Dyer Creek, and he grew some of the best oysters in the world there. They were the biggest oysters I've ever seen. When he'd open them, you would have to cut them in three pieces to eat them. Twelve would fill a quart jar. Big as the palm of your hand. The ones you buy in the store today are common. They don't taste anything like what we used to get."

THE AUGUST STORM AND HAZEL

"We were always worried about storms," says Mary. "My father-in-law would tie a long line—one end to the skiff and the other to the door handle—so we could get out of the house if the tide came up. We lived right down to the water's edge.

"I wasn't at New Point in 1933 when the August storm came, but my mother-in-law told me about it. The water came up in the house on the first floor, up to her chin. Now, she was a short lady, but still that was high water. They had seven hogs then, and they had to drag them upstairs to one of the bedrooms and put a bureau in front of the door to keep them from falling down the stairs and breaking a leg or neck. During that storm, the family got in the skiff and went across to a neighbor's house to stay.

"I've seen it plenty of times when water was beating up under the house, and water came in one time when I was there. We didn't have electricity then, and we'd go down to my brother-in-law's house on Saturday night to watch television. When we got ready to go home, we couldn't get to our car for high water.

"We spent the night there, and the next day I put on hip boots and walked home. The tide had fallen some, but at places, the water was over my boots. The tide had been in the house and left a slick mud all over everything. I had just wallpapered and painted everything upstairs and down. The dampness made the wallpaper roll right up on the wall. I was a month getting it all cleaned up.

"Hazel [1954] is the storm I most remember. The wind must have blown a hundred miles an hour right up that creek. I was in bed up in the attic when my father-in-law came up and said, 'You best get downstairs because this house is old.' I could feel the bed moving with the wind.

"In no time, every bit of the water had been blown out of our creek, nothing in it but black, slick mud. Two things happened after that. All the oysters died on my father-in-law's oyster beds, and it ruined the water in our well. I believe a spring led from the well to the creek and that storm broke it loose or something and got salt in it. I'd wash clothes with the water, but we couldn't even make tea or coffee with it. For years after that, we got our water from a neighbor."

THE BIG CATCH

"It was August 28 around 1946 that we got a big thrill at home. My father-in-law and two of my brother-in-laws had three pound-nets out in the Bay. That year had been one of the worst fishing seasons. Nobody had done anything, and some of the boys had already taken up their nets.

"At breakfast on this morning, the men talked about taking up their nets the following week if they didn't catch any king billies [croakers] soon. Well, they went on out to fish the net, and when they got a mile away they could hear the king billies in the net. There were so many fish in the pound, they had to hire two or three other boats to help.

"Now, do you know that man [buyer] at Sandbank Wharf heard about them catching all those fish before they got there. He called Ballard in Norfolk [a fish-buying firm], and they lowered the price before they got to the dock. This is the truth, now, they lost three thousand dollars from that catch by them lowering that price. They still made thousands and thousands of dollars on that day.

"Those boys who had taken up their nets were some kind of sick when they heard about all the fish we caught. With the money he made, my father-in-law built a new barn, put new windows and floors in the house, built a wood house, and we still had plenty of money left over. I was glad to see that wood house. It kept me from having to cut wood in the rain.

"My husband didn't own the pound. He worked for my father-in-law and brother-in-laws for forty dollars a week, when everyone else was getting fifty dollars a week. They said they would make it up to him if they had a good catch. They did. We did all right that winter."

BIG EATER

"When my mother-in-law died, I started doing the cooking. My father-in-law weighed over three hundred pounds, and he was a solid man. There wa'n't no flab on him. For supper, he would eat five or six of them big spot. And I mean big spot, near 'bout as big as your foot. He would take three or four corn cakes and pile cabbage and potatoes as high as he could get it on his plate.

"Then he would get up and eat five or six eggs for breakfast, take several cold corn cakes, and split each one open and put butter on it. Then he would take cold cabbage from the night before, with grease still on it, and a chunk of fatback and eat it all down like it was ice cream.

"He was one of the strongest men around. Mr. Pugh had a big pound net bateau, which is bigger than a skiff—not as big as a deadrise workboat, though. I've seen him pull it up on the shore and lift one end up and put a barrel under it, go down and lift the other end and put a barrel under it. He could do it by himself, where it would take three of his sons to lift one end.

"I've seen him tie a piece of rope to a post and tell my husband and his brother to move it. They would pull and pull, but they couldn't do anything with it. He would go out and chock his heels in the dirt and pull on that rope until it would snap in two. He was one strong man."

GOOD YEARS

"My father-in-law worked the pound net until he got real old, and then I stayed there and looked after him. When he was young, he was a huckster and he would sell fish from his horse and wagon. He would take a tumble cart and go over to Sandbank Wharf and buy ice and bring it back, ice his fish down and go out into the countryside and sell.

"Sometimes it would be nine o'clock at night before he would sell all his fish and get home. The next morning he would get up two or three [in the morning] and fish the pound. He was a hard-working man.

"There wa'n't as much money in those days, but you didn't have somebody sending you bills every time you would go to the post office. The doctors and hospitals wa'n't as high. I remember when a doctor's visit cost thirty-five cents, and they brought the medicine to our house. There wa'n't no going to a drugstore.

"I washed clothes on a scrub board, but it wa'n't so bad, and two of my three children were born in the attic. My sister came over and helped me. The last child, I had in the hospital because the doctor was worried about me.

"There wa'n't as much money as it is now, but it was better times for everybody. I really believe that. In the summertime, I would lie out in the yard and sleep in the hammock. We would go down to Mr. I. P. Hudgin's store and get a soda. There has never been no colder or no better drink than Mr. Hudgin's sodas.

"Mr. Pugh would bring in jumping mullet and maninose [small soft-shell clams] for me to fix up. I'd cut the snout out of the maninose to get the sand out, and sometimes we'd put them in fresh water overnight and old maninose would spit all the sand out.

"I miss the old people. My mother-in-law and father-in-law took me in and gave me a home. There were hard times, I have to admit that. But somehow we all got through it and we all did it together.

"We worked together for a common cause. Today, everybody seems to be for themselves. But not then. We knew we had to work together or none of us would make it."

DOROTHY NORRIS

Dorothy (Norton) Norris, ninety-two, was born in Deltaville, Virginia, in 1902. Her parents were William Hervey Norton and Olivia Jane (Ailsworth) Norton. Dorothy was one of eleven children.

She married Hugh Norris of Deltaville in 1926. Captain Hugh was a boatbuilder and waterman. He also served as captain and mate aboard many of the sailing vessels on the Bay.

Their marriage ended Hugh's sailing career, but the ways of the water were still his main source of livelihood. Both her father and her husband have passed, but Dorothy recalls with fondness her life as a daughter and a wife of Chesapeake Bay watermen.

Dorothy Norris displays photos of her father and mother. She was both a wife and a daughter of Chesapeake Bay watermen.

"Papa was born in 1861 to William Henry Norton and the former Evalina Harrow," says Dorothy. "Papa was a Civil War orphan. My grandfather was twenty-nine years old when he was shot dead at the Second Battle of Cold Harbor in 1863. He left two little boys at home, Hervey (my papa) and John (my uncle)."

"Both of them grew up to be good men. Papa was a waterman, and he tonged oysters from a sailing [log] canoe. He also owned other canoes and had men work them.

"Papa would send his oysters in barrels by steamboat to Baltimore. We were raised on oysters. Papa used to buy some oysters in the fall of the year and plant them on his oyster grounds up close to the shore. When the creek froze over, he would go out on the ice and cut a hole and take oysters off the bottom with nippers [short-handled shaft tongs].

"If the steamboat was able to run, he'd ship those oysters, and that's when he would get big money because nobody else could get out and catch a mess. When everybody else was home by the fire, Papa could still get to his oysters."

DAY-TO-DAY LIFE

"When I was a child, we lived in a two-story clapboard house on Jackson Creek. There was no electricity and no refrigerators. In the wintertime, we would dig holes on the south side of a little hill there close to the house to store our turnips, Irish potatoes, and sweet potatoes. Over the holes, cornstalks, pine needles, and straw were stacked like tents, and stovepipes were placed in the center of each hole to allow air in. Mamma would say, 'Go out to the turnip mound and get a turnip.' One time, moles got into the mound and hulled out our entire winter supply of turnips.

"Later, we got an icebox and put it out under a pear tree near our garden so the wintertime weather would keep the food cold. In the summer, we used ice and put it down in sawdust to make it last longer inside the box.

"Papa killed four big hogs every year and stored them in the meat house. He never smoked hams, but he had his own recipe for salt-curing them. We salted herring, spot, and trout. We had plenty of fowl and we had plenty of oysters because that was the way Papa made a living. We always had plenty to eat.

"My favorite way to fix oysters is stewed in its own liquor with a little butter and pepper. My sister likes them stewed in milk, but I don't.

"We didn't have much money, but we had good times, and we had it in the home. I remember the first time we went to a movie. It was a silent Western film, and my brother got scared and started screaming. He was scared the horses would come out the screen and run overtop him. We had to take him home.

"In the summertime, Papa would take us fishing, and we would pack a lunch. The boys would go out early in the morning and catch peelers around the shore for bait, while the girls would finish the breakfast dishes.

"We would go out in his big boat and he would pull a skiff behind. We'd fish from the big boat, and he'd get in the skiff and paddle away from us because he said we made too much fuss. I know those fish didn't hear us because we would have never caught anything, as much noise as we were making.

"At lunch, we would go over to Stingray Point Lighthouse and eat what Mamma had packed for us. There were watchmen living on the lighthouse then. They always enjoyed some company, and we shared our food with them. We would eat watermelon and throw the rind overboard and watch it float on down the Bay. We were all barefoot, with our feet dangling over the side of the walkway.

"I wish they would have restored that lighthouse rather than tear it down."

Stingray Point Lighthouse was dismantled in 1965 and was replaced by a small automatic beacon.

HUGH NORRIS

In August 1926, Dorothy married Hugh Norris. "Hugh worked aboard the sailing vessels, but I told him I didn't want to marry a man who was going off to sea all the time," she says. "So in January of 1926, he made his last trip on the old ram the *Corapeake.* After that, he worked the water and built deadrise workboats.

"Hugh oystered in the winter, crabbed and fished in the spring and summer, and later quit working the water to build boats here in the yard. He would hand tong or patent tong for oysters, trotline for crabs, and gill net for fish.

"He gill netted in the spring and summer. He would set his nets for a short while and then bring them in and dry them out on his gill net reel. Some of the men had reels on shore, but Hugh had his in the creek so he could pull his skiff right up to the reel and turn it.

"I used to go with him trotlining. That was fun, dipping those crabs up and watching the line go over that roller. Once a year, Hugh and a bunch of the men in the neighborhood would go to the seaside of the Eastern Shore and go trotlining. He would stay for several weeks, and he would make big money on that trip. One time he brought home seventy-five dollars, and we thought we were rich. Those were Great Depression days. People don't believe it now, but a carpenter was making ten cents an hour then—a bricklayer fifteen cents—and they were happy to get that.

"Hugh, Alvin Yates, Luther Walden, Tom Parks, David Shreeves, and Johnny Norris, all from Deltaville, would go to the shore to crab. Hugh would take his feather bed [mattress] and sleep in the boat. They all looked forward to going to the seaside because they all lived right here in a huddle together. They were all good friends.

"The first year he went crabbing, he had to buy his trotline on credit, but he paid for it the first year and made money, too.

"Hugh loved the water. I sure miss him. [Hugh died in 1991.] When I'm here by myself I think a lot about the past. Near about all the people I were raised with are gone now. This world is a different world than when I was coming along."

BOATBUILDING

"Hugh quit the water in 1951 when he started building boats here in the backyard," she recalls. "He learned to build boats by working for Rob

Dudley and Lee Deagle [Both noted Deltaville boatbuilders]. One time when he came home from the seaside, Mr. Dudley had hired another man to help him, so Hugh decided to go on his own.

Dorothy pulls out a boatbuilding ledger, which listed sixty-two deadrise workboats and skiffs Hugh built by himself from 1951 until 1982. The first boat listed, built for Gordon Crockett of Crisfield, Maryland, was a thirty-eight-foot round-stern deadrise workboat.

"Hugh usually built three boats a year, but one year he built four. That was the year it seemed like it never rained. When you are building in the backyard, the weather tells you when you work and when you don't. Some years, he didn't get but one built."

The ledger states that Hugh built boats for Maryland and Virginia watermen. In 1954, he started listing the price he received for boats. James E. Anderson of Crisfield paid $750 for a thirty-four-foot round-stern deadrise boat delivered in February of 1954.

The ledger shows the distinction between the races that was pervasive in the fifties and earlier. Hugh listed the names of all white buyers, but for black buyers he wrote, "Colored man, Tidewater, Virginia, September 28, 1955" and "Colored man, Syringa, Virginia, June 1955," and so on.

The most he ever received for a boat was $3,300. This was for a thirty-eight-footer he sold to Virgil Miller of Deltaville in September 1976. In very fine pencil, he wrote, "my last bateau."

After his last round stern, Hugh built flat-bottomed and deadrise skiffs until 1982. His last boat was a skiff. The ledger read, "1982, Huck, $500."

"I can hear him now out there chopping on a round stern all day long with a foot adz," says Dorothy. "I didn't think he would ever get through. But he did, and we did all right. We had a good life together.

"He always said, if he had it all to do over, he wouldn't change a thing. I don't think I would, either."

Dorothy ends the interview with a smile.

HELEN CROUTHAMEL

Helen (Hubbard) Crouthamel, seventy-six, was born at Walnut Grove, an eighty-acre farm on Back River Neck in Baltimore County, Maryland. Her father, Clarence J. Green, was a farmer, fisherman, and market hunter and trapper.

Helen Crouthamel was born and raised on an eighty-acre farm on Back River Neck in Baltimore County. Her father was a fisherman, trapper, and farmer.

Walnut Grove had been a gunning club in the 1800s, and the large three-story structure with full basement was a great place for Helen and her three brothers to grow up.

Her grandfather John Green had bought the house and land right after the Civil War. Clarence later inherited the farm and settled there with his wife, Helen Savier Green, who was from Queen Anne's County on the Eastern Shore of Maryland.

Helen recalls growing up in what was then a rural countryside setting.

"When I was a little girl, it was all farms close to us. My father was a truck farmer, hunter, trapper, and a fishermen. He fished and trapped in Back River in the winter and fall and farmed in the spring and summer," Helen says. "We always had good market for everything because we were so close to Baltimore City. You know, the country folk fed the city folk in those days—at least we did until the Great Depression came."

HUNTING

"Dad had been a market hunter before the law stopped it. [The Migratory Bird Act of 1918 put a stop to the occupation of killing wild ducks and geese to sell.] He would shoot ducks and sell them on the streets of Baltimore City. He killed wagonloads of ducks and would haul them in horse and wagon to the city and go up and down the streets selling.

"When the law came, he stopped selling them, but he and my brothers didn't stop killing them. We had plenty of ducks to eat," says Helen. "They would go out and shoot them, and my mother and I would stand and pick the feathers off. I'd get so sick of picking those little coot ducks [American Coot]. Mother had a lot of recipes for ducks. They were good, but I got so tired of duck that to this day I won't eat one.

"There was woods on the farm where wild rabbit and partridge were plentiful, and Dad and my brothers would kill a-plenty. They would kill partridges like nothing, and that was good eating."

FISHING

"Dad and his partner, Edward Hughs, would fish for rockfish [striped bass], catfish, and carp in Back River. They fished from a twenty-foot flat-bottom skiff my dad made. It was powered by two sets of oars, and it would solid fly. It was wide and heavy, and he built it in our backyard out of cypress wood.

"He fished with anchored gill nets, and he would buy the twine and knit his own nets. What worried my mother the most was that he couldn't swim a stroke. She was scared he would fall overboard and drown.

"In fact, his fishing partner did drown. Mr. Hughs and my dad had a policy of never going out alone in the boat, but on this day for some reason, he went out by himself. Naturally, no one knows what happened, but we think he fell overboard and got tangled in the net. He was a good man, and my dad hurt real bad when he died.

"Dad never got another partner after Mr. Hughs. He got my brothers and uncle, my mother's brother, to help him after that.

"Rockfish brought the most money, but sometimes carp brought good money, too. On certain holidays, Jewish people wanted the carp, and Dad knew just when to fish for them.

"He would sell his fish in Baltimore City at Lexington Fish Market. He would leave home about twelve midnight to get to the fish market real early. They would start buying around two or three in the morning, and the first fishermen there would usually get the best price for their fish.

"If there was a glut of rockfish, they might not know it at two in the morning, but as more and more fish were brought to market, the price would go down. Dad always got there early to get that good price."

TRAPPING

"Walnut Grove had marsh on three sides of it, and in the winter, all the men and boys would trap muskrats. In the fall, each one would go out and scout for muskrat leads. Well, not my younger brother—he was too young—but my two older brothers, my uncle, and father would go out into the marsh.

"At the start of the season, each one was assigned a portion of the marsh so there would be no fussing and fighting over territory. When the season started, they would go and set their traps, and every morning, before daybreak, they would go out and bring in whatever they caught.

"Because they took pleasure in whatever they did, they had side bets each day on who could skin the prettiest muskrat, who would catch the most, who would get stuck in a muskrat lead—there were bets on everything.

"Each one had their own skinning post. They would skin the muskrat, and the meat was taken to a local country store and sold for ten cents apiece. Of course, we kept some of the meat to eat. In those days, most everyone ate muskrat. There were two country stores around, and during trapping season, muskrat meat was a big seller.

"My mother would parboil the meat, dip it in batter, and fry it up. There is a saddle across the back of a muskrat that is especially tender. It is a real dark meat, like deer.

"Wild rabbit was also sold at the country stores back then, but I liked muskrat meat better than rabbit.

"The muskrat hides were turned inside out and stretched on hide boards to dry. There was a big wood stove in our kitchen, and sometimes the pelts would be lined up all the way down by the wood box to dry.

"In those days, muskrat fur was bringing $3.00 to $3.75 a pelt. That was real good money. Black muskrats brought better money than brown muskrat, but once or so a year we would catch a silver muskrat, and that was like money in the bank.

"We had two buyers who came to our house to buy fur. One was a Mr. Cohen, and the other a Mr. Davidson. They were both Jewish. We always hoped they wouldn't come at the same time because they fought like tooth and nail.

"We liked Mr. Davidson because he always gave us something. He came all during the year, even when there were no furs. He would bring a great big suitcase loaded with all kinds of pretty things that my mother was interested in. She would buy stuff from him. He had the most beautiful table linens and lingerie. He always gave me fancy pins or a little bit of jewelry. My brother would get mad because he didn't always get anything, and one time he threw my pins down the heat register.

"Mr. Cohen and Mr. Davidson would bargain for the hides, and Dad would take the best offer.

"Mr. Davidson would walk everywhere he would go. I can see him now, walking out our lane with pelts slung over his back. He would catch a streetcar back to Baltimore City. Mr. Cohen came in horse and buggy, and later he got an automobile. But Mr. Davidson always came on foot. Mr. Davidson was a nice old man."

PETE THE MUSKRAT

"My dad had his own little plot of marsh, and he would go out each morning to trap. One day, he went out and he came back with a live muskrat that had been caught by its front leg.

"He said, 'I'm going to keep it,' and he put it in a basket and built a pen for him. The pen was made of wire, and he put straw in it for the muskrat to sleep on.

"We children would watch him every day. One morning the darn muskrat chewed off his front leg where it had been broken. Dad was worried it would get infected. But it didn't.

"Dad fed the muskrat roots, carrots, and things like that. He also had a big pan of water in the pen for him. The ol' muskrat would wash every bit of food before he ate it. He would scrub it all up and then sit back and eat it.

"My dad named him Pete. At first, he had to put gloves on to feed him. Later on, he didn't need gloves, and Pete would run all up and down his shoulders.

"Pete was a great weatherman. You could tell when it was going to turn cold because Pete would scoop straw up into a big pile. Then he would scoop out the inside of the pile and crawl up in it.

"My dad kept Pete for a long time. When he [Pete] finally died, the whole family was sad."

HAUL SEINING FOR SOFT-SHELL CRABS

"Today everybody is crazy over hard crabs. But when I was a child if one got in the boat we would stomp it dead. Nobody much ate hard crabs.

"Once in a while, mother would bring enough in to make crab soup, but we never steamed crabs. She would boil them and pick the meat out.

"We did eat a lot of soft crabs, though, and my brother and I would catch them in a crab haul seine. The seine was about fourteen feet long and five feet tall. Each end was tied to a pole. I'd get one end and my brother would get the other. We would wade out into a couple feet of water and just haul the net along through the grass. The net would nudge the crab off the bottom and it would get caught in the belly of the net. We ate many a good soft-crab sandwich from that haul seine.

"I remember on July Fourth, we would always have a big gathering, and mother would send us out in the morning to haul seine for soft crabs. By noontime, we would have more than we could all eat."

THE GREAT DEPRESSION

"Things went bad for us when the Great Depression came. Dad raised corn, tomatoes, cabbage, spinach, and cantaloupes and would truck it to Baltimore City, but when the depression came, he couldn't sell his produce anywhere. Nobody had any money.

"He could no longer make a living. Sometimes he would dump the produce on the ground. It just wasn't worth taking to market. Dad just kept putting good money after bad, and it had to come to a stop.

"Eventually, he had to sell the farm, and that was hard on the family. Walnut Grove had been a special place to all of us. At that time, Dad owned part interest in a lumber company, and he went to work there.

"We never went hungry during the Great Depression, because we could still kill ducks, trap muskrats, and grow vegetables, but there was no money to do anything else much.

"I don't really look at those days as hard times, though. When I think of good old days, I think of Walnut Grove and riding in the snow in a horse-drawn sleigh, catching soft crabs for the July Fourth gathering, and Mr. Davidson coming up to our door with all his goodies.

"It was a simple life compared to all the things we have today, but it was a good life!"

✻ *In 1990, Edwin Ruark of Deltaville, Virginia, suggested I write a story on his two cousins, Edmond and Talmadge. Edmond had owned the sailing schooner* Columbia F. C., *and Talmadge sailed extensively on the* Maggie, *also a commercial sailing schooner.*

The article appeared and was well received. When considering chapters for this book, I remembered the excitement I felt interviewing these two old salts.

For this chapter, I decided to go back to the Ruarks, but this time I included Charles Alvin ("Duck"), younger brother to Edmond and Talmadge, and their cousins, Rufus and Edwin. I felt just as much excitement the second time around as I did the first.

28 : A Sailing Family

THE RUARKS hailed from Hooper Island on Maryland's Eastern Shore. Sometime in the late 1800s, Alfred W. ("Captain Al") Ruark, and his cousin, Millard F. ("Captain Phil") Ruark, moved to Deltaville on the western shore of Virginia.

Both were sailing men who came from a long line of watermen, boatbuilders, and sailors. Phil's father, Captain Thomas Henry Ruark, died in 1869 on Hooper Island. Court records from the Cambridge, Maryland, courthouse list Captain Tom's possessions at his death. One item was a partially completed schooner in his backyard.

The Ruark family has saved a touching account of the passing of Captain Tom that was written by a friend. It tells of his faith in God and shows his strength and courage to the last breath.

> After a short but painful illness, Capt. Thomas H. Ruark, age 48, . . . came to teach us, that in the midst of life, we are in death.
>
> After the doctor had visited him for the last time, he asked me how much longer I thought he had to stay with us. I told him his time with us was short, that he was gradually approaching Jordan of death, and that he would soon cross over.
>
> He said, "Thank God for it."
>
> I asked him, if he felt that all was well, he exclaimed, "All is well, my peace is made with God. . . ."
>
> His brothers and sisters, and many of his friends approached his bedside, and [he] bade [them] farewell by giving to each one his dying blessing, with the request that each one should strive to meet him in heaven.

> During the silent watches of the night, his aged mother approached his bedside, and wept over him. She said, "My dear Thomas, what shall I do when you are gone?"
>
> He replied, "Dear mother, you can come to me."
>
> He said to a dear old sister, who had recently lost her husband, "Dorinda, what shall I tell your angel if I meet with him on the other side?"
>
> She replied, "Tell him that I am striving to meet him."
>
> His hope of eternal life and immortal glory grew brighter and brighter, as he drew nearer the river and as he entered its chilling waters he was sweetly singing,
>
> "Home sweet home, savior conduct me to heaven, my home after which the conflict ends."
>
> He sweetly fell asleep in the arms of Jesus.

Captain Tom left a house full of orphans. One of the children was Phil Ruark. As the Ruark children grew up, one by one they turned to the water to earn their livings. Captain Phil went to work aboard a schooner, spending much of his life on the old workhorses of the Bay.

Sometime in the late 1800s, Captain Phil was sailing near Deltaville, and as so often happened in those days, he went ashore to do some courting. There he met his wife-to-be. After he was married, he moved to Deltaville near Fishing Bay. His first cousin Al had already moved to Virginia.

The Ruarks were well established at Fishing Bay by the turn of the century. United States postal records show that a post office by the name of Ruark was established on Fishing Bay in 1898. The first postmaster at Ruark Post Office was none other than Captain Al. Ruark Post Office remained open for fifty-seven years, closing in 1955.

Captain Phil was married twice. He had four boys (Lanny, Rufus, Tom Henry, and Willie) and four girls (Lillian, Mary, Blanche, and Laura). All the boys but Willie worked aboard the boats. Tom Henry had three sons (Edmond, Talmadge, and Duck) and a daughter (Dorothy). Rufus and Edwin are the sons of Rufus.

Tom Henry spent a lifetime sailing on the vessels throughout the Chesapeake and owned the schooner *Maggie.* Built in Dorchester County, Maryland, in 1871, the *Maggie* measured eighty-seven by twenty-three by nine feet. Edmond, Talmadge, and Duck all sailed aboard her. After Tom Henry sold the *Maggie* in 1946, she went north and became a "dude cruiser" in Maine.

Edmond owned the schooner *Columbia F. C.* She was named for the District of Columbia Fishing Club and was built at Mundy Point, Virginia, in 1874. The vessel was sold in 1947 and went south to Cuba.

The heritage of the Ruark family is steeped in a sailing tradition. As far back as anyone can trace, the family, originally from Hooper Island, Maryland, has either worked the water or captained or crewed aboard the old sailing vessels that once plied the waters of the Chesapeake. Pictured are, from left, Edwin, Edmond, Talmadge, Duck, and Rufus.

The subsequent interview speaks of a time when wind and sail were man's best tools for powering the vessels of the Chesapeake.

EARLY DAYS AND HARD DRIVERS

Rufus: "Daddy [the elder Rufus] used to talk about the wind coming down and almost snapping the mast right out of the boat, and he used to say Uncle Lanny was the daredevil of the boys. When it was blowing a darn hurricane and no one else would leave the port, he'd head on down the Bay and unload and get back before anybody else had left."

Edmond: "That's a true story. Lanny was a hard driver. He was up in the Great Wicomico, loaded down with lumber in the old *Simmons.* The *Gracie May* was there and a lot of other boats. The *Simmons* was a little boat about the size of the *Columbia.*

Edwin Rufus Ruark stands at the wheel of the *Maggie* with his brother, Tom Henry Ruark, next to him. This photo was taken in the 1930s on a sailing party in the Chesapeake Bay. The Ruarks made extra money by carrying parties on day cruises. (Courtesy of Edwin W. Ruark)

"While everyone was sleeping, Lanny went on out and got under Point Lookout where the wind favored him more. It was smooth sailing around that shore, and he had a good run up to Baltimore. When he got to Baltimore, the weather broke bad. So he unloaded, and by the time he got back down there, they were still laying there. It was just one of those things. He took a chance and hit the wind just right."

Talmadge: "A lot of those old boys were hard drivers. I remember old George Duncan. I was with the old man [Tom Henry] in the *Maggie.* We were laid up in the Great Wicomico, and Captain George was in the *Columbia.* He would raft the lumber up on the deck. I ain't lying to ya, her deck board was dragging the water, and all you could see were the night-head anchor, yawl boat, the cabin back aft, and the deck rail. There was water across the stern, and he had corked the cabin doors to keep the water from flooding her.

"Early in the morning, I've seen him get her under way, and when he went across the Potomac, he'd get that yawl boat underneath the stern and battle her up that shore trying to get up the Bay. Captain George was a good seaman, but he took a lot of chances. She was damn near sunk, but he didn't care."

Edmond: "Old Lanny was a bird in this world. He ran the boats like the rest of us. He'd run lumber, fertilizer in the spring, canned goods and watermelons. He also ran seed oysters out of the James River in the old *Brownstone* and the *Minnie Emma.*

"One time, he went down to Gloucester [County] and got this guy who knew every darn oysterman in Guinea Neck to help him buy oysters.

"Lanny would come from Hooper Island here loaded down with whiskey. He got that guy, and they went to the James River, and he bought every damn oyster down there, near about.

"The other buyers couldn't figure out how Lanny took all their business. They didn't know he was giving the boys some free whiskey."

Talmadge: "All of Captain Phil's boys worked on the vessels at one time or another. The only one that didn't follow the water was our Uncle Willie, and he didn't stay on the water because of Lanny.

"Lanny was a hard driver. And on one trip, he pushed Willie hard, and Willie told him, 'Darn if you are going to drown me in the Chesapeake Bay,' and he left and went to work in Baltimore."

Edmond: "There used to be a lot of West Indian colored who cooked and crewed aboard the boats. Some of them were mean, too.

"The old man [Tom Henry] had a crew of them one time. He was in the *L. E. Williams.* She carried two topmasts, so he would carry a larger crew on her. He was up one of them rivers, and one of the crew broke into his quarters and stole three hundred dollars.

"He got real mad. He knew they stole the money. So he blew the foghorn. Finally, someone came down, and he got them to go get the sheriff. They searched the boat but couldn't find anything.

"The sheriff said, 'Well, Captain, there is nothing we can do if we can't find the money.'

"The old man had a lot of nerve. He headed on out towards Baltimore, and when he got a good ways out in the Bay, he called them all out on deck. 'I know damn well one of you stole my money,' he said, and he pulled out his pistol and shot down at their feet to make a point. Then he said, 'One damn wrong move and it's going to be some damn dead bodies floating in the Bay.'

"One of them had the nerve to say he was going to get the old man."

"He [Tom Henry] said, 'I don't sleep much, boy, and I got the thing right here that will stop ya,' pointing to his pistol.

"He searched the boat and found his money underneath a washtub down in the pump hold.

"He went on to Baltimore and got rid of that bunch."

Talmadge: "Daddy [Tom Henry] was something. One time we went down the Chickahominy River to get a load of barrel staves. The Chickahominy is the most crooked river I've ever seen. Daddy had been up there about twenty years before. I wanted him to get a pilot because there were trees all over the place, but he said, 'Hell, one trip is all I need and I can get back there every time.'

"We made it and didn't hit once. He didn't use a chart or nothing. Daddy had a photographic memory. If he went there once, he could get you there twenty years later."

SEA OATS AND SAWDUST

Edwin: "You all remember Bobby Warthen? He told me this story about Daddy [Rufus, Sr.] on the *Maggie.*

"Bobby was just a boy, and he was soft crabbing around the shore on Ferry Creek when the *Maggie* was going by.

"He yelled over to Daddy and asked if he could go to Baltimore with him.

"Daddy said it was all right with him, but he had to ask his mamma.

"He rowed home and asked his mamma.

"She said, 'Yeah, if you are going with them you'll be all right.

"So he packed his bags and rowed his skiff to Holland Point [on the Piankatank] where Daddy and Uncle Tom were getting a load of lumber.

"When he got there, Daddy and Uncle Tom Henry gave him a bucket and said, 'Boy, go up to that sawdust pile and fill that bucket up with sawdust.'

"He went up there and got a bucket and came back.

"'Now, walk around the boat and throw it overboard,' Daddy said. As they loaded the lumber and the *Maggie* settled down, water was running right down in the cabin, but when that sawdust went into the seams, it chinked her right up and the water stopped."

Talmadge: "Yeah, we used sawdust sometimes, too, but the best stuff was sea oats. It is the same stuff people use to pack soft crabs to ship to Baltimore. We used to get it around Fishing Bay Bar. We would take a long-handled crab net and fill it with dry sea oats and shove it under the bottom. The water pressure would suck it in the seams that leaked."

Edmond: "I recall one time old Captain Springfield was in the *[Edward L.] Martin.* Dr. Spencer owned her, and she hadn't been loaded in years. Her seams were all opened up. We were up on the Patuxent [River] and when he went to loading her, water just poured in through the open seams. They didn't have a gasoline pump. All they had was a hand pump to keep her afloat. The old man [Tom Henry] and I got in the yawl boat, went ashore, and got some sea oats. It did the trick. It plugged her right up."

CAPTAIN PHIL

Talmadge: "Our granddaddy, Captain Phil, was in the business during the heyday of sail. It's funny the little things you remember about the old people. I just barely remember Captain Phil's wife, Grandma Ida, we called her.

"She was a great big woman, and she had some kind of disease in her legs that made them swell up big. He would carry her to Baltimore. She couldn't walk onto the boat, so they'd put her in a great big chair on the shore, hook a block and tackle to her, and hoist her up on deck.

"Do you remember that big chair, Edmond?"

Edmond: "Yeah, Granddaddy kept it down in the cabin."

Duck: "The only thing I remember about Captain Phil was the day we buried him. I was a little boy, and I had a white sailor suit on, and I walked behind the hearse. When they started it up, black smoke came out of the exhaust pipe and went all over me. My white suit wasn't white anymore." He laughs.

Talmadge: "Captain Phil used to always say he wanted to die on Hooper Island with his boots on, and damn if he didn't. He died out in his yard cleaning fish, [and he had his] gum boots on.

"Lanny went up to Hooper Island to bring him back to Deltaville for burial. He went up there in the *Virgie.* She was a thirty-eight-foot deadrise workboat with a Ford engine in her. Coming back, he ran into a northeaster, and she was blowing a gale. Captain Phil's casket was in a wooden box, and it got to sliding around, so Lanny nailed it down to the deck.

"He damn well didn't want to lose him overboard. The whole family would have killed him.

"Captain Phil's last trip was a rough one. Lanny brought him around to the steamboat dock on Fishing Bay and unloaded him."

WOMEN AND FAMILY ABOARD THE BOATS

Edwin: "Mamma stayed right much on the boats the first eight years they were married, didn't she?"

Edmond: "Yeah, she did. She was on the *Maggie* with Rufus all the time. She was on there when we were running barrel staves over there to Cape Charles and Onancock.

"I remember that corn bread she used to fix. She could solid make it, I'll tell you the truth. I think she used sour milk or something, but it was really good."

Talmadge: "The Ruark women were on the boats a lot. I remember one time we had a birthday party for Aunt Mary on the *Maggie*. It was in the summer and we were all going to Baltimore.

At a family reunion in 1946, three Ruark brothers, all sea captains, and two sisters posed for this photo. Pictured are, from left, Tom Henry Ruark, Laura Ruark Harrow, Edwin Rufus Ruark, Ida Blanche Ruark Evans, and Lanny Filmore Ruark. (Courtesy of Rufus Ruark)

"Aunt Blanche had baked a cake and hid it back aft in the stern locker. We used the locker for storing old junk stuff. We could have had a berth back there, but the *Maggie* had side berths on each side of her.

"The locker was no place to be hiding a cake, because we had ants and roaches all over the *Maggie.* They would come aboard on the lumber and stuff we would haul. Well, those ants got into that cake and tunneled all through it, and when Aunt Blanche brought it out, it looked all right, but when she cut down into it, there wa'n't nothing inside." He laughs.

Edmond: "When they were first married, Mamma stayed on the boats. During World War I, the old man [Tom Henry] went on the *Thomas B. Taylor.* Mamma used to go there and cook for the crew. She told me this story. She had a Victrola at home, and one time she said to me, 'You know where I got that Victrola?'

"I said, 'Daddy bought it for you, didn't he?'

"'No, indeed,' she said. 'I was the cook on the *Thomas B. Taylor* and made that money, saved it up, and bought it.'

"A boy by the name of Jarrett was in the *Thomas B. Taylor* before Daddy, and he had to go off to war. When he came back, Daddy had to give the vessel back to him. The *Thomas B. Taylor* belonged to C. C. Paul and Company in Baltimore."

Duck: "Going on the *Maggie* was just an everyday thing for us. We started going when we got old enough to get off the bottle."

Edwin W. Ruark was just a toddler when this photo was taken of him aboard the *Maggie* in 1942. (Courtesy of Edwin W. Ruark)

Talmadge: "Yeah, that's right. When we were small, we would take two or three trips in the summertime to Baltimore on the *Maggie*. Edmond was the oldest so he was the first to go with Daddy full time. And later I went with him.

"In those days, Daddy was always taking somebody to Baltimore. Anybody in the community or in the family who wanted to go, he'd say, 'Come on aboard.'

"We had seventeen head aboard the *Maggie* one time, and I remember Paulene Norris told Mamma she was making too many pancakes. 'Don't you make nare 'nother one, Aunt Susie. Them boys are up there just seeing who can eat the most.'

"Mamma was down there in the forepeak, hot as I don't know what, making those pancakes, and we were eating them just as hard as we could go—making pigs of ourselves."

MAGGIE STEW, GOOD VITTLES, AND COOKS

Talmadge: "Boy, Mamma was a good cook. All them old people back then were good cooks. We didn't have much refrigeration on the boats. We had them old iceboxes. We'd get ice in Baltimore.

"We would get codfish—salted and dried—and have canned food, mostly. We would get little cans of Boston mackerel, and we'd get oysters all the time to eat, but my favorite was Maggie stew."

Duck: "Darn, if I don't remember that. I can smell that Maggie stew coming up out of that forepeak now. It was some kind of corned beef hash. I don't remember much, but I remember it was damn good. If it had something to do with eating, I remember it."

Talmadge: "Maggie stew was corned beef, potatoes, and onions all mixed together. We also had slab bacon and codfish, and we would almost always have a ring of cheese. We drank coffee and water.

"We had black molasses and flour. The molasses we bought by the gallon in a jug, and the flour was always kept in a tin. We always had bugs bad. They would come on the lumber. Ants were the worst."

Edmond: "I first started going on the *Maggie* with the old man when I was a kid. The first thing I learned was to cook. I learned to fix my first biscuits between Windmill [Point] and Stingray [Point]. The first batch I ever made I forgot to put yeast powder in them. When they were served,

Daddy took one look and carried me right back to the galley to show me how it was done. I did a lot of cooking when I first started."

Rufus: "Daddy was cooking full time on the *Maggie* with Captain Phil when he was nine years old."

Edmond: "Yeah, none of us went to school long, and when we quit, we went on the boats. We had some good colored cooks. There was old Ed; he stayed with the Ruarks for over twenty years. He was a good cook. I forget his last name. We just called him Ed."

Talmadge: "There was Alec Easter. I remember him. One time the old man [Tom Henry] got mad at him and left him at West Point [in Virginia, on the York River]. We went on up the Pamunkey [River] to Whitehouse to fetch a load of lumber. Rufus and I was sitting on the deck there at Whitehouse and I looked over and said to Rufus, 'That looks like a damn tramp coming down the railroad track.' He had a little pack over his shoulder, like a hobo.

"'That ain't no tramp,' said Rufus. 'That's old Alec.'

"We had a long wait, and there was a little pond, and Alec said we ought to go catch some frogs for breakfast. I'd never eaten frog legs before, but we went that night and caught two dozen big bullfrogs. Alec cooked them for breakfast and it was mighty good. His best were corn-meal muffins. I don't know what he put in them, but they were sweet.

"Alec would always say, 'I might be dirty in some ways, but I'm clean in my cooking.' He was a fine cook."

WOOD AND COAL

Edmond: "It would get hot in that hold in the summer when that Shipmate wood cookstove was fired up. We would keep a fire in the summer with some of the lumber we were hauling, but in the winter, we would get heavier wood because the lumber would burn up too quick. We had a coal stove and a wood stove, but we'd burn more wood because we couldn't afford much coal. There was always a buck saw aboard to cut up cordwood for cooking and heating."

Talmadge: "The man who owned the lumber didn't like us burning up his wood. He was selling it to Baltimore, so the smart ones would have their men load a few extra slabs for burning."

Edmond: "We cut up a lot of the man's lumber, though, to use in the Shipmate. It used a narrow board, but those big galley stoves would go right through the narrow stuff."

CAPT. RAYMOND BRISTOW AND THE GREAT DEPRESSION

Edwin: "Didn't Captain Raymond [Bristow] have a boat?"

Talmadge: "Yeah, he had the *Gracie May*. He had it built up in Seaford, Delaware. She would carry about a hundred thousand board feet. When she was loaded, you could sit up on the wheel box and you could see her knightheads. She never did pile very high." [A knighthead is a thick, strengthened portion of the forward deck above the hawsepipe. The hawsepipe is a metal opening in the bow through which the anchor chain moves.]

Edmond: "Old Harvey Conway ended up with her and changed her name to the *Ruth Conway*.

"I remember the time we were running out of Suffolk. Captain Raymond was getting old, and he told the old man [Tom Henry], 'I ain't got to make another trip. I got enough money to run me.'

"Well, he went on and sold his boat and he lost everything he had in the 1929 stock market crash. He went to bed a rich man and woke up penniless.

"He had to go back to the boats, but he never was the same. Before he lost his money, he always had a necktie on, even when he was on the boats. But after the crash he became a regular bum. He ended up in the *Charlie Joyce*.

"He got so when he wa'n't on the boat, he was in those joints in Baltimore drinking beer. I don't think he ever took a drink before the crash.

"That was the difference between the Ruarks and the Bristows. We drank before the crash."

They all laugh.

Duck: "Yeah, we were already prepared for the crash."

They laugh again.

Rufus: "We didn't have nothing to lose, like Captain Raymond."

Edmond: "Captain Raymond and the old man were good friends. I heard the old man tell the story that they used to try and steal away from each other in the harbor.

"They were both running lumber up there to Johnson Lumber Company in Annapolis, right by the Naval Academy. The old man had the *Maggie* loaded, and Captain Raymond had the *Gracie May* loaded, and they laid over in Annapolis for the night.

"Mamma was on the boat, and real early in the morning she heard the *Gracie May*'s hoister engine start up.

"'Tom Henry! Wake up! I hear the *Gracie May*'s hoister engine. Captain Raymond is trying to beat us to Baltimore.'"

They all laugh.

Talmadge: "When that stock market crashed, lumber went from eighty-five dollars a thousand feet to fifteen dollars, and we were hauling for a man in Baltimore who had a million feet cut and ready to go. Damn if he didn't take a beating, too."

HORSEPLAY

Talmadge: "We had a lot of fun on the boats. One time we were drifting around one night waiting for the wind. It wa'n't no wind at all. I was up on deck lying around and Daddy was down in the cabin with his mouth wide open, sound asleep.

"I said, 'Damn if I ain't going to get him.'

"So I crawled over there and took a piece of wire and stretched it over to the plug wire on the yawl boat. I hooked the other end of the wire to the screen door handle on the cabin. I went to the steps and rolled that old Palmer [engine] over and shoved the switch up.

"I yelled down to Daddy, 'Come up here a minute.' He came up and when he put his hand on that screen door, I shot the juice to her. It lit his hand up like a neon light.

"'Oh, damn it,'" he yelled. 'That's all right, you'll pay for this.'

"And damn if he didn't get me back. About a week or so later, he caught me asleep in the bunk in Baltimore. He took some copper wire and coiled about four or five inches around my big toe.

"I think he hooked two batteries and two coils to me, and when he put the juice to it, he just about electrocuted me in that bunk. I was screaming, trying to get the wires off my toes, but every time I touched the wires, it would circulate the current through the rest of my body. I damn near beat myself to death trying to get out of that bunk.

"Another time, we were loading up lumber over at Holland Point and this fellow Sears had a dog there. He thought the world of that dog, but every day he [the dog] would come aboard the boat and steal lunches from the stevedores who were loading us up.

"The stevedores would lay their lunch bags up there by the house, and that dog would steal lunches pretty near every day. Mr. Sears would go and buy bread and baloney to replace their lunches, and he got tired of that real quick.

"The old man [Tom Henry] told him he knew a way to stop the dog from stealing lunches.

"'You're not going to hurt him, are ya?' he asked the old man.

"'I'm not going to hurt him, but I can't promise he won't hurt himself.'

"Daddy took a piece of tin, laid it down on the deck, and put the lunches in a wooden box on the tin. He ran a wire from the yawl boat to the tin, got in the yawl boat, and waited for the dog to come along.

"That dog went over there and stuck his nose in one of those bags, and about that time the old man shoved the juice to it. This is the truth, now. The hair on that dog stood out like he had a permanent wave. He went off that deck, and—this is no lie—he left toenail marks in the deck, trying to get away from that current.

"We didn't have no more trouble with him. He never put his paws on that deck again."

THE BUSINESS

Edmond: "We hauled mostly lumber, but also carried fertilizer, coal, empty tomato cans, watermelons, and barrel staves. We'd get between $1.50 and $3.75 per thousand board feet, and the *Columbia* would carry about seventy-five thousand board feet. It would carry nine thousand cases of tomato cans and we got about 1½ cents a case. And we could haul up to fourteen thousand watermelons."

Talmadge: "It wa'n't great money in it. The only time you made good money was when you could make a down trip. If you could carry a load of lumber to Baltimore and have a few tons of fertilizer, say fifty to seventy-five tons, or so many cans to bring back to one of the factories, then you could make a little money.

"You see, there were canning factories all through the county [Middlesex] in those days. Earl Daniel and Bernard Wood had factories, and there were certain times of the year they would hire us to bring them cans.

"If you had to come back from Baltimore light, you didn't make much money."

Edwin: "Your expenses weren't much, were they?"

Edmond: "No, not really. If we carried a crew, we paid each one a dollar a day—thirty dollars a month. We didn't always get a full load, though. The *Columbia* would hold seventy-five to eighty thousand board feet of lumber on the average. But I've seen it when she wouldn't hold but fifty thousand. That was real green, wet stuff."

Edwin: "Well, sixty thousand at $3 a thousand, that's $180. That wasn't bad money then. How fast could you make a trip?"

Edmond: "Well, I've seen it when we could sail from Deltaville to Baltimore in twelve hours, but that wasn't often. Sometimes, if you made a trip in a week, damn if you wa'n't doing good. In the wintertime, when there were ice-ups it might take three weeks. I remember one year, I don't think the old man hauled but one load of lumber the whole winter. There wa'n't nothing moving."

FOUL WEATHER

Edmond: "We never knew what the weather was going to do. I remember one time, we left Deltaville and we had a good southwester blowing. I wanted to get to Baltimore some kind of bad because I had a girlfriend I wanted to see.

"We were going to be up by the Patuxent early in the day [12:00 P.M.] so I thought we'd get to Baltimore by 9:30 P.M. Then the old man got to checking the glass [barometer]. 'We ain't going to get nowhere,' he said.

"I said, 'Damn, Daddy, we got a good wind. Let's keep her going.'

"'It's going to jump down here and blow tonight and we're going to catch hell,' he said.

"After a while, the glass stopped dropping, and it went back up a little bit. He told me, 'Go up there and tie that topsail up.' I went up and tied it up and came down and I don't think it was ten minutes before that storm came down on us.

Tom Henry Ruark captained the *Maggie* for many years, and his sons, Edmond, Talmadge, and Duck, learned the skills of sailing from their father aboard this vessel. This photo was taken in 1946 in Deltaville, Virginia, by the Ruark family doctor, Dr. A. L. Van Name, Jr. (Courtesy of Dr. A. L. Van Name, Jr.)

"The *Maggie* didn't steer too well, anyway. She was wild steering, but the old man could handle her. The seas come up there so big the yawl boat was floating to the davits. We had a gasoline pump going, and we were pumping by hand as hard as we could go to keep her from sinking.

"We shot her up under Drum Point that night, but we had to get that main boom over on the starboard side to go in the Patuxent. We had another hand on board, and the two of us had to put everything we had into it to move that boom. We set up all night pumping, and after a while, it slacked off.

"During the worst of it, the only thing the old man said to me was 'I'd rather be home under the bed eating cat shit than let the Chesapeake drown me.'

"After that, I never said no more. If he said, 'I think you ought to go in the Patuxent,' I went in the Patuxent.

"The next day, we went up to Solomons Island and got a newspaper. A tugboat pulling a barge had gone by us and, be damn, it had sunk. The newspaper story said a ship had rescued the family on board the tug.

"There was a man, woman, and baby aboard the tug. To save the baby, the man put the baby down in a five-gallon paint can."

BIG FREEZES

Rufus: "Daddy told me one time about a big freeze, and there were two or three schooners laying out here in Fishing Bay all winter. It was his job to go out with an ax and cut the ice from around the schooners—to keep pressure off the hull.

"He said it was frozen so thick that when he chopped down into the ice, the ax head was down under the ice and the end of the handle was flush with the top of the ice. Now, damn if that wa'n't frozen. It was frozen as thick as the length of that ax."

Edmond: "That must have been the big freeze of 1917–18. The whole Chesapeake Bay was frozen solid for fifty-two days.

"I seen it in 1936. It wa'n't that thick, but we could have skated to Mathews [County]."

Duck: "I heard some of the old-timers say they hauled lumber in ox carts from Mathews to Middlesex across the ice in the 1917 freeze."

Rufus: "Daddy told me you could skate right out of sight of land."

HOOPER ISLAND

Edwin: "I used to hear Daddy talk a lot about when he was on the boat and he would go to Hooper Island to visit relatives. Uncle Lanny lived up there, and they would go gunning at night and shoot a boatload of ducks and geese."

Duck: "I went there once on the *Maggie*, and all I remember is Lanny had a mule, and that damn mule had eaten the barn up. I can remember them holes right now."

Talmadge: "They built the barn out of drift lumber from dead vessels. It wa'n't Lanny's barn; it was old man Travis's barn who lived next door to Lanny. The driftwood had been in the water and had taken in salt. The mule was eating that wood to get that salt out of the wood. He damn near ate the whole barn up."

Edmond: "Yeah, he did. I seen it myself."

Edwin: "In those days, they didn't worry about the law on Hooper. It was so isolated. Hell, when they came to Deltaville, they thought they had come to civilization."

Talmadge: "There are a whole lot of Ruarks buried on Hooper and right many still living there. Travis and Simmons are other names there. Daddy used to talk about Charlie Simmons."

Edmond: "Yeah, Aunt Virgie was a Travis. Then there was Edmond, Alvin, and Tom Simmons. Tom Simmons owned the *Maggie* when she had two topmast in her. One of them Simmons was on the *William H. Van Name* when she was lost up the beach [ocean side] running oysters to Long Island."

DELTAVILLE

Rufus: "Now, Deltaville was pretty isolated, too. I remember Daddy saying the first time he went to the courthouse in Saluda [overland about seventeen miles from Deltaville] he was eighteen years old. He sailed in the *Maggie* to Urbanna and walked to Saluda from Oaks Landing [a three-mile walk]."

Talmadge: "Yeah, we were isolated. When the boats played out, Edmond and I got a job working with the railroad on barges in Newport News. This was the late 1940s.

"We would go to Mathews, and if we left Lee Hall in Mathews by 5:00 A.M. we might get to the boat in Newport News by dark. Now you can drive down there in an hour."

Edwin: "The ferries held you up so. The first car Daddy had was a 1929 Chevrolet with a rumble seat in the back. There was a ferry across the Rappahannock and the Piankatank. It just took a long time to come and go. The roads weren't the best."

GROWING OLD

Edwin: "The thing I remember most about Tom Henry was when he got old, he didn't wear shoes in the summertime and he always had his false teeth out." They all laugh.

Talmadge: "Yeah, when the boats went out, Daddy started taking fishing parties out in the summertime. He was barefooted most of the time, and he kept his teeth in his shirt pocket.

"Mamma used to say, 'Tom Henry, put your teeth in your mouth.'

"He'd say, 'Susie, one time them damn things hurt so bad and I couldn't do nothing about it, but with these false ones, Tom Henry can do something about it now.'"

RELIGION

Edwin: "The Ruarks were pretty religious people. Our grandmother helped build Clarksbury [United Methodist Church in Deltaville]. She was a pillar of that church. Grandpa Phil didn't go to church much. I think a lot of the guys on the boats were Christians and belonged to a church, but they were never here, whereas the wives played an integral part of the churches."

Edmond: "Towards the last, Tom Henry started going. Of course, he wa'n't sinful or nothing before that."

THE END OF AN ERA

Edwin: "I remember the day the *Columbia F. C.* left here for the last time. I was sitting over on the hill, and she went on out into the Bay. I remember what your mamma said to Uncle Tom. He left some blankets on her, and as she was going down the creek, Aunt Susie said, 'Tom Henry, did you get those blankets off the *Columbia?'*

"'No, and darn if I'm going after them now,' he said.

"She was hot about that thing. He gave her blankets away."

Talmadge: "Yeah, that sounds like Mamma. They were probably some quilts she had made. When the *Columbia* left, that was the end of it for us. Damn if Ruarks hadn't been sailing for a long time, though, I'll tell ya that. And boy, did we have some times."

Edwin: "By 1947, the trucks had just about run you out of business, hadn't they?"

Edmond: "Yeah, that's right. It wa'n't much to it when I bought the *Columbia F. C.* I was figuring on cutting her up and putting an engine in her.

"She was a nice vessel. Towards the end, there just wasn't much to do except haul seed oysters.

"Everything plays out, just like all them boats that used to go to the James River to bring seed oysters up to Urbanna."

The *Columbia F. C.* heads from Baltimore to Amburg, Virginia, around 1945. Edmond Ruark, owner and captain of the vessel, had her loaded down with nine thousand cases of tomato cans. He delivered the cans to the H. T. Daniels and Son tomato factory in Amburg. "We had her covered from end to end, but those cases were light," says Edmond. "She was way out of the water when we took that photo." (Courtesy of Edmond Ruark)

On a trip to Baltimore, Edmond Ruark is writing in his log in the cabin of the *Columbia F. C.* (Courtesy of Edmond Ruark)

Talmadge: "We hauled a lot of lumber, but when the big lumber mills played out and the truck came along, that did us in. The lumber people went to these little portable mills. They could cut a truckload of lumber and take it by truck just as soon as they cut it. They could bring in a bunch of little trucks and haul it real quick, whereas we needed a bigger load to carry, and if the wind wa'n't right we didn't move too fast.

"When big mills were around, it took a week to move the mill because you had to move the big boiler. They didn't move unless they had to. Mostly, they hauled logs in ox carts to the big mill, and as they cut it, they stockpiled the lumber. You couldn't move much with a horse and wagon. The best way to haul was over water."

Edmond: "After the war [World War II], a lot of boys bought those government surplus trucks. They bought them for little or nothing and started hauling stuff. When highways improved, the trucks could move faster than we could. They just took it over. It was just a thing of the past—just a passing thing. You know, just like everything else."

The interview ended as the Ruarks one by one departed from Edwin's home on Fishing Bay.

After Edmond sold the *Columbia F. C.*, he oystered for several years and then went aboard tankers for Standard Oil. Today he runs fishing parties out of Deltaville.

Talmadge worked for the New York and Pennsylvania Railroad on barges that carried railroad cars from Cape Charles, Virginia, to Little Creek, Virginia. He also spent time oystering and crabbing.

Duck is retired from the Virginia Marine Resources Commission, where he worked as an enforcement officer and was captain of several marine police boats.

Rufus is part owner of Shores and Ruark Seafood, one of the largest oyster-shucking and crab-picking houses in the state of Virginia.

Edwin holds a doctorate in biochemistry and nutrition. He also has a captain's license and real estate and appraisal licenses and owns the real estate firm, Ruark & Associates of Deltaville.

✻ *The first time I learned that anyone would eat a muskrat was around 1955. It was very early spring. I was six years old and was playing down by a shanty on Urbanna Creek. A black man named George Goldman was poling around the shore looking for some soft-shell crabs.*

I knew that George lived in a shanty near the mouth of Boney Finger at the headwaters of Urbanna Creek and that he was very poor by our standards. His only transportation to town each day was a rough deadrise skiff. In the bottom of his boat, he always carried along a large, holey burlap sack, which he slung over his shoulder when he would walk up into town.

The older children would scare us by saying George picked up children, put them in his burlap sack, and carried them off. At six years old, that was a frightening thought. One of the older children said to me, "I'll bet you a banana split that you won't go up and ask him what's in that sack."

The rest of the children all chimed in, "Yeah, I bet you won't."

In those days, a thirty-five cent banana split at Marshall's Drugstore was so good it would make you want to kiss your grandma. It made that bet well worth taking.

I edged my way down to the shore and yelled over to George, "Whatcha got in that sack?"

George stared at me for a moment and then began to pole toward me. I was scared but I stood my ground. He reached down in the sack and pulled out two furry muskrats.

"My supper," he said.

29 : Cooking Muskrat

LIVING ALONG the shores of the Chesapeake during the early part of this century, finfish, crabs, and shellfish were not the only food sources that came from the Bay's waters and around the water's edge. Particularly during cold-weather months, many people would trap muskrats to provide meat for their tables. The fur provided extra income as well.

Maxwell Chandler, eighty-seven, recalls that muskrat meat was as choice as a good round of beef. Max has been eating and preparing muskrat since 1917.

"I remember the first muskrat I ever fixed," he says at his home in Revis, Virginia. "It was 1917, and I went down the road to Bernard Cumner's

For centuries, muskrats have been trapped for their fur and meat. The meat was a regular dish on the tables of many rural homes in the Tidewater area. Today, however, only a few old-timers can even recall that muskrat tasted mighty good.

house and bought two fat rats for twenty-five cents apiece. I took them home and fried them up, and I've been eatin' muskrats ever since.

"City folk don't like the thought of eatin' them because of the 'rat' in its name. They think you're talking about a barn rat. But if you just tell them they're eatin' a marsh rabbit, they'll love it.

"Part of the problem is people don't always skin them right," he continues. "You got to be careful because if the gall in the liver happens to bust, it will make the meat bitter." Gall is a bitter, greenish fluid secreted by the liver of an animal and stored in the gall bladder.

Max enjoyed eating muskrat so much that he started buying them on a regular basis from Bernard Cumner and Willie Ward, another trapper who lived just down the road.

"They were both good trappers, and back then, there was plenty of market for the meat. The trappers skinned and cured the hides and sent them by steamboat out of Burtons Wharf in Urbanna [on the Rappahannock River] or West Urbanna Wharf in Remlik to a buyer in Baltimore.

"I cook them different now from back then. Years ago I would fry my rats on a wood cookstove, and nothin' tasted better than food cooked on an old wood stove," he says. "I'd soak my muskrats overnight in salty water and parboil them for an hour the next day. Then I'd take them out and let them drain and dry off, cut them up like you do a chicken, and deep-fry them with a little flour.

"We ate muskrats like some people eat beef now. It was a Sunday dish. We didn't get it every week, mind ya, but we had it right much.

"It was a lot better than opossum, I'll tell ya that. Years back, my mother used to cook opossum, and we'd have to eat everything that was on the table—like it or not.

"Opossum ain't so bad if you clean him out, but he ain't as good as a muskrat. We'd catch the opossum live and feed him for a while on bran and persimmon before we'd kill him.

"We'd catch him in the day mostly, because at night they'll bite ya. I can pick a opossum up by its tail in the day, but at night they'd bite the tar right out of ya. The old people used to say they [opossums] were ashamed [of themselves] during the day. That's why they don't bite ya by day."

At twelve years of age, Max went to work on the Rappahannock River culling oysters for his father on a sail-driven log canoe. His father died in 1914, and Max, at fifteen, bought his own boat, a twenty-eight-foot log canoe that cost him $150. He worked the canoe in the winter, and in

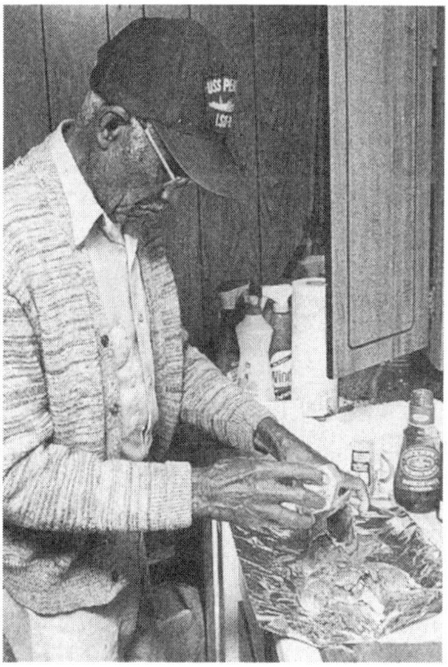

Maxwell Chandler prepares to cook up a meal of muskrat at his home in Revis, Virginia.

Max ate his first muskrat in 1917. In those days, the meat was usually fried, but today Max prefers it baked in the oven.

the spring and summer, he farmed the land around his home with a pair of horses.

"Man, a lot of wind has blown on me. I can tell you that. Years ago, the river and the land were all we had," he says. "There wa'n't no great amount of education, and even if it was—what would you do with it?

"Our lives were centered around home and the river. You've got to understand there wa'n't the big jobs in Newport News, Richmond, and Washington, D.C., like there are today. You lived off the learning that was passed down from your daddy, that he learned from his daddy. . . .

"We learned to eat what we could catch and kill. We didn't ask for much more of life than to have a good meal at dinner time and the strength to get up in the morning to work the horses.

"During the depression years, people in the cities were in soup lines, but we didn't go hungry in the country," recalls Max. "We raised everything but salt, pepper, and sugar. There were people in the cities who would have liked to have had some of those muskrats we were eatin'."

After the depression, Max moved to Philadelphia, where he worked as a butler and a cook. He moved back to his family's home place in Revis in 1956, bought a boat, and went back to working the water.

Several years later Max was approached by a local furrier about coming to work in a skinning house. The furrier hired him to skin game and, as an added duty, to cook up some muskrat meat to give to potential customers that were coming by. It was then that he developed his locally famous recipe for baking muskrat.

"Nobody was hardly eatin' rats until I went up there and started cooking them," says Max. "We'd give the trappers that were coming and going a little taste, and pretty soon we had a good business selling muskrat meat. Some of those boys would say it tasted like roast beef."

Max retired from working for the furrier, but he still enjoys eating muskrat. He has graciously agreed to disclose his recipe. He used two muskrats that were caught that day on Urbanna Creek. After he skinned and gutted the muskrats, they were soaked in salt water for twenty-four hours. The next day, Max salts and peppers the uncooked muskrats and sprinkles meat tenderizer on front and back. He then lays the rats down on their backs in front of him with the chest cavity open. For each muskrat, Max places inside the chest cavity a half-stalk of celery and a pinch each of sage, parsley, and paprika. Two "blobs" of Thick N' Spicy Hickory Smoked Barbecue Sauce are added, followed by a slice of onion. Max then sews the cavity shut with a piece of wire and wraps the muskrat in aluminum foil. The meat is baked at 350°F for 90 minutes and at 400°F for another 60 minutes. When done, the muskrat looks like a cooked squirrel.

"You best believe it's better than any squirrel," remarks Max. "Muskrats are some of the cleanest animals alive. They eat roots and clover, and they wash everything they eat."

All the meat on the muskrats is dark and sure enough, it does taste a little like roast beef. It is better than squirrel.

"Now, didn't I tell ya it was good to eat?" says Max. "Part of it is just knowing how to cook it. Young people today don't know anything about cookin' muskrat. Like I said before, most of them can't get by the name. But they're missing out on a real treat."

"Am I right?" he asks as I taste the meat.

Max was right! It tastes great!

✻ *During the 1950s, my grandfather, Raymond Blake, moored his oyster boat on Locklies Creek on the Rappahannock River. One Saturday, when I was staying at his farm, he took my cousin and me with him down to the creek.*

While he worked on his boat, the two of us just passed the time walking along the shore. A short distance down the shoreline, we heard a lot of talking and commotion. We decided to go and see what was behind the singing and loud "aaa-mens."

We moved closer to the sounds of people. When we came to a small knoll, we lay down on our stomachs and peeked over the hill. We could see the beach lined with black people all dressed to the hilt in their Sunday "go-to-meeting" clothes.

We stayed and watched as the preacher told the people that this was a harvest of souls and that the water would wash away their sins. The baptismal ceremony lasted for over an hour; we did not leave that spot until my grandfather came looking for us.

"Get up, boys. Let's go down and see what's going on," he said.

Down by the water, we were greeted by all. When we were riding home in Granddaddy's truck, he said to us, "Now, that's real religion there, boys."

30 : Harvesting of Souls

THE WATERS of the Chesapeake have provided a livelihood for generations of watermen. Since man first laid eyes on the Bay, we have looked to it for food and nourishment. When the Baptist movement first began in Virginia in the early 1700s, new members of this denomination looked to the rivers and streams to provide a spiritual type of nourishment. Baptist followers would literally gather at the river for baptisms.

At the start of this country, our founding fathers agreed that church and state should be separate. Their reason was in part based on lessons learned from Great Britain's religious policies in Virginia. In the days before the Revolutionary War, the Anglican Church, known as the Church of England, ruled much of Tidewater Virginia with a firm hand. The church could levy taxes and pass laws. Church laws required colonists to attend church and prohibited drunkenness, betting, and "profaning the Sabbath." If a person was involved in any of these atrocities, fines could be levied, and offenders could be banished from the church—a fate worse than death. Throughout Tidewater Virginia, the church was stern and powerful. However, as the population began to grow and move inland, it became more and more difficult for the church to levy control over the colony. Also, other denominations began pulling people from the Anglican flock.

The Baptists were one of those groups. The Baptist faith was first brought to Virginia in 1714 by English immigrants who moved to the southeast part of the state. About 1743, another party came from Maryland and formed a settlement in the northwest. When early Baptist preachers began spreading the Word of their faith, officials of the Church of England fought back by having those ministers jailed for preaching without licenses. One notable case was John Waller, a pioneer Baptist preacher, who in 1771 was imprisoned in Urbanna, Virginia.

The Anglicans were dismayed, however, because Waller carried on his ministry from the window of the jail and supposedly had more listeners than the Church of England had on a good Sunday. Finally, the local hierarchy of the church had jailers beat on drums to try to drown out the sermons of Waller and his followers.

Waller was eventually released from jail but returned a year later to help the Dissenters from the Church of England organize Glebe Landing Baptist Church, one of the earliest Baptist churches in the Tidewater area. When independence came in 1776, the Baptist movement spread even more rapidly across the state. For black Americans, however, it came much slower.

SLAVES AND WORSHIP

During slavery, the owner of the plantation decided whether religion was to be taught to the slaves. Some masters felt it was their obligation to convert their slaves to Christianity. Others believed that any type of knowledge was bad because it might give slaves the courage to try to run away. The latter owners would not allow their slaves to attend church, have a Bible, or be baptized.

As some black people were allowed to attend church, they began to spread the Word to other slaves that there was a better life to come, but it meant becoming a Christian and being baptized. Along with this movement, a quiet form of rebellion began to take place along wooded streams and in the high marshes that fed the coves, creeks, and rivers of the Chesapeake as slaves baptized one another.

A SLAVE'S LEGACY REMEMBERED

Clemon Brown, eighty-three, is the grandson of a slave who retained clear memories of that era.

Clemon Brown was baptized at Canoe House Landing on the Rappahannock River in September of 1920. It was a day Clemon would never forget.

During slavery, many African-Americans were denied the opportunity to participate in organized religion. When freedom came, they organized and built their own churches. Since most African-Americans in the Tidewater area became Baptist, an annual part of their worship was a spring baptism in the river. In the late 1980s, these children of Grafton Baptist Church in Hartfield anxiously await their turn at being baptized in the Rappahannock River. Grafton Baptist is one of the few churches around that still carries on the tradition of holding baptisms down by the river.

"My grandmother Judy Brown was a slave on old Nesting Plantation, which was in Jamaica District in Middlesex County, Virginia," he recalls. "She was born a slave on the plantation and was the cook, nurse, and housekeeper for Massa Eubank and his wife.

"My grandmother told me that some massas wanted their slaves to become Christians because they were afraid of facing St. Peter and having to say they had kept someone from knowing Jesus. There were others, though, who felt that the more we knew, the more likely we were to run off. This is hard to say, but a lot of white people didn't want black people to know anything about God or anything else.

"Grandmother would tell the story that when she and others were alone, they would take an iron pot, turn it upside down, and sing and pray into it. The iron pot would drown the sound and keep the sound from going outside so Massa could hear. Anything iron will draw your voice in so it won't go outside and be loud.

"There were good whites, too, now. Wives of massas who would not tell their husbands about what was going on because they knew he would hurt the slaves.

"Grandmother told me that some Baptist massas allowed their slaves to go to Glebe Landing Baptist Church, and they [slaves] would enter through a separate door that went up to the balcony.

"If you look closely at the church, you can see where there was a door that has been bricked up on the side of the church. That was the slave door.

"Churches that did not have balconies would have separate pews for us to sit on," Clemon recalls his grandmother saying. "Even though some massas would allow their slaves to go to church, they did not like for them to meet together and worship alone.

"Grandmother said that sometimes slaves would attempt to meet together, and the massa would send pat-rollers to spy on us. I think the word 'pat-roller' came from the word 'patrolman.' Sometimes the pat-roller would be a white man, but just as many times it would be another slave.

"There were a lot of slaves that weren't allowed to go to church, but the ones that went began talking around about a better life to come. They were all hoping that one day, life would be better, and this began to give people a little hope.

"Some massas came down real hard on their slaves to keep them from getting any religion and had pat-rollers spying all the time, but it didn't work.

"Grandmother said they would find out who the pat-roller was and would find ways to keep them out of the marshes when a baptism was happening.

"There were chairbackers [ministers without any education] who would sneak onto the farms to baptize the slaves. My grandmother was baptized back in the woods in a mill pond. Others were baptized in springs and marshes—anywhere that the massa could not see.

"When freedom came, we continued to worship in the whites' churches for a while, but then we started worshiping alone at bush arbors [outdoor meeting places] and later we got our own churches."

Even though President Abraham Lincoln's Emancipation Proclamation freed the slaves in 1863, real freedom did not come to many African-Americans in Tidewater Virginia until after the Civil War in 1865.

BEING BAPTIZED

"I remember the day that I was baptized," Clemon says. "It was the first of September in 1920. I was baptized at Canoe House Landing near Bayport Steamboat Landing on the Rappahannock River. Canoe House Landing was a landing where lumber and other things were hauled out from shore on lighters [barges] to awaiting schooners and other sailboats.

"It was a Saturday, and I got up early and went down to our spring and got washed up. Our spring was on the same path that went through the woods to Canoe House.

"My family met me at the spring, and we all walked through the woods together down to Canoe House. It was about two miles away, I guess.

"When we got there, the whole beach was loaded with people, and horses and buggies and ox carts were tied to tree limbs along the dirt road. I can remember looking inside the buggies and carts and seeing bundles of fodder [cornstalks] for their animals to eat."

Clemon said that it was common practice for the people in his neighborhood to carry along a couple of bundles of fodder to keep their animals from getting hungry when they planned to be away from home for a while. "They would strip the fodder down from the stalk, and usually take two big handfuls, bunch it up, and tie it together by twisting the blades around and around," he explains.

"The men took us boys behind a rick of lumber and helped us change into a white gown. The women took the girls behind another one, and they changed their clothes. It was a gang of us children.

As the children were led out into the water, family and friends stood along the beach singing, clapping, and swaying to the tune of an old Negro spiritual.

The walk back to shore was wet, but a towel and hugs and kisses were awaiting the children when they stepped onto the beach. There were expressions of both relief and fulfillment on their faces.

The Reverend Dr. C. E. Mann of Grafton Baptist Church in Hartfield, Virginia, carries on a tradition of baptizing in the river. Grafton, like many other African-American churches in Virginia, was founded right after the Civil War. For over a hundred years, members of Grafton Church have been baptized in the Rappahannock River.

"Reverend Henry Green took us out into the water and began baptizing us, and I'll never forget it when Mason Lomax and Saul Morris got scared and took off running right in the middle of everything. You see, when Reverand Green dipped the first one down into the water, he came up coughing. So, those two got scared and took off. I wish you could have seen the chase that went on then. The old people could not catch them, so they yelled for us to help.

"We ran out of the water and cornered them between two big stacks of railroad ties, and then the men came and grabbed them. One man said to them as they dragged them back into the water, 'We got to get the Holy Ghost in you, boys.'

"All the people started singing the ol' hymn, 'Wading through the Water,' and them old people would get happy and start shouting. Those old people knew how to serve God," says Clemon with a sigh.

"After all of us had been baptized, we went back behind the stacks of wood and got fresh clothes. We then went to the church and had the biggest feast. I remember, I caught a ride to church in an ox cart, and the other people in the cart were all patting me on my back, saying how proud they were of me. Everybody was so excited for me and the rest of the children, and I could hardly wait until the next [Sunday] morning, because it would be the first time I would be able to take communion.

"At the church, we had a big meal and played games. Boy, we were poor, but we ate like kings.

"Late in the afternoon when the meal was done and all the fun was over, we [his family] all walked home together. Mamma was so proud of me.

"The church was the only hope that some people had back then. The old people had all been slaves, and the hope that they found from freedom was that life would be better for their children and their children's children. They knew life on earth would not change much for them, but God and the church offered them hope for the future. I guess that's what we all look for in life. Don't you think?"

Index

A
Aberdeen Proving Grounds, 174
African-American, 140, 147-48, 238, 294-99
Alexandria, Va., 102
Amanda F. Lewis (sailing pungy), 82-92
Amburg, Va., 285
American Civil War, 142, 199, 233, 257, 261, 296
American Revolution, 19-20
American shad (*Alosa sapidissima*), 11-17, 29, 43, 111, 238
Ampro Fisheries, 76, 81, 97, 101, 201
Anderson, James E., 260
Annapolis, Md., 278
Anne Arundel (steamboat), 241, 248
August storm of 1933, 73, 187, 253-54

B
Back River Neck, 260-62
Back River, 8
Baker, Walter, 214
Baltimore, 26, 65, 139-42, 145-48, 151-52, 155, 174, 202, 231, 235, 237-38, 244-47, 257, 261-62, 264-65, 269, 270-80, 285, 288
Baltimore and Ohio Railroad, 140
Baltimore and Rappahannock Steam Packet Company, 232
Baltimore County, 174, 260
Baltimore Orioles, 174
Baptist, 239, 292-93
Barker, Christopher, 94
Barnes, Mildred, 244-45
Batoe Service, 131
Bay Line steamers, 69
Bayport Steamboat Landing, 296
Bergman, Scott, 28, 34
Beverley, Robert, 19, 102
Big Gut Canal, 188
Blackbird (schooner), 133
Blacksmith, 118, 149
Blake, Minnie Heath, 242, 244
Blake, Raymond, 292
Blue crabs, 156, 166, 169-77
Bluefish, 59, 75, 100
Boothbay Harbor (Maine), 81
Boston, 142
Boston mackerel, 275
Bottom-line crab potting, 169-77
Bow fenders, 217-30
Bowler's Steamboat Wharf, 25, 245
Box stern, 197
Bradshaw, Carroll, 208
Branch herring (*Clupea vernalis*, Mitchill), 20
Bristow, Raymond (Captain), 277-78
British Civil War, 19
British salt, 19
Brooklin, Maine, 73, 94, 170-71
Brooks, Charlie, 85
Brown, Clemon, 293-99
Brown, Judy, 295-96
Browne, Ross J., 93
Brown's Store, Va., 37
Brownstone (schooner), 270
Bruno & Stillman, 171, 173, 175
Buckroe Amusement Park, 73
Buckroe Beach, Va., 19, 64-68, 73-74
Burhans Steamboat Wharf, 248-49
Burroughs, Walter Cole, 62
Burtons Steamboat Wharf, 114, 151, 242, 288

C
Calvary Baptist Church, 247
Calvert (steamboat), 152, 239-40, 248
Calvert Marine Museum, 116
Cambridge, Md., 146-47, 266
Canada, 18
Cannon, Willis, 217-30
Canoe House Landing, 296
Cape Charles, Va., 19, 273, 286
Cape Hatteras, N.C., 101
Cape Henry, 7-8, 165

Cape May, N. J., 105
Captain Thomas (tour boat), 231
Carey, George G., 116
Carll, David, 133
Carlton, Oleathia Heath, 242, 244
Carp, 262
Carter, George, 114-15
Carter, Mason, 148
Cast iron pots (kittles), 27-33, 35
Catfish, 102-11, 174, 238
C.C. Paul and Company, 274
Cessna aircraft, 93, 96-97
Chandler, Maxwell, 287-91
Charles P. Payne Power Plant, 175
Charlie Joyce (schooner), 277
Charnock, John, 183
Chase, Md., 169-70
Chesapeake Bay Bridge, 175
Chesapeake Bay Bridge-Tunnel, 10, 164, 167
Chesapeake Bay fishing bateaux, 64-74
Chesapeake Bay pungy, 87
Chesapeake Bay retriever, 41
Chesapeake Bay, 50, 58, 64, 75, 77, 81, 91, 93, 96, 100-3, 105, 112, 119, 129, 130-31, 139-41, 154-56, 162-68, 169-78, 199, 214, 270, 281
Chesapeake Corporation (West Point, Va.), 138
Chester River, 105
Chester, Va., 104
Chestertown, Md., 103, 110
Chickahominy River, 271
Chowning, Emily, 242-43
Christ Church, Va., 247
City Island, N. Y., 133
Clam rakes, 156-61
Clams, 154-61
Clara F. (log canoe), 8
Clarke, John C., 213
Clarke, Morton, 212-16
Clarke, Morton Emory, Sr., 213-14
Clarksbury United Methodist Church, 284
Cod Harbor, 86
Codfish, 275
Coleman, Captain Dick, 135
Collamore, John "Chip", III, 102
Collins, J. W., 4
Colonial Beach, Va., 174
Colt revolver, 117
Columbia F. C. (schooner), 266-69, 279-80, 284-86
Columbia, South America, 164
Conch fishery, 162-68
Connecticut, 140-41
Conway fleet, 146
Conway, Harvey H., 146-47, 277
Conway, Harvey H., Jr., 146
Cooper, Willie, 82-85, 89-92
Corapeake (sailing ram), 259
Corn herring, 143
Crab pot, 75, 169-77
Crisfield, Md., 140, 180, 185-86, 204, 260
Croaker, 45, 71, 75, 254
Crockett, Bobby, 184-89
Crockett, Gordon, 260
Crockett, John, 180
Crockett, Mary, 178
Crockett, Shad, 89-91
Cromwell, Oliver, 19
Crouthamel, Helen (Hubbard), 260-65
Crowley, Michael, 169
Cumner, Bernard, 287-88

D
Daniel, Earl, 280
Davenport, Cathy (Winegar), 199-211
David Carl (schooner), 133
Davis, Buddy, 240
Davis, John, 241
Davis Creek, 166
Daytona, Florida, 175
Daytona Diesel Engine Corporation, 175
Deadrise workboat, 178-98, 214
Deagle, Lee, 260
Deal Island, Md., 189
Defiance III (fishing vessel), 169-77
Deihl, Kendal, 59
Delaware Bay, 12, 100
Deltaville, Va., 11-12, 102, 106, 185, 194, 199, 244, 256, 259-60, 266-67, 272, 280-84, 286
Dermo, 184, 210
Diamond stern, 196-97
Dickinson, Fielding, 111-12, 232, 234-39
Diggs, Isaac (Ike) W., 29, 41
District of Columbia Fishing Club, 267
Dize, Melvin, 82-83
Dize, Mitch, 86, 88, 89
Dolphin oil, 94
Don's Crab Carryout Seafood, 174
Dorchester (steamboat), 239
Dorchester County, Md., 267
Doughty, Charles, 27
Dowell, Courtney (Cody) Neale, 245-46
Dredge, 162-68
Dredging for crabs, 163, 167, 183, 194
Drum Point, 281
Dudley, Rob, 259-60
Duffy and Duffy Boats, 170-71, 173
Duncan, George (Captain), 269, 270
Dunlevy, Grayson, 213

Durant touring car, 143
Dyer Creek, 250-51, 253
Dymer Creek, 200

E
Easter, Alec, 276
Eastern Shore of Maryland, 142, 195, 261, 266
Eastern Shore of Virginia, 19, 72, 76, 84, 155, 168, 179, 183, 189, 200, 259
Edmonds, Richard H., 140-41
Edward L. Martin (schooner), 272
Edward's Menhaden Plant, 88
Eel pot shaft tong heads, 119-20
Eeling, 170
Elburn, Mark, 105, 107, 108
Elizabeth City, Va., 6
Elk River, 175
Elliott, Charles, 38, 64-74
Elliott, Matt, 64-65
Elliott, Obediah, 72-73
Ellyson Creek, 55
Emancipation Proclamation, 296
England, 4, 18-19
English, 11, 16
Essex County, Va., 4, 25, 232, 239
European immigrants, 140
Evans, Ida Blanche Ruark, 267, 273-74

F
Factory Point, 73
Fairbanks Morse engine, 145
Fancy Hill fisheries, 12
Faulkner, Bobby, 16
Ferry Creek, 271
Field, A., 140
Fish gig, 3
Fishing Bay, 267, 273, 286
Fishing Bay Bar, 272
Flounder, 166, 253
Fox Hill, Va., 19, 38, 64-65, 68, 69-70, 72-74
Fredericksburg, Va., 235-36, 239-40
French and Indian War, 131
Frog Pond, 236
Frye, John, 82, 95-96

G
Gardner, Reverend Joe, 232, 235, 239-41
Gardner, John, 131
Gaskins, Diane, 63
Gaskins, Eddie, 37, 49-63
Gaskins, Edward, 58
Gaskins, Fred, 231
Gaskins, Paul, 58
Gatling gun, 116-17
George, Dale, 81
Georgia, 104
Glass, Va., 171
Glass Marine, 171-72, 175
Glebe Landing Baptist Church, 293, 295
Gloucester County, Va., 70-71, 131, 137, 142, 158, 163-64, 270
Glut herring (*C. aestivalis*, Mitchill), 20
Goldman, George, 287
Goode, George Brown, 4, 20, 39, 94-96, 140-41
Gough, Wayne, 59
Grace (buy boat), 144
Gracie May (schooner), 268, 277-78
Grafton Baptist Church, 294
Grandview Beach, 64-68, 73-74
Grandview Development Corporation, 68
Gray, Louise, 18, 21, 23-26
Gray trout, 45, 252
Great Britain, 18, 292
Great Depression, 259, 261, 265, 277
Great Freeze of 1917-18, 187, 244, 282
Great Wicomico, 268-69
Green, Clarence J., 260-61, 264-65
Green, Helen Savier, 261
Green, Rev. Henry, 298
Gregory, Joseph F., 178
Guinea horn timber, 197
Guinea Neck, 8-9, 142, 164, 210, 270
Guineaman, 71, 115
Gulf of Mexico, 59, 76, 100
Gulf shrimp trawlers, 75
Gwynn Island, Va., 27-28, 31-32, 41

H
Hampton, Va., 19, 38, 64, 69, 164
Hampton Roads, Va., 155
Harris Creek, 74
Harrow, Evalina, 257
Harrow, Laura Ruark, 267, 273
Harryhogan, Va., 75, 117, 169
Harvey H. Conway (schooner), 146
Haul seining for soft-shell crabs, 264
Haven Bar, 48
Hayes, Va., 168
Hazel (hurricane), 253-54
Heron Gut, 85
Herring, 43, 238, 252
Hilda Crockett's Chesapeake House, 188
Hinton, Meade, 38
Historic American Merchant Marine Survey, 64
Hole-in-the-Wall, 42, 48
Holland Point (Piankatank River), 271, 279
Holmes, Sherman, 247-49
Hook-and-line fishing, 3-10
Hoop nets, 102-110
Hooper Island, Md., 193, 266, 268, 270, 272, 283

Hooper Island drake tail, 192-93, 197, 215
Horseshoe crabs, 106, 163, 166
Horton, Frank, 74
Horton, Hugh, 74
H. T. Daniels and Son tomato factory, 285
Hubbard, Chris, 169-77
Hubbard, Don, 169-77
Hubbard, Jeff, 174
Hubbard, Joan, 174
Hughs, Edward, 262
Hulls Unlimited East, 102
Hummel Airfield, 93, 101, 190
Humphreys, Raymond, 200
Hunt, Alex, 8
Hurley, J. Boyd, 143, 148-50, 153
Hurley, J. W., 115, 142-46, 148, 153
Hurley, Virginia, 144
Hurley, Walter Boyd, 144, 147

I
Icehouse, 237-38
Indiana, 103-4
Ingersoll, Ernest, 154-57
I. P. Hudgin's store, 256
Irene and Pearl (buy boat), 9, 183
Irvington, Va., 56
Isaac Fass (buy boat), 9
Iva W. (buy boat), 183

J
J. Boyd (buy boat), 144
Jackson Creek, 244, 257
Jamaica District (Middlesex County), 294
James, Bette, 18, 21, 23-26
James River, 18, 27, 121, 145, 270, 284
Jamestown, 3-4, 188
Jersey Beach skiff, 131
Johnson, Alex, 235
Johnson Lumber Company, 278
Jones, Marty, 84-86, 90-91
J. W. Hurley & Son, 114, 139, 142-53

K
Kate Tilghman (schooner), 221
Kelley Seafood, 76
Kelley, Jimmy, 76, 78, 81
Kellum, Billy, 163-68
Kellum, Stillman, Sr., 164
Kelly Marie (deadrise workboat), 163-64, 166
Kentucky, 103
Kilmarnock, Va., 81, 207
King, Leon, 162-68
King & Queen County, Va., 16, 21
King Charles I, 19
King George County, 236
King William County, 245
Kingfisher (Curtiss flying boat), 95

L
Labrador herring, 29
Lackey, Henry, 12-14
Lagrange Creek (Rappahannock River), 149
Lancaster (steamboat), 239, 241
Lathrop engine, 71, 203, 214
Lawson, Charlie, 214
LeCompte, Billy, 116-17
Leedstown, Va., 236
Lee Hall (Mathews County, Va.), 283
Leolyn, 205
Lester Manor, Va., 245
L. E. Williams (schooner), 270
Lewis, Benjamine F., 75, 169
Lewis, Frank, 58
Lewis, Shelton, 151
Lewisville, Va., 21
Lexington Fish Market, 262
Little Creek, 286
Little Wicomico River, 55, 58
Locklies Creek, 212, 292
Locust Hill, Va., 248
Log canoe, 3, 179, 191-93, 196, 199, 212-13, 215, 257, 289
Lomax, Mason, 298
London, England, 162
Long, Archie, 151
Long Island, N. Y., 157, 283
Long Island (tugboat), 221
Long Island Sound, 157
Loretto, Va., 111, 234
Lorraine's Diner (Tangier Island), 187
Lower Middlesex County Volunteer Fire Department, 11, 13
Lynn Haven Bay, 6

M
Mackerel, 4
Maggie (schooner), 266-67, 269, 271, 273-74, 276, 278, 281, 282-83
Maggie stew, 275
Maid King (pound boat), 46-47, 48, 50
Maine (tugboat), 221
Maine lobstermen, 76
Maine sardine carriers, 75, 81
Maltby, C. S., 140
Man-a-Way (schooner), 145-46
Mann, Dr. C. E., 298
Maple Creek, 112
Marsh, Charles L., 156
Marsh, Leonard, 188
Marshall's Drugstore (Urbanna, Va.), 178, 287

Marshall's Oyster House (West Point, Va.), 137
Martha Virginia, 51, 55-56, 58-61
Mary Duncan (drake tail workboat), 193
Maryland (tugboat), 221
Maryland, 6-7, 100, 102-3, 118-21, 129-30, 139, 141-42, 155-56, 169-77, 191, 231, 293
Maryland and Virginia line, 55, 180
Maryland Oyster Police, 113, 116-17
Massachusetts (tugboat), 221
Master's Lumber Company, 239
Mathews County, 26-28, 62, 64, 70, 112, 115, 250, 252, 282-83
Mathews County Courthouse, Va., 30
Matilda (steamboat), 242
McDonald, James, J., 154
McDonald, Marshall, 6
Menhaden, 75, 172, 174
Menhaden fishery, 73, 75-101
Menhaden spotters, 93-101
Middlesex (steamboat), 151-52, 239, 241, 245-46
Middlesex County, 3, 248, 280, 282
Midnight (pound horse), 37-40
Migratory Bird Act, 261
Miller, Charles, 214
Miller, Virgil, 260
Minnie Emma (schooner), 270
Mississippi River, 217
Mitchell, Bret, 59
Mitchell, Buddy, 28, 31, 32
Mitchell, Nelson, 56-58
Mobjack Bay, 26, 112, 115, 155
Model A Ford, 203
Monhegan Island, Maine, 81
Moon, Va., 42
Moore, Jim, 8
Morattico Bar (Rappahannock River), 146
Morris, Saul, 298
Mount Vernon, 20, 22
MSX, 184, 210
Mundy Point, Va., 267
Muskrat, 263, 287-91

N
Nanticoke dam, 7
National Museum of American History, Smithsonian Institute, 65
Native Americans, 3, 11, 118, 154, 156, 162
Naval Academy, 278
Naxera, Va., 118, 120
Neale, Robert G., 245
Neale's Store, 26
Nellie Crockett (buy boat), 195
Nereid (Maine sardine carrier), 81
Nesting Plantation, 295
New England, 5, 18, 88, 141, 155, 157, 163, 171, 172
New England cod fishery, 173
New England dories and wherries, 131, 173
New Jersey, 27, 100-101, 168, 199-200
New Jersey (tugboat), 221
New Point, Va., 47, 50, 155, 250-51, 253
New York, 27, 100-101, 103, 141, 142
New York and Pennsylvania Railroad, 286
New York Bay, 157
New York City, N. Y., 131
Newport News, Va., 283, 290
Nippers (short handled oyster tongs), 119
Nomini Creek, 113
Norfolk, Va., 6, 101, 139, 140, 142, 146, 155, 231, 244-45, 250, 254
Norris, Dorothy (Norton), 244, 256-60
Norris, Hugh, 256, 259-60
Norris, Johnny, 259
Norris, Paulene, 275
Norris, Ruby Lee, 113-14
Norris, Willard, 194, 197-98
North Carolina, 75, 93, 100
North End Steamboat Wharf, 244, 247, 248
Northeast River, 175
Northern Neck, 49, 55, 73, 75, 199-200
Northumberland County, Va., 37-38, 40, 76
Norton, Hervey, 244, 256-58
Norton, Olivia Jane (Ailsworth), 256-58
Norton, William Henry, 257

O
Oaks Landing (Urbanna Creek), 283
Ocean City, Md., 106
Ocran, Va., 199
O. E. Wentworth Packing House (Baltimore), 151
Ohio, 103, 104
Old Point Comfort, 69
Onancock, Va., 183, 273
Only Daughter (schooner), 73
Ophelia, Va., 49, 55, 57
Opossum, 289
Owens, Grover Lee, 185-86
Owens, Harry, 252
Oxford, Md., 193
Oyster cocktail, 152
Oyster shucking houses, 139-40, 210
Oyster thievery, 136
Oysters, 113, 118-53

P
Pacific Northwest, 119
Palmer engine, 144, 214
Palmer Fisheries, 95-96
Palmer, Alfred, 242
Palmer, Charlie, 242

Palmer, John Armistead, Jr., 95-97
Palmers Steamboat Wharf, 242
Pamunkey River, 276
Parker, Lawrence, 214
Parks, Charles Roland, 180-82
Parks, Mel, 82, 85
Parks, Micky, 180-84, 189
Parks, Tom, 259
Patuxent (steamboat), 232
Patuxent River, 146-47, 272, 280-81
Payne's Crab House, 116
Payne, Jonesey, 144, 148-51
Pennsylvania, 103
Perch, 111, 238
Perkins Creek, 242
Perry, Lynn, 136-38
Pete (muskrat), 264
Philadelphia, Pa.,12, 65, 247, 290
Piankatank River, 113, 121, 271, 283
Pierce, Joe (blacksmith), 149
Pile drivers, 43-45, 66
Pittsburgh, Pa., 140
Plantagenet, Beauchamp, 162
Pocomoke Sound, 155
Point Lookout, Md., 269
Pole huncher, 53, 54
Poquoson, Va., 8, 196-97
Poquoson stern, 196
Porpoise oil, 94
Port Clyde, Maine, 81
Portsmouth, Va., 101
Pot pie stern, 193-95, 197
Potomac (steamboat), 152, 244-45, 248
Potomac River 37, 50-51, 54-55, 113, 116, 270
Pound nets, 27, 75
Pound stakes, 41-54
Pound stake maul, 41-42
Powhatan (Indian chief), 154
Powhatan (yankee skiff), 135
Price, John, 67
Price, L. P., 144
Prince's Bay, N. Y., 130, 133
Prince's Bay skiff, 130
Princess Anne County, Va., 6
Pruitt, Clyde, 183
Pruitt, Jerry, 182, 188-90
Pruitt, Sherman, 208
Pruitt, Thomas Raymond, 188
Pruitt, William (Bill), 208
Pugh, Johnny (Boy), 251, 253-56
Punch Bowl, Va., 145
Purse boats, 76, 79-80, 89, 97-99
Purkins, Grandpa, 21, 23
Purtan Bay, 137-38

Q
Queen Anne's County, Md., 261

R
Rainbow Lakes, 104
Rappahannock (steamboat), 232
Rappahannock River, 4, 25, 41, 101, 111, 139-40, 142-43, 145, 151-53, 212, 217, 231-32, 240, 242, 244-45, 248, 283, 288-89, 292, 296
Razorback clams, 174
Reed, Elijah Warren, 73, 94
Reedville, Va., 69, 73, 88, 89, 95, 97, 100-101, 180, 185, 201, 208
Regent, Va., 212-14
Remlik, Va., 149, 288
Revis, Va., 287, 289, 290
Revolutionary War, 72, 292
Rhode Island, 94
Richmond, Va., 144, 215, 245, 290
Robins, Jack, 8-9
Robinson, Otho, 121
Rock Hall, Md., 105, 107
Rock, Lydia, 16
Rockland, Maine, 81
Rodgers, Ray V., III, 123-27, 160, 222-30
Rollins, William, 197
Round stern, 194-95, 215
Rowe, Achilles, 7, 143, 150
Rowe, George Vernon, 27-28
Rowe, Julian, 27-28, 34
Rowe, Ralph Hall, 7
Rowe, Shelly, 27-28, 34, 41-43, 45-48, 50
Rowe, Wilson, 27-36
Rowe, Woodland, 3, 7-10, 114, 139, 142-53
Royall, Anne, 102
Ruark, Alfred W. (Captain Al), 266-67
Ruark, Charles Alvin (Duck), 266-68, 272, 274-75, 277, 281
Ruark, Edmond, 146, 266-68, 270, 272-86
Ruark, Edwin Rufus, 267-69, 271, 273, 276
Ruark, Edwin W., 266-69, 271, 273-74, 277, 280, 282-84, 286
Ruark, Lanny Filmore, 267-70, 272-73, 282
Ruark, Lillian, 267
Ruark, Mary, 267, 273
Ruark, Millard F. (Captain Phil), 266-67, 270, 272-73, 284
Ruark, Rufus, 266-68, 276-77, 282-83
Ruark, Talmadge, 266-73, 275, 277-79, 281-84, 286
Ruark, Thomas H. (Captain Tom), 266-67
Ruark, Tom Henry, 267, 269-79, 281, 283-84
Ruark, Willie, 267
Ruark & Associates, 286

Ruark Post Office, 267
Ruth Conway, 277

S
Salt herring, 18-26, 143, 152
Salt Pond, 19
Salt, evaporating, 19
Saluda, Va., 21, 26, 283
Sand dollars, 166
Sandbank Wharf, 251, 254-55
Sassafras River, 102, 105-6, 108
Saunders, John, 232-34
Saunders Steamboat Wharf, 112, 231-41
Scalloped oysters, 152
Scanlan, Ed, 136-38
Scanlan, Mike, 136-38
Scroggins Creek, 113
Sea Bright skiff, 131
Seaford, Delaware, 277
Second Battle of Cold Harbor, 257
Seed oysters, 130, 145, 194
Segar, Beverley, 115
Seneca Creek, 173, 174
Severn River, 164
Shad planking recipe, 14
Shad planking, 11-17
Shaft tongs, 118-29
Shores and Ruark Seafood, 286
Shreeves, David, 259
Sickal, Bernard, 121-22
Simmons, Alvin, 283
Simmons, Charlie, 283
Simmons, Edmond, 283
Simmons, Tom, 283
Simmons (schooner), 268
Slaves, 20, 22, 26, 293
Smith, John, 18, 102, 188
Smith, Lennie, 46-47, 50
Smith Island, Md., 186, 188, 231
Snapper rigs, 75-92
Snediker, George, 27
Snow Hill, Md., 185
Soft-shell crabs, 272
Solomons, Md., 116, 156, 281
Southern States Cooperative, 153
Southside Sentinel, 11, 217, 231
Spearing fish, 3
Spot, 45, 252
Square stern, 197
St. Mary's, Md., 231
Standard Oil, 286
Standard Products, 81, 201, 208
Starfish, 166
Starvation Farm (Gloucester County, Va.), 132, 135-36
Staten Island, N. Y., 130-31, 133
Staten Island skiff, 130-33, 135, 137-38
Stepaside II (deadrise workboat) 106, 109
Stingray Point, 275
Stingray Point Lighthouse, 258
Strachey, William, 11, 162
Striker house, 143, 152
Striped bass (rockfish), 59, 111, 113, 238, 262
Strong, Albert "Buffalo," 102-10
Sturgeon, 253
Sunnybank, Va., 55
Susquehanna Democrat, 6
Susquehanna River, 105, 175, 177
Swain's Memorial United Methodist Church, 188
Syringa, Va., 260

T
Talbot (steamboat), 239-40
Talbot County, Md., 193, 195
Tallman, John, 94
Tangier Island, Va., 75, 82, 84, 178-90, 208, 231
Tappahannock, Va., 231-32
Taring pound nets, 27-36
Thomas, Mary, 250-56
Thomas B. Taylor (schooner), 274
Thomaston, Maine, 81
Thompson, Ralph, 37-40
Three Rivers, 239
Tidewater Virginia, 26, 179, 260, 288, 292, 296
Topping, Va., 93, 101, 113, 180, 190
Trap-pole horses, 37-40
Treading for clams, 154, 156
Trotline, 75
Tuck stern, 193-95
Turkey Point Lighthouse, 175
Turner Creek, 105
Turtle Point, 149
Twilight (sailing pungy), 82, 85, 89, 90-92

U
Union Baptist Church, 9
United States Navy, 95, 100
U. S. Postal Service, 214
Urbanna, Va., 114, 116, 139, 142-43, 151, 217, 241-42, 244, 284, 293
Urbanna Creek, 146, 217, 287, 291
Urbanna Oyster Festival Foundation, 217

V
Valerie Faith (deadrise workboat), 182-83
Van Name Brothers, 131

Van Name, Arthur, Sr., 132, 135-36
Van Name, Dave, 131, 132-33
Van Name, Dr. A. L., Jr., 87, 130-36, 281
Van Name, Ethel Coleman, 130
Van Name, Jacob, 131
Van Name, Peter, 131
Van Name, William H., 131
Vermont (tugboat), 221
Virgie (deadrise workboat), 272
Virginia (tugboat), 221
Virginia conch landings, 162
Virginia Dare (buy boat), 203-204
Virginia Institute of Marine Science, 156-58
Virginia Live Fish Company, 104
Virginia Marine (Police) Resources Commission, 43, 117, 162, 208, 286

W
Wakefield, Va., 12
Walboro, 21-23
Walden, Luther, 259
Waller, John, 293
Walnut Grove, 261, 263, 265
Walter Boyd (buy boat), 144-45
Ward, Willie, 288
Warthen, Bobby, 271
Washington, D. C., 65, 109, 152, 231, 290
Washington, George, 19-20, 22
Water View, Va., 145
Waterview Farm, 213
Watts Island, Va., 85
West Coast, 76, 124
West Indians, 270
West Point, Va., 135, 136-37, 145, 152, 276
West Point Grammar School (West Point, Va.), 138
West Urbanna Steamboat Wharf, 151, 242, 288
Westmoreland County, Va., 236
Whales, 93-94
Wharton, James, 18, 20
Wheatland, 111, 232-33, 237-38
Whelks, 162-68
White Stone, Va., 187
William Floyd (Menhaden steamer), 94
William H. Van Name, (schooner), 133, 283
Williams, Charles H., III, 96-101
Williams, George, 118-29, 154, 158-61
Wilson, Willis, 199
Windmill Point, Va., 145-46, 275
Winegar, Joe, 200-211
Winegar, John Chrysler, 200-1
Winegar, John Joseph, 201-3
Winegar, Joseph David, 201-4, 206-7, 209-11
Winegar Fish Plant, 201
Winegar's Marine Railway, 199-212
Wisconsin air-cooled engine, 46, 49
Wolf Trap Lighthouse, 89-90
Wood, Bernard, 280
Wood Cross Road, Va., 137
Woodward, Philemon, T., 21
Workboat sterns, 191-98
Works Progress Administration, 64-65
World War I, 244, 274
World War II, 71, 241, 286
Wormeley, Ben, 144

Y
Yamacraw (deadrise workboat), 208
Yankee (northern) oystermen, 113, 130-31, 139-40
Yankee skiffs 130-38
Yates, Alvin, 259
Yeomac (Chesapeake Bay buy boat), 76
York River, 16, 25, 130-135, 137-38, 140, 152, 163, 164, 276
York River Seafood Company, 168
Yorktown, Va., 101, 155
Young, Henry, 236

Z
Zapata Haynie, 76, 96-97, 100-101